OPENING OUR ARMS

Helping Troubled Kids Do Well

KATHLEEN REGAN

BULL PUBLISHING COMPANY
BOULDER, COLORADO

OPENING OUR ARMS
Kathy Regan

Copyright © 2006 Bull Publishing Company

Bull Publishing Company
P.O. Box 1377
Boulder, CO 80306
Phone (800) 676-2855 / Fax (303) 545-6354
www.bullpub.com

ISBN-13: 978-0-923521-94-3
ISBN-10: 0-923521-94-1

Manufactured in the United States of America

Distributed in the United States by:
Publishers Group West, 1700 Fourth Street, Berkeley, CA 94710

Publisher: James Bull
Production: Dianne Nelson, Shadow Canyon Graphics
Cover Design: Lightbourne Images

Library of Congress Cataloging-in-Publication Data

Regan, Kathy.
    Opening our arms / by Kathy Regan
        p. cm.
    Includes bibliographical references.
    ISBN-13: 978-0-923521-94-3
    ISBN-10: 0-923521-94-1
1. Child psychotherapy—Residential treatment. I. Title.

RJ504.5.R44 2006
618.92'8914—dc22   2006027846

CONTENTS

Section Two: Reaching a "Tipping Point" 77

ACKNOWLEDGMENTS

This book could not have been written without the help, support, and understanding of many people. First and foremost, I owe my gratitude and thanks to all the staff of the Child Assessment Unit. There are no words that can accurately describe my appreciation of their talents, their intelligence, and their commitment to and love of the children in our care. It was their hard work that made the writing of this book possible. I also make special mention of Jeanne Ford, whose behind-the-scenes support helped me in countless ways.

Close in line behind the staff of the unit are Doctors Ross Greene and Stuart Ablon. Ross provided the approach for our change in focus in the way we viewed the behavior of children, and he provided direction for us to better serve them. His "Collaborative Problem Solving" approach resonated within me and became hard-wired to my synapses. Ross and Stuart were wonderful mentors and teachers. They facilitated our growth and learning as we struggled to gain mastery over new skills. They provided guidance for us as we dismantled one structure after another and built a new structure to support our care for the children of the unit. To them we owe much, and from them we gained much.

I am extremely grateful to my nursing mentor, Mary Milgrom. Her trust and belief in my ideas, ideals, and goals made a complicated process much easier. She was a source of direction, strategy, and advice that I needed and sought out on a regular basis. I am grateful to Carol Collord (the former NCO) for her support and for her trust in my decisions and leadership. I am grateful to Dennis Keefe, our CEO, for his support and belief in the value of nursing and nursing leadership in the improvement of patient care services. I am also grateful to Dr. Jay Burke, the Chairman of Pyschiatry at Cambridge Health Alliance, for his trust and support in our efforts to better psychiatric care for children. His encouragement was instrumental in our receiving the Psychiatric Services Award for Excellence in 2003 from the American Psychiatric Association. I am grateful to Dr. Bruce Hassuk for his support and enthusiasm in our work to provide humane care to children. I am grateful to wonderful past leaders of the unit; first and foremost being Dr. Joel Goldstein, whose dedication and commitment to children bestowed on the unit a rich history of providing the highest quality of services to children and their families. Likewise, further back in time, the unit was enriched by the leadership of Doctors Tim Dugan and Peter Chubinsky, along with the first leader, John Wechter, Ph.D. Their commitment to the children is evidenced by their continued involvement as mentors and teachers to the present day. This is true also for Dr. Maria Sauzier. Doctors Elizabeth Weidmer-Mikhail and Aruna Rao have joined our ranks and have continued our work to the present day. My friend and colleague, Heidi Schliesske, also joined us later in our endeavor and quickly helped us continue the work and started our first CPS Parent Support Group with David Whelan, who was loved by staff and children alike. I am very fortunate to have found Jim Bull, the President of Bull Publishing. He saw something of value in my manuscript and turned it into a published book.

I am grateful for the support I received from Nan Stromberg, Michael Weeks, and Janice Lobel from the Massachusetts Department of Mental Health, as we moved out of a traditional framework to create a different model of care. I am also grateful to Kevin Huckshorn, the Director of NASMHPD, the technical assistance arm of SAMHSA, for her support and for encouraging other programs to contact us so we could share what we have been doing and continue the dialogue about better services for children.

I am indebted to Julie Regner, who agreed to be my official reader; her suggestions were invaluable and of great assistance in providing clarification and suggestions for editing. She also provided the charts in the Results section. I am also grateful to Dianne Nelson of Shadow Canyon Graphics. Her copyediting was seamless and made a potentially tedious task seem effortless. Last, but by no means least, I am grateful to my husband, Mark, and to my children, Mark, Andrew, and Beth. Their support was evident daily and was manifest in their never complaining at my obvious preference for writing rather than for housework.

A special note:
I am at a loss to convey the depth of my appreciation to the children and their families who taught us so much. I am acutely aware of the grace in which families bestow upon us their trust by allowing us to care for the most important individuals in their lives—their children. This was manifest time and again in their patience as we struggled to understand the difficulties their children were facing. It was also evident in their tolerance of our mistakes and changing perspectives as we worked to deepen our understanding of their children and worked to formulate strategies and approaches that would be more successful.

To all the children of the Child Assessment Unit I owe much. The ability to love and be loved by the most innocent and tender is a gift beyond any other and one that I treasure and never take for granted.

INTRODUCTION

I wrote this book so that I could put to paper the changes and processes in which we became involved as we went down a road to make major changes on our unit. I believed that the recording of that journey was a useful work in itself. I believed that in reflecting on our steps, our successes, and our challenges, I would develop a better understanding and perspective. I also thought that our journey might prove interesting to other child programs that were beginning to question the humanity of some of our current child welfare practices. A larger motivation was that I wanted in some way to make public the deep admiration and respect that I had for our staff. We could not have made the journey or achieved the rewards and recognition that we did without the staff who work on the unit. I was blessed to have energetic, questioning, bright, compassionate, and loving staff members who genuinely cared for and enjoyed the children for whom we provided services.

Every step we took to develop new practices was met with quick understanding by the staff. There was an undaunted, repeated willingness and desire to provide the best care possible. The staff as a team of people working with a common purpose had a desire to excel in the continuing mastery of skills that would influence the care we provided to kids and their families.

This story was written from my perspective as the nurse manager and as one of the leaders of the unit. It is my view, and others on the unit might have a somewhat different perspective. Despite differing views, I was consistently met with an openness and willingness to consider almost any idea. On occasion, there was some minor eye rolling, as if to say, "There she goes again!" but that exasperation never got in the way of considering what might be best for a child or a parent. This made the changes we implemented seem effortless at times. There were other times when we were challenged by behaviors that we did not as yet feel we had the tools to manage, nor did we have the immediate answers to what was needed at the moment. We plodded on through the difficult times because of a strong commitment to keep going and reach the other side—to make it over the hump.

Some of our most difficult moments had to do with resistance of coworkers and our own lack of self-confidence in the beginning stages of our efforts. We made it through those difficult times, and it was a credit to the staff that, even in the worst of times, the difficulty was almost unanimously attributed to our own failings or lack of expertise and not to a negative outlook about a child who was presenting the challenge.

I hope that retelling our story will prove interesting to readers and will add to the dialogue about the way care for children should be provided. It is the story of one psychiatric unit, and I do not presume that our story is the defining work on the care of children.

I do believe that our values of providing child- and family-centered care in a way that is collaborative, humane, and trauma-sensitive are on target. I hope that this story will encourage others to question the way they do things and to embark on their own journey.

The format of this story is in some ways unique. The book is a narrative of our experience, and in that sense, it is like narrative nonfiction. This story also gives detailed information regarding our processes and thinking as we made changes in the culture, structure, and model of care that we were providing. In that context, it resembles a how-to workbook. The story is told through the discussions we had in our group supervision sessions; in that perspective, it is a story about process. From my own viewpoint, I think of this book as a bird's-eye view of a group of people undertaking major change. It describes how that process unfolded and took root. From that vantage point, the book resembles a case study on the application of change and leadership theory in a particular psychiatric setting.

This book is not written in an academic style. Although it makes use of psychiatric jargon, it is intended to be told in everyday language so that people who are not familiar with the operations of a psychiatric unit will be able to follow along easily and be able to understand the context. It is meant to be readable by front-line staff and by child welfare providers from a variety of settings. My hope is that it will also be helpful to parents who are interested in exploring different views on management of children's behavior.

I have frequently used the term *kids* instead of *children*. This has been intentional on my part and I did so because children most often use the term *kids* when referring to themselves and each other. *Kids* is less formal and more familiar than the term *children*. Use of this term is not meant in any way to be derogatory or disrespectful.

I hope that you enjoy our story. It was a tremendously exciting venture for all of us.

—Kathleen Regan
June 2006

This book is dedicated to Mark Tomás.
His life and struggles have been the fuel
for my passion to create better services
for children and their families.
He has forever had my love and respect.

SECTION ONE

Beginnings

CHAPTER 1

ANTICIPATION

• Malik •

"All meaningful and lasting change starts first in your imagination and then works its way out. Imagination is more important than knowledge."

— *Albert Einstein*

One of my first memories of this job, as the nurse manager of a locked child psychiatric unit, stands out vividly. I had been on the unit less than six weeks and was still learning how the unit operated. I wanted to try and understand as much as I could: the structure, the culture, the staff's perceptions, their fears, the unit practices, and the influence of the unit's past and recent history on current unit events. The staff had shared some of their concerns in my group interview with them prior to my hiring. They had let me know that they were afraid; they felt the unit was unsafe. A number of them described an alarming, fatalistic attitude. One milieu counselor poignantly described the prevailing ethos in the following way: "It's a matter of waiting for your number to be up. When I see one of my coworkers assaulted, it's not a sense of relief that it's them and not me. It's a feeling that since one more staff has been hit, it is getting closer to when my number is up—it's just a matter of time." I also had a series of interviews with administrators of the psychiatric department within the hospital, as well as with the present administrators of the unit (all of whom were leaving). Everyone had shared their various perspectives on the issues the unit faced and the role of the nurse manager who would be co-leading the unit.

I had six interviews, which involved some people more than once. The bottom line was that the chief nursing officer (CNO) and the nursing site director (NSD) wanted me to be very clear about the challenges I would face, and they wanted to feel confident that I was up to the task. They were sensitive to the staff's perception that they had been "abandoned" and felt unsupported due to all the leadership changes and the staff turn-over. I felt ready for this challenge and had taken the job with the hope of being able to do something worthwhile for children. I had ample quantities of energy and even more of passion, and I was ready for something important. I had seen firsthand in my own life that services for children were sorely lacking, and I had lots of thoughts and opinions on the way care should be provided to children and their families. I felt up to the task.

I started the job with much enthusiasm. My first task was to identify which staff members seemed to operate in a manner consistent with my values about the care of children. I also wanted to know who was competent, but more importantly, I wanted to know who was curious and wanted to learn. At the same time, I wanted to identify who would be my challenges: Who did I think would be the stumbling blocks in the months ahead?

After only six weeks on the job, I already had a tremendous appreciation for the nurses and counselors of the unit. They were caring for the children twenty-four hours a day, seven days a week. Decisions made by the clinicians were often played out on the unit; kids would receive bad news, such as hearing that they would not be going home but to a residential program, or they would have an upsetting family meeting. Some would disclose to their therapist some horrible experience that they had been through, and then they would return to the unit. The overwhelming emotions that had been stirred up would often result in emotional explosions on the unit. Frequently, the staff had no warning, no heads up, that Johnny was in for a rough time. The staff were left with the aftermath and with an expectation to keep a sense of order at all times. They had a limited set of tools with which to manage a group of kids who had been hospitalized because they were unable to control their behavior and were deemed "too dangerous" for the community at this time. At its worst, the fear of any psychiatric unit was that of several kids exploding at once and the contagion effect taking over the unit. I sensed that there was an undercurrent of everyone anticipating a worst-case scenario. It is easy to imagine that if enough close calls occurred, or if staff members were being assaulted on a regular basis, the result would be a group of people who were hyper-alert and hyper-vigilant; they were looking to stomp out any sparks of smoldering emotional distress.

It was a spring afternoon. I was in the nurses' station talking with one of the nurses, and change of shift was about to begin. Change of shift was a daily practice on hospital units, and it was a time when one shift gave a summary of the important events that had transpired on their shift (which included information on new admissions, kids who were being discharged on the evening shift, new data learned at the clinical rounds meeting held in the morning, and visits or meetings scheduled for the shift). Most importantly, it included the children's behavior and staff observations of the children for the shift. At change of shift, a lot of staff were present, because the one shift was already working as the next shift came in to hear the reports before going on the floor. When the reports were finished, the new staff came out onto the floor to replace the people who had been there. Staff members from the previous shift were getting ready to leave. Our nurses' station was a small, crowded area that had work space with computers around two walls made of glass looking out at the living room and the corridor in front of the living room. The third wall was covered with a big white board that listed the rooms, the patients' first names, and the doctor and therapist assigned to them. The fourth wall was filled with built-in cubbies that served as individual mailboxes for all the staff of the unit.

I don't know what made me turn around to face the window looking out at the living room. Maybe the conversation I was having had ended and I was getting ready to move on to another task. I was standing there watching as Malik approached the nurses' station window. He was a stocky, eight-year-old African-American boy with great big brown eyes that sometimes were clearly focused and sometimes seemed glazed and faraway. Colleen was following right behind him, and she casually asked him what he needed. Before my very eyes, Malik turned and, with full force, threw a punch, haymaker style, into Colleen's face. There was a loud crack and then blood everywhere. The next few minutes were confusing as Colleen screamed in pain. The children in the hall had witnessed this event; some were yelling at Malik and some started crying. Staff were rushing to the scene from all directions. Malik was approached, taken down on the floor, then carried to the Quiet Room. He was put on a mattress on a steel frame, and leather cuffs were wrapped around his wrists and ankles, securing him to the bed so that he could not move. (This procedure is referred to as the application or use of mechanical restraints. It is also referred to as 4-point restraints.) A staff person stayed with him, sitting in a chair outside the room about twelve inches away, and the door was kept open. Malik was initially cursing and then quieted.

In the nurses' station, various staff were attending to Colleen, and I called the emergency department (ED) to let them know that we were bringing Colleen there for medical treatment. She was crying and in a lot of pain. A staff person accompanied her off the unit to the ED. The rest of the staff met with the children in an impromptu community meeting to discuss what had happened and to try and assure them that we could keep them safe. The children were able to state that they felt angry with Malik. They were afraid of him and wanted to know why he had hurt Colleen. Truth to be told, we did not know why he had hit Colleen. It appeared to be totally unprovoked.

Events that *seem* totally impulsive and unpredictable lend credence to a belief that an environment is unsafe and dangerous. They can also result in a reactive stance; they contribute to a belief that you need to put more structure in place to prevent unpredictable acts. This then leads to a sense of needing more consequences. All of this is based on the assumption that if you make the punishment hard enough, it will discourage behaviors that you do not want to see.

Could we have predicted this event as a possibility? What did we know about Malik? He was considered impulsive, violent, and intermittently psychotic. He had a severe abuse history, with many placements in foster care and residential programs. He had come to us from a residential program where he was increasingly violent and was not able to return there. Our job was to try and determine why he was so violent, provide treatments that would decrease his violence, and secure another placement for him. Hopefully, we would develop an understanding of him that was greater than the reasons for his violence. A comprehensive picture needed to include not just his vulnerabilities but, even more importantly, his strengths.

Malik had been on the unit almost three months when this event occurred, and it followed a number of previous assaults on staff that were less severe in nature. We knew that he was very wary and untrusting of adults. He had developed a belief system that life was not fair, and this was certainly an accurate assessment in his case. Life had not treated him fairly at all; horrendous things had happened to him as a young child. It was hard to form a relationship with him due to his pervading sense of mistrust of adults, and there was a natural hesitation in getting too close because of his assaultiveness. Although he was only eight years of age, he was very strong and quick. Most people were to some degree afraid of his unpredictability, and this reticence affected how much we gave to him emotionally. What had happened that day that might have had a bearing on Malik's emotional state or potential for violence? The staff were not able to identify any significant events that had occurred.

Despite this crisis, the staff continued to do their jobs. They worked hard to calm the unit, restore order, reassure the other children, and occupy them with activities.

My first priority at that time was to ensure that we were giving Colleen all the support we could. Then I needed to reassure the staff that I genuinely appreciated their fears and concerns and that I would take that into consideration in my actions. Colleen was treated for a nasal fracture and was sent home on paid leave. She was encouraged to avail herself of some trauma counseling and to take as much time as she needed before returning to work.

On an administrative level, my boss, Maryanne, the nursing site director (NSD), and Corinne, the chief nursing officer (CNO) were notified, and they were highly supportive. We temporarily froze admissions (we had three vacant beds at the time). This reassured the staff that we were not at risk of receiving another child who might be out of control while we were trying to resolve this crisis. Maryanne suggested that I contact our victims of violence team located at one of our outpatient clinics, which I did. I let them know of our situation and asked for their assistance. They encouraged me to have Colleen contact them.

They also suggested that we hold a special violence debriefing session on the unit for all staff and that we use this specific incident as the focus of our discussion.

All staff were encouraged to attend and were assured that they would be paid to come in if they were not scheduled to work. Colleen agreed to participate in the debriefing, and it was scheduled for two weeks in the future, giving staff enough time to make arrangements for this meeting and for Colleen to have enough time to feel comfortable with the meeting.

The debriefing session was helpful in many ways. It helped everyone deal with the latest occurrence of violence, it provided an opportunity for everyone to show their support to Colleen, and it provided a space for everyone to share their fears and anger at the current state of things.

I was struck by an outcome that really helped us with the work ahead. The perspective of looking out for oneself, which tends to grow in situations where people feel vulnerable and unprotected, was replaced by the camaraderie of being in this together and having a sense of working together to help one another as a group. This shift was not overtly expressed in words, but there was a different feeling among staff.

The staff also expressed feelings of anger and of being let down by the administration. This recent assault was interpreted as further evidence of being undervalued by their bosses, their reasoning being that they felt the incident was a reflection of employees being expected to tolerate dangerous situations. The sharing of these perceptions provided a sense of validation and it further generated expectations from the group that there should be some help from the hospital system in making the conditions better for them.

This incident was unfortunate, but it also proved to be a sentinel moment, the center around which events were about to take place. I had already assessed that the staff as a whole appeared traumatized by the episodes of violence that had occurred on the unit over the previous two to three years. In order to think about how things might change, the staff needed to be attended to first. They needed to feel supported and heard, and they needed a sense of being in control of their environment rather than feeling like prisoners in it. They had tried to gain control by increasing the structure of the unit with various rules that were established after adverse events had occurred. They had become increasingly rigid and reactive. Despite all these rules and protocols, the unit was no less dangerous; in fact, it was more dangerous. But there did not seem to be any other way to do things.

So again, what about Malik? Malik, who had a pervading sense of life's unfairness and a well-based wariness of adults as people who could not be trusted, was thrust into an environment where he was viewed as the cause of danger. The victim had become the perceived victimizer. There are lots of psychological explanations for this development. Yet, in my opinion, a psychodynamic understanding of why Malik became violent was lacking in vision. It was looking at Malik and his difficulties to explain events. It did not look beyond Malik and his aggression, even when giving it validity. For me, an important consideration was that we had not created an atmosphere where he did not have to fear others or fear his own feelings of rage.

We were not unusual—we were the norm. Most other psychiatric hospital units were doing the same things we were doing. We had all been taught that we needed to provide containment for children who were in need of this because they were lacking the inner controls themselves and thus were dependent on us to provide this for them. It was not just about us and about Malik. It was about all the Maliks out there and all the other child-treatment units and centers.

The aftermath of this crisis was positive for our unit. It mobilized us to change. It was an event upon which I capitalized. For a few weeks, our staff meetings focused on what had happened, then moved to a broader view. The staff were encouraged to talk about what they liked about the unit and what they didn't like. They were encouraged to voice what specific policies they disagreed with and the reasons for their disagreement. They were encouraged to describe the way they would like to work and the type of place the unit should be. They were encouraged to brainstorm new ideas and to question traditional practices that we had all learned. They could wonder aloud if there was another way.

Creating a climate that allows questioning involves, to some degree, going out on a limb. It takes courage to open discussions regarding current practices by being critical yourself about traditional, accepted standards. You are risking people calling into question your sanity, your training, and your competence. But *not* to question has an even greater price—one of missed opportunities to grow and to change.

Sensing that the time was right for change was an important factor. The crisis with Malik led us to pull together. I had gained trust with the staff by stating openly that not only were the children of the unit victims of trauma, but the staff, too, were victims of trauma. I sensed that the staff viewed me as trying to understand their plight and doing something about it. I was able to capitalize on this trust to move us ahead and look at how we could change things.

It was important in our discussions to point out, first and foremost, that what had already been tried was not working. All the rules and protocols had not provided safety. In fact, a closer look would show that the level of violence had increased as more structure was imposed and as the list of rules and consequences grew. We really had nothing to lose by looking at things in a different way. These discussions took place over approximately three months. During that time, we kept the old structure in place but began to see it differently. And we began to talk about change as having the potential to make things a lot better for the kids and for us.

Back to Malik. What was his outcome? I can't say with any surety that there was a happy ending for him. He was the force that led us down a path to change, but that occurred months down the road. Malik was not there to benefit from the changes we made. In fact, part of my gaining credibility with the staff was pushing for Malik to be transferred to an intermediate-care unit within the state system. The process had been started prior to my arrival. I was able to push the process along quickly due to the violent incident, which prioritized Malik for a quick transfer. I did learn that Malik spent a year or so on a state intermediate-care unit, then went to a residential program. About one year after that, his picture appeared in the local paper under "Wednesday's Child," a newspaper column that highlights a child awaiting an adopted family. I do not know if he moved into an adoptive family, but for him to be considered for adoption meant that he had been very successful in his program and was stable enough to be placed in a permanent family setting.

CHAPTER 2

MALIK
IN PERSPECTIVE

*"History, although sometimes made up
of the few acts of the great, is more often
shaped by the many acts of the small."*

— Mark Yost

In thinking about Malik and all the "Maliks" out there, I thought it might be useful to think about Malik from different points in time.

If Malik had been born in 1850, no one would have considered that he was suffering from emotional or mental health problems. In fact, if anyone noticed his out-of-control behavior, it would have been assumed that he was "morally deficient," and—what's more—so were his parents in that they were unable to control the child. He would have been viewed as an extension of his parents, as children were seen as possessions of parents with no

13

real identities of their own. He would have been expected to work long hours in the fields, laboring on his parents' land if he lived in an agrarian community, or he would have been expected to work those same long hours in a factory if he lived in an industrial society.

If he was not able to do that, his parents might have easily abandoned him, and, most likely, they would have felt justified because he would have been viewed as defective. If he had any luck, he might have ended up in an "alms house" (a poor house), where he would still have been expected to work long hours each day. But he would have received some measure of food several times a day, and he would have had a bed to sleep in and a roof over his head. As he grew, and if his behavior continued, as an adolescent he would have been considered an adult and would most likely have ended up in jail. During his life, he would have regularly experienced beatings and punishment as interventions aimed at rectifying his behavior. His life would have been miserable. He would have received little understanding, and, if he made it to adulthood, his life experiences, filled with layers of trauma, would likely result in an adult who knew no other way than to strike out and vent his rage before someone did the same to him.

If Malik was born in the early 1900s, he might have fared slightly better. There was still little consideration given to children, and Malik would have been considered the property of his parents. They would have been judged as deficient because of his acting-out behavior. If Malik's parents were unable to care for him based on their own problems, he would likely have been placed in an orphanage. In the early 1900s, there was a beginning public concern about the conditions prevalent in orphanages, and there were the beginning developments of a foster-care system. Malik might have been given an opportunity to live in a foster home. If he exhibited acting-out behavior, he would have undoubtedly been returned to the orphanage. It is likely that no further attempt would have been made for him to live in a family setting. Dorothea Dix had raised awareness in the mid-nineteenth century about the conditions of mentally ill adults. By 1900, there might have been a fifty-fifty chance that Malik's behavior would have been recognized as a symptom of his emotional distress. There were few resources available, and he would most likely have been placed in a state institution along with other children with disabilities, cognitive limitations, and physical deformities. These asylums were often overcrowded and poorly staffed by untrained employees who had little understanding of aberrant behavior. It is likely that Malik would have suffered further abuse and would have received little therapeutic treatment.

By 1950, Malik would likely have fared significantly better. The awareness of mental illness and serious emotional disturbance in children was much greater. The prevalent theories stressed social treatment, and there would have been emphasis on milieu treatment. Malik would have been placed in a state institution, and he would have had a reasonable chance to be considered for long-term residential treatment. Malik might have met with some hope and positive interactions. Two authorities at this time, Redl and Wineman, wrote in 1952 about therapeutic environments for severely emotionally disturbed children and advocated for treatment settings to provide: (1) programming that recognized a child's need to have fun; (2) "a high amount of basic affection from adults" to establish treatment rapport; (3) group programming that was flexible and kept small; and (4) "freedom from traumatic handling" (i.e., institutional policies designed to prevent retraumatization rather than based on conventional customs or other considerations).[1] Malik may have fared even better in the 1950s than in the present day. Granted, there would not have been the range of interventions that are available now, but there would not have been the pressure from managed-care insurance companies for his health-care providers to come up with a quick fix. He would have moved around less. If his problems appeared extreme, he would not have been expected to make multiple transitions through a myriad of attempts at foster care and to move in and out of hospitals quickly. His health-care providers would not have felt pressured to achieve quick medication stabilization and then move him on to the next program. Once it had been determined that his family was unable to care for him or to provide the type of care he required, the child welfare system would have been responsible.

There would have been less understanding in the 1950s of the various diagnoses Malik carried, and in some states he would likely have been viewed as incorrigible. But if he lived in a fairly progressive state that had access to nonprofit organizations and philanthropies, he might have ended up in a program that was caring and committed to him for the duration. He may have been allowed to grow up in one program. He would not have been expected to improve and then, once improved, have to move on to yet another program. In this era, there may have been less bureaucratic tension among the agencies responsible for children who needed placements for treatment of their mental health and emotional needs.

But Malik was born in the 1990s, and he was born into an era that was sophisticated regarding the emotional needs of children. He was born in a time that had good understanding of the biopsychosocial nature of children's mental health. This was an era that had access to extensive research on the impact of trauma on young children and its impact on growth and development. It was a period that was well aware of the importance of nurturance in children's development and in their developing sense of self. This was an age that understood the difference between a disability and a defect. This was an environment that believed in a recovery model of mental health. There was a continuum of services for children that included, on a community level, outpatient mental-health counseling and school-based services, as well as home-based services that were available to families for treatment.

There was also an extensive array of out-of-home services and placements that ranged from group homes (where a child received intensive mental-health treatment but was able to attend community schools) to residential programs that provided mental-health services and schooling as part of the program. There were options of partial hospitalization, where a child would receive intensive mental-health services by day and return home at night. There was another option of acute residential treatment, a program that lasted for two weeks to several months. It was similar to a hospital program but had fewer nursing and medical staff available twenty-four hours a day. Lastly, there was the most intensive option—that of a psychiatric hospitalization. Most states had a number of hospitals or units that were dedicated to children and adolescents.

On the school continuum, schools provided a number of increasingly sophisticated options that ranged from supportive help within the regular classroom to a separate, specialized classroom for one or more periods during the day. The range continued to separate behavioral classrooms within the school to community-based specialized therapeutic schools that provided extensive mental-health and behavioral support on-site as part of the schooling.

Child-welfare agencies also evolved a complex assortment of services for children and families. The philosophical bias was to preserve and support families. If that was not possible, then state welfare agencies were expected to make permanent plans for children. This included efforts to secure permanent families for children within their care. They created programs that included helping parents raise their children with community and specialized supports and providing a network of foster homes, ranging from emergency homes, to general foster homes, to specially trained foster parents who were expected to raise children with more complicated medical and behavioral needs. The child-welfare agencies also funded a range of residential programs for children who were not able or ready for a family situation.

But the system is not perfect. The system is underfunded and in many ways dysfunctional. Services for children are separated and housed within several agencies. Bureaucratic tension and turf battles occur between agencies providing care to children and families, and services often are not available in sufficient number or in a timely manner. Funding for services is dependent on politics and on the values of the majority of citizens at this particular time.

Despite the limitations of services in the beginning of the twenty-first century, Malik would be considered fortunate to live in this era. Yet, Malik had not had an easy life; it was one of severe early abuse and trauma. He had experienced many moves and failed placements. He was expected to modify his behavior in order to achieve success. Yet, he had no tools with which to meet this expectation. And to further hinder his chances of success, he was poorly understood. Our knowledge and interventions had come a long way, but we still had a long way to go.

CHAPTER *3*

GETTING STARTED

• *Alexander* •

*"It is not so much what you believe in that matters,
as the way in which you believe it and proceed
to translate that belief into action."*

— *Lin Yutang*

We embarked on a journey to change the status quo. It proved
to be a huge task and a complex process that involved a number
of things coming together. The first steps were to develop a culture that would support the changes. The culture would act as a
catalyst for further shifts in the way we were providing services to
children. Our new culture would also serve as the bedrock upon
which we would build a new model of care.

Getting started involved obtaining administrative support
from the very top of the organization for the changes to come.
For our institution, it also involved discussions with several unions

to coordinate training and supervision. I would outline with my boss, Maryanne, the ideas we had come up with and the details of what we wanted to do. Maryanne understood the hospital inside and out and had been through many turnovers in administration, centralizations, and decentralizations. She knew the history of the institution, and she knew the players who held both direct and indirect power. She was my Lao-Tzu—my strategist. I would present an idea, then she would entertain it and let me know the steps that had to be taken to lay the groundwork before I could proceed with implementation. Her behind-the-scenes coaching and mentoring were very important in our success.

Above her, we received the support of the chief nursing officer (CNO), Corinne. She would hear from Maryanne what the unit's next step was, and she and Maryanne would coordinate the administrative tasks that needed to occur. This support was essential; we were stirring things up and breaking a lot of rules and traditional practices. These two administrators needed to be forewarned each step of the way in order to let other departments know when problems arose, such as employees complaining to the Human Resources Department. Corinne kept the CEO informed when we were at a juncture and were instituting new policies and procedures. Maryanne and Corinne contacted our legal department and the unions to which our staff belonged.

Preparing for change involved more than the necessary step of lining up administrative support for the project ahead. It also meant taking a strong look at the staff who would be involved in this changeover and assessing the strengths and weaknesses of the workforce. A number of seasoned staff had left en masse the prior year to work at another unit that was opening. They were able to be recruited not just by the offer of more money. They were ripe for the picking because they were disenchanted with the state of the unit. They felt unheard and did not feel good about the work they were doing. Tension and strife, differing factions, and a vacuum of leadership ensued due to the ongoing conflicts among the staff.

Some talented people already had left, among them a senior milieu counselor, Miguel. He was a big bear of a guy with an even bigger heart, and he was friendly and funny. But more than that, his life's work was all about helping kids and making sure they knew that someone cared about them. He had worked on the unit for years and was a natural at engaging the children. He believed strongly in the power of nurturance and was a strong staff leader. Miguel had their respect; he was wise as well as funny and down-to-earth. He was also a politically astute go-between for the voice of the milieu staff with the leadership of the unit. He had heard via the worker grapevine that things were changing on the Child Assessment Unit (CAU), and he approached me about wanting to return. We had a few conversations by phone, followed by a formal interview. We found that we were in agreement about the direction the unit needed to take, and we had the same feelings and beliefs about the needs of the children we cared for. We had a clear understanding that Miguel's return involved joining with me to help implement the changes ahead.

A few months after his return, another seasoned milieu counselor, Evan, was rehired and returned to the unit. He lent his own unique style to the unit and had a way with kids, especially kids who were mistrustful of white, middle-class staff. He was able to do wonders with some angry kids who had built tortoiselike defenses around themselves to keep others at a distance.

The staff present on the unit when I arrived consisted of a mix of long-time staff and recent hires. The second group had been hired in the last year and a half, and most of them were milieu counselors. This latter group was young, enthusiastic, and eager to learn but had started out at a loss. With the turnover in nurse managers and the vacancy before my arrival, they had not received much supervision and training. Daniel, one of the milieu counselors, was very helpful to me in my beginning days, and his immediate support of me was helpful for me in learning the ropes and increasing my credibility with the other milieu counselors. When the group was initially skeptical, Daniel was welcoming and willing to give me the benefit of the doubt right off the bat. He also filled me in on the lay of the land and shared his perspective of critical issues that needed attending. He had stepped into the leadership vacuum and taken on the staff self-scheduling so that it would continue despite the exodus of staff the previous year. He was funny and outspoken and loved practical jokes. He still had much of the kid left in him, and the kids sensed this. They gravitated to him and to his playfulness.

As a group, the nurses on the unit were understandably more wary. The nurses included several people who had been on the unit for many years—some since the day the unit had opened in 1989. In the more recent past, they had seen three nurse managers come and go, and then the position remained unfilled for eight months. Each of the nurse managers had very different styles and priorities. The nurses appeared to be withholding judgment until they saw what I would do and if I would stay. Some of the nurses had played a strong role on the unit in the years they had worked there, and they were highly skeptical of my beginning to voice my vision of what the unit could become.

One nurse was brutally direct in letting me know that I would not automatically have her support. In fact, her words to me were: "I was here long before you, and I will be here long after you." This nurse had a lot of indirect power on the unit and had been a strong presence for a number of years. My assessment of the situation was that I would have an easier time winning over the hearts and minds of the younger milieu staff than I would of the nursing staff.

It was relatively easy to stand back and look at our unit and then try to explain our existing culture with a few descriptive adjectives. We looked like many traditional psychiatric units and programs and had the same core values as they did. We were all taught some basic precepts in our education and training. The values that we espoused were those of safety, consistency, and structure. It was hard to imagine a conversation about the structure of a psych unit where safety was not the focus and the most repeated word. And who could dispute that you need to have a safe environment and protect the patients for whom you are caring? Who could dispute the importance of being consistent—the rules should be the same for everybody. In the same vein, where would we be without structure? We would have chaos.

From a different perspective, if you had a desire to work with kids, it was usually because there was something particularly appealing about children. Children often were more honest in their responses. They had a sense of playfulness, and they learned through play. They enjoyed interacting with others. They were able to experience the moment and use it as an opportunity to learn. They were responsive, spontaneous, curious, and open to new ideas. They were also pragmatic—they loved to know how things worked. They loved the "why" of things. They saw opportunity and adventure in many places. They had a great ability to spot insincerity and disingenuousness. They had built-in phony meters. They often learned by testing out rules. They were always stretching the boundaries of their universe because they were curious and open to figuring out how things worked for themselves.

If we wanted to genuinely help children, we needed to create a child-friendly environment. In fact, we needed to go further than that. We needed to provide child-centered care. This meant that we needed to be clear in identifying core values that we were prioritizing; the first and foremost consideration was that we be nurturing. This would take precedence over all other values. I believed that, for children to grow and develop to their potential, they needed to be nurtured and treasured. That was at the heart of a safe environment. I believed that an essential part of our job involved ensuring that each child perceived himself or herself as special. It would be our interactions with the children for whom we cared that would help create this perception within their minds. We needed to create a culture that was built around learning and teaching. Tied to these values was the need to provide choices. Providing choices is a natural byproduct of creating a learning environment; one is intertwined with the other.

Identifying these new values and putting our ideas into words was facilitated at a meeting of the then chief of child and adolescent psychiatry and my boss. The medical director and I were asked to put into words and describe simply how we envisioned a change in the culture by identifying these overriding values. In that meeting, we described the core values that would be at the heart of the environment we were seeking to create. These would be prioritized over traditional values.

A problem I encountered when thinking about the existing culture on our unit was that the priority on safety, consistency, and structure had been elevated to some higher level where they became the end product rather than tools to be used to achieve some greater goal. The staff had been trained, and most believed, that to help children, you needed to treat everyone the same. And you had to stand firm on the rules to keep everyone safe. This meant that the children needed to endure the structure imposed on them so that they would succeed when they returned to the community or to another program.

But children who end up in psychiatric units and in residential programs were already expected to follow rules and an imposed structure in the community. Despite being in environments that were considered safe, consistent, and structured, these children did not succeed; in fact, they got worse—so much worse that they ended up in a psychiatric hospital! The kids were viewed as out of control, and the environments from which they came to us felt ill equipped to be able to handle these children.

What did these children have in common? Ninety-nine percent of children admitted to our unit were admitted for "out-of-control" behavior at home, in school, or both. This means that they were aggressive and explosive, and their behavior usually involved hitting, biting, kicking, threatening verbally, refusing to comply with adult wishes, not following the rules, etc.

Something else that almost all of the children had in common was that they had a history of trauma. Research was growing at a rapid pace indicating that the children found on psychiatric units and in residential treatment programs had, by and large, suffered serious trauma either directly or by witnessing traumatic events. The statistics were so high, in fact, that it should be assumed that if a child was admitted to a psychiatric unit, it was likely that the child had suffered trauma. The Massachusetts Department of Mental Health had estimated that 84 percent of children and adolescents who were hospitalized in psychiatric units within the state had experienced trauma.[2] The implications were that the units and programs entrusted with caring for these children needed to make sure that care was not only nurturing, but also restorative and healing. Programs needed to ensure that they were in no way retraumatizing children. Neuroscience had shown us that trauma (direct and indirect) played a significant role in the developing brain of a child. And severe trauma or repeated trauma could have lasting effects on that developing brain if care was not provided to mitigate the damage done to children by these extreme life events and their aftermath.[3] If we were creating child-centered units and programs, then part of our job was to help restore children and undo to whatever extent possible the effects that trauma had played upon the child's evolving neurological system.[4] If we did not attend to this when we had the opportunity with children when they were young, then we would be condemning many of them to less than their full potential for having satisfying, productive lives as adults.

When I thought about the children we served and the problems the unit faced, I was seeking a philosophy or model of care that all the staff would be able to embrace and one that would be compatible with the children we were treating. Finding such a philosophy proved to be an easy task. A few years earlier, I had gone to an all-day presentation sponsored by an urban school system in conjunction with the community mental-health clinic for which I worked. The presenter that day was Dr. Ross Greene. He had published the book *The Explosive Child* and was presenting his "collaborative problem-solving approach" to a huge auditorium of teachers, guidance counselors, and outpatient clinicians. The audience seemed quite jaded; some teachers were open in expressing their frustration with the state of their schools and with violent kids disrupting their classrooms. Dr. Greene went on to describe his perspective on these explosive kids. He elaborated on an effective way for adults to view the explosive behavior of children, understand it, and be able to help kids by teaching them the skills they needed to successfully master the sources of their frustrations. He won over this difficult audience. And he won me over, too. What he had to say resonated with my experience of explosive children. I bought his book that day and felt I had learned a lot.

Here I was, three years later. I was thinking about identifying a model that would work for us on the unit—a model that all the staff would be able to learn together and that would help us to provide better care for the children. I was looking for a model that would accommodate three separate needs: acceptance by the staff, being a good match with the children for whom we were caring, and success in terms of our being able to implement the plan. My thoughts drifted back to that lecture and I had one of those defining "Ah ha!" moments. This, I thought, was the approach we needed. I discussed my idea with some of the about-to-be-departing leadership on the unit. One doctor reported that she actually knew Ross Greene and was willing to call him and make an introduction. The rest became our history. After some mutual checking each other out, we came to an agreement. Dr. Ross Greene would provide initial training for all the staff of the unit and provide ongoing supervision with his associate, Dr. Stuart Ablon, for six months. We would provide the subjects for a research study, testing the effectiveness of Dr. Greene's collaborative problem-solving (CPS) approach on an inpatient psychiatric unit. The subjects of the study were not the children, but rather the staff of the unit. They would be trained in CPS—trained to see children through this new perspective. They would learn the CPS theory and skills and would then be able to teach the children the skills they needed to manage frustration more successfully.

Plans were made for us to have an initial training of all staff—top to bottom—from the nurse manager and the medical director to the most recently hired per-diem milieu counselor. There were two training times set—one in the morning and one held the next day in the afternoon. One part-time milieu counselor told me that she could not make it, as she worked full-time at a school and could not get the time off. Everyone had been given six weeks notice, and the unions had agreed that mandatory training was in order, as we would be changing our model of care, and the staff members needed the training to develop competence. When this staff person told me she had no intention of coming, I told her that her *not* coming was deciding that she no longer wanted to work on the unit. I let the union representative on our unit know of this. A representative from the union then called her and advised her to attend, stating that she would have no cause for grievance, as she had been given sufficient time to make arrangements for her other job. She was present for the afternoon training. We had spent a lot of time preparing for this and were pleased with a 100 percent turnout of all staff who worked on the unit.

Following the training, ongoing supervision was arranged to take place twice a week for six months. There was a Monday group supervision session held from 2:30 to 4:00 (to catch two shifts, with the evening shift coming in one hour early to attend the supervision) and a Thursday morning time scheduled after morning clinical rounds.

The training provided the basics of CPS and the rationale for this approach. Supervision would prove to be the place where we made it work. It was in the group sessions where we mastered the skills we needed and where we could speak frankly about our failed attempts. They were the place where we could support one another and also raise questions. But the group supervision sessions were more than that—not only did we learn together, it was a great leveling factor. We were all initially ignorant and started on the same playing field. It was a wonderful opportunity to dissipate the power inequities within staff relationships. It made no difference how much schooling or how many years of experience you had, or what your job description was. Here we were all learning together, and we all started off at 0 and our knowledge base grew from there.

We had agreed that this was a pilot program, and all staff were asked to suspend their skepticism for the next six months so that they could master the skills they would need to implement the model. If it was successful, then it would be a permanent change. If it wasn't, then we would evaluate the program, look at why it was not working, and determine if it was it fixable. In order to critique the new model, all staff were expected to learn the basic skills and use them. You would have no credibility criticizing the changes if you did not make any attempt to master the skills you would need to be successful in this approach.

Ross Greene's CPS approach was based on the premise that "kids do well if they can." That was a major shift in perception from the belief that "kids do well if they want to." One implies ability, and the other implies motivation and attitude. Unfortunately, the state of things in children's mental health in recent years has been leaning toward the "want to" premise rather than the "if they can" premise. The underlying assumption regarding "kids do well if they can" was that if they were not doing well, it was the job of the adults to find our why the children were not doing well, then teach them the skills they needed so that they *could* do well.

This approach was about assessing and identifying the thinking deficits causing the child to become frustrated, then angry, then explosive. And this focus on determining thinking deficits in no way eliminated our understanding of children via identifying their symptoms to develop a DSM IV diagnosis. (This is the standard text used to define and formulate psychiatric diagnoses.) In fact, the CPS perspective greatly enriched our understanding of a child. It expanded our formulations and was much more specific in nature. Once we were able to determine the cause of the frustration, we could then work on determining what skills were lacking. We could further break down those skill deficits by identifying all the steps involved and use these little steps to begin to teach the child a more successful approach to managing frustration and problem solving. It was about developing a deeper pragmatic look at a child and at his or her skills, strengths, and vulnerabilities. Our job was to act as advocates in getting kids back to baseline by helping them gain skills to manage frustration that would prevent them from experiencing major meltdowns.

The CPS approach was also lacking in blame. It did not blame the child, for if you believed that explosions or meltdowns were the result of not having the skills to master a situation and solve problems, then it made no sense to hold a child accountable for lacking the skills needed to master a situation effectively. This approach did not blame the parents either. It acknowledged that adults, too, were doing the best they could. And if they were contributing to the child's distress and frustration, it was because they did not know any better way, and we needed to teach them the skills *they* needed in order for them to help their child problem solve.

This approach was about teaching the adults a different way of looking at a child's behavior. It was considered behavior in a more humane way. We talked often in our supervision groups of look-ing at children's behavior with a different lens and about shifting our focus. We learned to become detectives, and we became astute observers of interactions. We learned to do situational analyses and looked for antecedents leading up to a child's meltdowns. We learned a new language, too. We worked hard to put aside the blaming, judgmental, mental-health jargon that we had once worked so hard to master. Now that old vocabulary got in the way of our formulations. We discarded words such as "manipulative," "attention-seeking," "secondary gains," "intentional," "gamey," and "provocative." This was a difficult task because the words were so ingrained into us. But these adjectives really said more about the person observing the behavior and about his or her analysis, rather than the words themselves being an accurate, fac-tual description of behavior.

Other words had already been brought into question. As we changed our culture to create a nurturing environment, we changed the way we interacted with the children. We were no longer a "hands-off" unit. Staff were encouraged to be nurturing in the real sense of the word—no air high-fives, please! Everyone was encouraged to hug kids and to tell them many times a day how great they were. Holding kids by the hand, putting arms around a child, having young children sit on the staff's lap, or car-rying a tot upon your shoulders were accepted as an integral part of our daily routine. For the real little guys and gals, female staff could be seen walking up and down the long unit hall with a little one straddling their hip as they did their five-minute checks on the children, locating and documenting where they were.

The preoccupation with "boundaries" was discarded. No one wanted or expected the staff to be inappropriate with the children, but common sense had gone out the window on many psych units, ours included. Everyone was so worried about the worst-case scenario (sexual or physical abuse—either an accusation or actual occurrence) that physical contact with children had been severely restricted. Imagine being a child and being hospitalized on a psychiatric unit, away from everything and everyone familiar—a frightening experience. Add to that your caretakers, strangers really, who were nice but reservedly so. If ever a child needed cuddling and caring, this was the time for it. The staff with the most confidence and common sense had always had doubts about the sanity of a hands-off policy, and many talked about the type of unit that they desired to work on. They talked of being able to provide comfort and support through physical contact. The measuring stick of treating kids the way you wanted your own kids or relatives to be treated was mentioned more than once. A number of staff even confessed that for years, when no one was looking, they would hug a child and cuddle him or her in their arms, especially when they were visibly distressed and scared. Thank god for their innate instincts.

In our first CPS group supervision, Ross went over the basics of our interventions with children. Adult interactions with children were basically broken down into three major types: Basket A, Basket B, and Basket C. Basket A was the imposition of adult will. It was saying "NO." It was evidenced by similar phrases: "You can't"; "you mustn't"; etc. Every adult was familiar with Basket A. It was the way most of us taught children rules and issues of safety. In the CPS approach, Basket A was reserved for imminent, enforceable, serious safety concerns. Grabbing a two-year-old child's wrist as he or she attempted to run in to the street was a Basket A response and an understandable one. Basket C was also very familiar to everyone. Basket C was essentially ignoring a behavior or action because you determined that it was not important. In the grand scheme of things, you could not be working on everything with a child, and a lot of what ideally might be good to cover, but was not essential at that point in time, was relegated to Basket C.

Basket B was the essence of the CPS approach. Basket B was where you "worked it out" with a child. It was where teaching took place. It was a two-step process: The first was empathy in its most basic form—concrete recognition of the child's concern in the child's own words. This could be a bit tricky. As adults, we liked to reframe what someone had just said. For the child to feel that we were genuinely listening and interested in his or her perception, our empathy was reflected in our repeating back what the child had just said. For example:

Johnny: "I hate Stephen; I wish he were dead."

Adult: "You hate Stephen."

(Notice that the correct response was not: "I hear you saying you are mad at Stephen," or "It sounds like you are really mad at Stephen.")

The second step was obtaining an invitation to work it out or to problem solve together.

Adult: "You hate Stephen. What's up?"

Or you could say: "Let's see if we can figure this out," or "Tell me more about that."

The step-one empathy response did not include comments such as, "Gee, you seem angry," or comments that immediately jumped to a lecture about wishing someone dead. The second step was an invitation to work on the problem together. After the invitation, the process moved to gathering information so that you had a grasp of what was going on. Your next intervention would be low-keyed attempts to find out more. "Can you tell me more?"

Johnny: "I wanted to play Gameboy and he took it out of my hand."

Adult:	"So let me see if I understand this. You were playing Gameboy and Stephen came up to you and grabbed the Gameboy out of your hands—just out of the blue."
Johnny:	"Well, it was kinda like that but not exactly. See, he had the Gameboy and put it down and I came up and took it off the seat and started playing it. It was just sitting there. Why'd he have to go and do that?"
Adult:	"Let me see if I understand this. The Gameboy belonged to Stephen? And you walked up to him and took it off the seat where he was sitting? Is that correct?"
Johnny:	"Yeah, but he wasn't using it. He took it from me because he doesn't like me."
Adult:	"Do you think that maybe he would have let you play with it if you had asked permission? Maybe he thought you were going to take his Gameboy and keep it? Maybe he was taking a break and wanted to continue playing it? What do you think?"
Johnny:	"I didn't think of asking, I just saw it there and jumped to grab it before someone else grabbed it."

What did we learn here? That there are a couple of areas to explore. Was Johnny impulsive; did he act without thinking? Did his behavior get him in hot water because he did not think ahead of time about acting and about the effect of his actions? Did he understand the connection between cause and effect? Was he able to learn easily from past experience? Did he have an awareness of social customs? Was he able to read social cues? Or was he socially clueless? Could he be lacking in an awareness of what other people may be feeling?

Based on this one interaction, it would be difficult to tell, but keeping track of observations of Johnny in his interactions over a short period of time should lead to identifying some patterns that might make you suspect that a thinking skill deficit contributed to his frustration and anger.

It was through our observations of a child's interactions that we learned where he or she had strengths and talents and where the child was having difficulty.

Once we understood the source of the difficulty, our remedy was to teach the child the skills he or she needed. We would do this live in Basket B interactions (called Basket B in the moment), or we could do it at a later time before a similar situation occurred and when the child was calm (this is called a Basket B intervention out of the moment).

Thinking skills were best taught out of the moment, when a child was calm, or when a child was just beginning to become frustrated and was only mildly upset (referred to as -5). At -5, a child was having some identifiable difficulty but had not reached the stage of total frustration or moved beyond that to anger or, in a worst-case scenario, to a full-blown meltdown. In CPS jargon, when someone was in a "meltdown," that person was said to be at -30. As we all know when we have lost it and are very angry or enraged, we are not open to reasoning, problem solving, or learning new skills. The best and only practical intervention at that time is to do whatever it takes to help calm things down. The goal here is to "restore coherence" as quickly as possible.

As you worked with a child, you learned what helped that child when he or she was very upset. Some kids liked space; they needed to be alone to calm themselves down. Other kids liked to work off the energy with some physical activity (shooting hoops, punching a punching bag), and some kids liked to rip up paper. Other children listened to music or played Gameboy or Playstation; focusing intently on these games was soothing for them. When a child was very upset, it was counterproductive to try and get him or her to talk. Very few of us are able as adults to do this, so why would we expect this of a child? The child may not even fully understand why he or she was so upset.

This brings up another premise of CPS, which is the belief that meltdowns are not good for kids. This means that, as adults, we want to be careful that our interactions are not precipitating meltdowns. Meltdowns do not increase awareness, they do not increase self-esteem, and they are not learning experiences. None of us like feeling that we have been out of control, and we like even less that others have seen us in that state. Usually, we feel terribly afterward. Often, meltdowns are accompanied by guilt, shame, and feelings of poor self-worth. And the more meltdowns a child has, the less he or she feels in control of things. This exacerbates a lack of positive self-esteem.

Our job as adults is to try and determine what happened before the child blew. What was happening prior to the meltdown that caused frustration? Our explanation of why a child is becoming upset is what will drive our intervention. For this reason, we are very interested in what happened before a child became upset, and it is also the reason why communicating observations between adults is very important in discovering patterns in situations that lead to frustration. This is how we will identify what thinking deficits are lacking and causing the problem. We are not interested much at all in what happens when a child melts down and what he or she does. After you have seen a few meltdowns, they are pretty much the same. And rehashing the actual meltdown and what it looked like does not provide any information for teaching the skills the child needs to prevent meltdowns.

Ross pointed out that what was important for us to remember was that Basket B wasn't an either/or situation. It was a process of negotiation. And it was a little different than the way most of us had thought of negotiating with a child. The negotiation did not consist of the adult presenting two or more choices for the child to choose. It was being open to an undetermined outcome that was worked on together. In fact, the child might and often would come up with the solution. The success of a Basket B intervention was in a decision being reached that was acceptable to both the child and the adult.

We also learned not to expect every Basket B intervention to have immediate success. Sometimes we would not be able to get the information we needed to determine what the problem actually was, and sometimes the child would not be able to engage in a Basket B intervention. Sometimes our efforts would be laying groundwork for future successful Basket B interventions.

We discussed some potential problem areas. One question was: "What do we do if a child does not want to go to our school group or refuses to do work in school group?"

Ross asked the staff member to identify what outcome we would be seeking. The answer was twofold: (1) we wanted to prevent a meltdown; and (2) we wanted to find out why the child did not want to go to school. Ross went on to explain that either setting a consequence for the child's school refusal or making the child stay in school were two possible alternatives. If we were to make the child stay in the classroom, he or she may continue to act up, he or she still would do no work, the disruption might well disturb the other kids, and the other kids could possibly even join in with the child's negativity. On top of this, we would not have learned anything about why the child did not want to go to school. And, we might be precipitating a meltdown. The same would apply with setting a consequence: We might precipitate a meltdown, and we would not learn why the child did not want to go to school.

The bottom line was, we would not have learned any valuable information. So what else could we do? We could let the child leave the classroom. This would get him or her away from the other kids so that they would be able to continue to work, and they would not see that the other child was not working. We could ask the child what else he or she would prefer to do. Staff could attempt a Basket B discussion with the child.

Staff: "You don't want to do schoolwork?"

Child: "I want to draw."

Staff: "Let's see if we can work this out."

The child might not be able to tell us today why he or she does not want to do schoolwork, but we would have set the tone by responding to this child's discomfort in the classroom and not penalizing him or her for not doing work. We would have acknowledged that the child has a problem in the classroom. We would not yet know what the problem is. It could be that the child was unable to read and has not told anyone. Seeing the child's response has already told us that it would be important to get information as soon as possible from the teacher in this child's previous school.

One of the staff raised a question that led to a discussion about our being creative in developing strategies to help kids cope rather than just putting a rule in place. The issue was whether or not our flexibility and creativity would prepare kids for the real world to which they would return after they left us. We talked about how one aspect of our job was to create a climate where we could learn what was going on with each child and then be able to pass on that information to the next care providers for each of the children. The reality was that being rigid and setting consequences were not necessarily conducive to creating a climate in which we would be able to learn as much as we could about a child in a very short time.

We also discussed when to use Basket C. A case in point was a situation with Alexander. One of the staff talked of Alexander, a nine-year-old boy, who had extreme difficulty settling on the previous night. The staff member explained that Alexander's normal bedtime routine was to take sixty to ninety minutes to settle and involved building a fortress of mattresses, cushions, etc. Another staff person chimed in that Alexander appeared terrified at bedtime, and it did not seem that he viewed his bedroom as a safe place. Megan, one of the nurses, reminded everyone that Alexander had recently learned that he would be leaving the unit to go to another program, and he was understandably anxious about this. The staff who had worked the night before had attempted numerous interventions to help him settle: offering fruit, cereal, and ginger ale; giving choices where he could move his mattress and pillow; offering to help him work on his Good-Bye Book; etc. At that point, it was 9:30 and there was little likelihood of Alexander being able to have a meaningful conversation. Everyone agreed that we had identified his being anxious as a major contributing factor to his being able to relax and fall asleep. Therefore, being able to distract him from his anxiety was a good alternative. Allowing him to go to the day hall and watch a movie until he was tired and would be more likely to fall asleep was a fine Basket C solution to this particular problem.

We had just finished our first group supervision. Initially, some people had worried that group supervision would be awkward and that it would be difficult to speak out and ask questions about how to use the Baskets approach in our interactions with the kids. It proved to be a non-issue. Once the first question was asked, the ball got rolling and more questions came. Before you knew it, the hour was over.

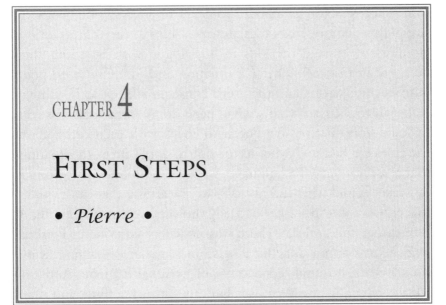

CHAPTER 4

FIRST STEPS

• *Pierre* •

*"Leadership should be born out of the understanding of
the needs of those who would be affected."*

— *Marian Anderson*

We were trying out our new knowledge and skills. It was fun, it
was challenging, and it was embarrassing. We were self-conscious;
we did not yet have any confidence in what we were doing. The
bravest among us just plunged in and gave it a try. They led the
rest of us onto the dance floor, and in a matter of days we were all
blundering through. And in the very beginning it felt (and
looked) like bumbling. In a self-conscious moment, I would say to
myself, "What in God's name are you doing?"

But the discomfort passed quickly and so did the feeling of
being totally inept. I think this was because we were meeting with

some success. Not great big moments of success—but we were stopping situations from escalating just by the very nature of our attempts to engage the kids in a dialogue with us about their behavior instead of viewing a situation and jumping in to point out what was wrong and then set a consequence. Quickly, some of us began to see that what we had been doing in the past was really counterproductive. We began to check with each other about the rules we had and whether or not to apply them to situations that arose. In our CPS language, we were defining what belonged in Basket A and what did not. We were learning that most things, in fact, were not in Basket A. Daily showers were not in Basket A. Remember the criteria: There was no safety issue here. Personal hygiene was important, but it was not a matter of life and death. Kids are not hospitalized because of personal hygiene. And personal hygiene issues were usually dealt with over time, and often they were an indicator of something much larger (fear of the bathroom, fear of water, feeling depressed and not caring, being psychotic and not paying attention, etc.).

So we asked: What should we do if a child refuses to shower? First, what was our agenda? We wanted to keep the milieu calm. Second, we wanted to understand the child by answering the question: What is this child's deal? We wanted to understand as fully as we could the difficulties he or she was having that led to the child being here on our unit. Third, we believed that meltdowns were not good for kids. So we would not force the issue and insist that the child had to take a shower. We would let it go. We would ask him or her to shower (we had expectations), but if the child refused, we would put the issue in Basket C. It could be something minor that led to the refusal. At home, the child may have taken showers in the evening and that was the routine. In the evening, he or she might agree without any resistance. If the child refused showers for several days, then it would become a Basket B issue. We would want to have some dialogue with the child to understand his or her resistance to showers. Once we had more information, we would be able to determine if we wanted to develop interventions to help with this. It was what we were doing with our unmet expectations that were different in our new approach.

In our next supervision, various staff brought in examples of their attempts at Basket B. Several of us were finding that we thought we were doing Basket B interventions but that they quickly deteriorated into Basket A. We were starting to enter into collaborations with the children, but if we were not immediately successful, then we were presenting two choices and asking the child to pick one of them. In the language of CPS, this was not a Basket B intervention; it was a "nice A." We had a friendly dialogue, but the bottom line was that *we* were presenting the choices. The child was not collaborating; the child was expected to pick one of the choices we presented. As nice as it might have sounded, it was still Basket A. It was still an imposition of adult will, albeit in a friendly voice with a smile on your face.

Mary reported an incident with Pierre. Pierre woke up early every morning at about 6 A.M. and was very loud. The night staff became worried that he would wake up all the other children. Mary asked him what he thought would help him talk quietly. He reported, "If you allow me to play Gameboy, I will stay quiet." When questioned by Dr. Stuart Ablon in Thursday supervision, Mary said that although she went with this, she really didn't feel it would work. By going with this suggestion from Pierre, she was buying some time and she would be back in the same situation, with Pierre talking and yelling loudly in a short time. Stuart's advice to us was that if you feel a solution has only a 30 percent chance of working, then you needed to keep the collaboration going until a solution arose in which you had greater confidence in its working. If a child started to become agitated in the negotiating process, then we needed to go back to Step One and be empathetic, then make another invitation to help solve the problem. It was also important for us to share among ourselves what we had learned about the child. In this case, we hoped our work with Pierre would result in Pierre getting the message via our Basket B interventions, and that he would be able to say to himself, "I am a wonderful kid, but I get really loud and sometimes that affects other people. So I will ask to play Gameboy and then ask if there is someplace I can go to play with Gameboy so that if I get loud, I won't disturb other kids." This would not happen overnight and would be the result of a number of interactions over time. A realistic limiting factor was that we often had children on the unit for only a short time.

It was essential that the observations gained from our interactions would give us information that we would be able to share with the child and with those who would be caring for him after us. If we learned that Pierre needed a highly individualized plan that allowed for preparations for any transitions he was expected to make, and then we learned that a potential program was highly regimented and structured, we might question if that was the most appropriate program for him. If we observed that he not only talked very loud but that he also turned the TV up really loud, that might lead us to question: Did Pierre have an auditory problem? Was it a sensory issue? Did we need to have an occupational therapist do an evaluation to sort this out and determine if sensory problems were one of his areas of difficulty? Did we need to order an audiology consult to rule out a hearing problem?

We learned that when we were dealing with a child who quickly became perseverative, we were encouraged to try aggressive empathy to avoid "the broken record" syndrome. We would dramatically exaggerate our empathetic response:

Staff: "Pierre, do you want to take a bath?"

Pierre: **"No, I want to play!"**

Staff: **"Pierre, you really want to play now, not take a bath!"**

Pierre: **"No."**

Staff: "Let's see what we can do about working this out."

Pierre: **"I want to play!"**

Staff: "Pierre, you want to play. What if you played for the next ten minutes, and after that you took a bath?"

Pierre: **"If I can play for ten minutes, then I can do that."**

Staff: "That sounds good. When the big hand is on the eight of the clock, then you will agree to stop playing and take a bath."

Staff   "Pierre, the big hand is on the seven now. You have five minutes left."

Staff: "Pierre, the big hand is on the eight now. It is time to stop and take a bath."

In this scenario, it worked for Pierre. We initially collaborated with him. Then we gave him advance notice, warnings, and time to make a transition. Many kids with difficult behavior often exhibit cognitive rigidity and need time and preparation in order to shift gears. Teaching meant verbalizing what was happening: "You have a hard time making a switch from one thing to another."

Pierre was one of the first challenges for us in learning new ways of viewing behavior and managing behavior on the unit. He was the focus of our next group supervision with Ross.

What did we know about Pierre? He was an adopted child, and his mother loved him greatly and was a wonderful and persevering advocate for him. He had a tragic early life; he was born to a woman who was substance abusing, which resulted in his being removed from his home shortly after his birth. His biological mother was unable to care for him. Next, he experienced a number of moves through a series of foster homes. At his last foster home he suffered neglect again. He was placed with his adoptive mother, and they made several moves over the next four years. Even with this, he was doing well.

Then he had a precipitous decline in his functioning that initially was observed at school. He began to have trouble focusing and paying attention. He continued to worsen at school and was having meltdowns daily, at which point residential treatment was recommended. He was placed in a residential program, and in the seven months he was there, he was restrained more than sixty times. He was tried on a number of medications, and the program diagnosed him as being schizophrenic. It was recommended that care be continued at a state hospital. He was then placed in a long-term care residence, but the staff did not feel that he was appropriate for them. Pierre was therefore transferred to another residential program, and the plan was for him to be returned home to his mother within eighteen months. Along the way, he received diagnoses of bipolar disorder and Asperger's disorder. The last residential program saw his difficulties as developmental in nature rather than a schizophrenic illness. He was assaultive in this program, and staff members reported that he "required restraints" and had injured two staff people.

He came to us with the admonition that "he sets up situations so that he can be restrained." Our unit was asked to perform a diagnostic assessment and formulation and to make recommendations based on this assessment.

Pierre was a handsome eight-year-old African American boy with a stocky build and great big brown eyes. When he smiled, his eyes lit up and glimmered. He had a wonderful laugh that was contagious. It started deep in his belly and sounded melodic as it came out of his mouth. He was very lovable and engaging despite his challenging behaviors.

We observed early on that it was difficult to involve Pierre in verbal conversations. He was highly impulsive and quickly would get stuck with the desire to do a particular activity. He was not easily redirected. Staff continued reporting on their observations of Pierre.

> He hates to wear shoes; he even hates to wear socks; he doesn't like the way certain of his clothes feel and refuses to wear them. Most often, no matter how cold, he prefers to wear shorts. After wearing a shirt for an hour or so, he usually discards it and walks around with his shirt off. He does not like any clothing binding at his waist. He is very fussy about the way food looks and the way it feels. In fact, he has a short list of the foods he will eat. He is impulsive and darts up and down the unit. He pushes his way to the kitchen counter, shoving past kids and staff alike.

It was reported that he was held a few times over the weekend for hitting children who were in his way or who would not do what he wanted them to do. Staff described running interference for him as he walked down the hall, moving other children out of the way or gently guiding Pierre over a few inches as he neared someone. Staff had observed that Pierre appeared unaware of where his body was in space, and he did not seem aware of how close he was to people. He even seemed unaware when he had elbowed a child in his efforts to get to the lunch counter.

When questioned for observations about his mood, staff members identified it as being very labile, with fluctuations throughout the day ranging from irritable to happy to very angry. He was sometimes observed rubbing his body up and down on the pillars we have on both sides of our long unit hall. Some female staff reported that there were times he approached them in a way that felt uncomfortable, and that his hugs felt like a "mauling," while at other times he was able to give appropriate hugs. He appeared unaware of many social cues. He exhibited little awareness of the impact of his behavior on others. He was observed to have a difficult time with transitions.

Pierre would seek out social interactions but in a way that annoyed the other children on the unit. He tended to do things that upset the other kids so that they would see him and say to staff, "Don't let him touch me." His ability to concentrate on any one task was of very short duration. We observed that he even had difficulty persisting with an activity he liked, such as roller-blading up and down the hall.

These observations gave us more specific information, rather than our relying only on diagnosis to convey a picture of Pierre. We were to diagnose him with bipolar disorder and with some degree of pervasive developmental disorder. But in CPS language, we would identify his pathways to frustration and aggression as those of mood regulation, concrete rigid thinking, executive skills, and social skills.

In the CPS approach to viewing explosive or rigid behavior, the task is to identify a particular child's pathways to aggression that are deficits in cognitive thinking skills. Greene identifies the following pathways:

- **Executive skills deficit.** This includes a myriad of thinking skills necessary to problem solve, such as the use of working memory, understanding the relationship between cause and effect, understanding the impact of your behavior on others, the ability to delay impulses, the ability to focus, the ability to concentrate and organize your thoughts, the ability to learn from previous experiences and use information from the past to solve a problem in the present, etc. Many children with attention deficit disorder exhibit a lack in a number of the components of this skill deficit category.

- **Mood regulation.** This is the ability to control your moods, have normal moods, etc. Being sad, depressed, or constantly irritable makes it very difficult to problem solve and to come up with options and choices. Being anxious or having post-traumatic stress disorder impact heavily the ability to problem solve.

- **Concrete rigid thinking deficit.** This is an inability to be flexible and adapt. These are skills that are needed to problem solve. Children with this deficit need to have routines, structure, and predictability in their day in order to function, and they are thrown by any variation to the point of having meltdowns.

- **Social skills deficit.** This means being socially clueless, not being able to put yourself in another's shoes, being unaware of social context, not understanding the importance of reading facial and body cues, etc. This deficit makes it very difficult to interact socially and to problem solve around social interactions. People with this deficit often upset people without having any awareness of what they are doing to upset others.

- **Language deficits.** These include expressive, receptive language disorders. Lacking a "feelings" vocabulary makes it difficult to problem solve and creates frustration when a person is unable to fully comprehend what someone else has said or is unable to express what he or she would like to convey. Language is the vehicle we use to problem solve; therefore, a deficit in this area limits this ability and generates frustration.

This is a very rudimentary explanation, and I encourage readers to go right to the source. *The Explosive Child* gives a more extensive explanation of the pathways to aggression and the skills deficits linked to them.

Even more important was what we observed as Pierre's strengths, or things that he had going for himself. Pierre liked telling stories. He was able to entertain himself for long periods of time when he was stable. He had a desire to help others. Even when he was very challenging and requiring enormous staff time to prevent his meltdowns, he had an awareness of the unit and the structure we were providing. When a new child would come on the unit, Pierre would approach him or her and give the child a guided tour of the unit. He would point out all the daily routines and describe them accurately and in great detail, even though he often was not able to successfully partake of them. When he was doing well, Pierre was an avid reader. He was able to engage in a dialogue with us if we were not asking him to identify his feelings. In the classroom on the unit, our teacher, Amelia, reported that he was able to concentrate on his work for up to forty-five minutes.

After we had given our observations, Ross went out on the unit and observed Pierre in action. His observations were that Pierre seemed to be "an immediate need" kind of kid. Pierre appeared very uninhibited. Ross described watching Pierre on the unit and the staff running interference to prevent his banging into other kids. He described it as the staff serving as his "Ritalin," being vigilant to prevent collisions. He appeared highly impulsive and excited by high stimulation but was unable to handle it. Ross suggested that we needed a better description from his mother as to how Pierre looked when he was doing well and more details about his precipitous decline.

Since his ability to negotiate verbally with us was limited, our interactions with him in Basket B would involve our acting as his "surrogate frontal lobe." This meant that he might not be able to participate in lining up alternatives to be examined, weighed, and decided upon. It would be up to us in our collaboration with him to provide a list of alternatives—to verbalize pros and cons of various choices out loud so that he could engage with us in making decisions and problem solving. Ross suggested that we prioritize a

few big areas to work on with him while he was with us. We identified his impulsivity, his instigating (getting the other kids going),
and his hyperactivity.

In dealing with Pierre's disinhibition, we needed to look at
what might be driving it. Was it that he was propelled by needing
to satisfy his immediate needs? Was he able to reflect, hold on to
insight, and have empathy? Before we designed interventions, we
needed more information. It was important for us to determine
his ability to be reflective. If he had a significant capacity for reflection and insight, then his prognosis would be much more opti-
mistic. We needed to determine at what times he had some understanding of his actions and at what times he showed empathy.
How long was he able to hold on to these qualities? Was it longer
than thirty seconds?

Ross said that to what degree we pushed the Basket B envelope was dependent upon our assessment of Pierre's capacity to
reflect and have insight. If Pierre was so uninhibited that he was
not able to hold on to anything, then we would need to create an
environment that was extremely anticipatory. We would start with
short parameters and widen them as we assessed that he was able
to do more. We would try to keep him in line with unit goals and
activities without pushing him so hard that he would have a meltdown. An example is: "Pierre, I know it is going to be hard to stay
in group. Let's give it a whirl. How much time do you think you
can last? Ten minutes?"

Our job was to identify how to help Pierre break out of his
explosive cycles without resorting to restraints. What had we
found helpful so far? The more neutral we were in working with
him, the more information we would be able to obtain. This
would help us with our interventions.

Pierre was with us for more than four months. He then went
to an intensive residential treatment program for about a year. We
heard that he did very well there and returned home to live with
his mother.

CHAPTER 5

OPEN HOURS:
Working With Parents

• *Sam* •

*"Coming together is a beginning. Keeping together is
progress. Working together is success."*

— Henry Ford

In our discussions about creating a nurturing environment for
the children, the issue of parents' presence on the unit came up.
I had been trying to steer the conversation in the direction of
looking at what creates a child-centered program. Parents are
the most important people in a child's life, and they belong with
the child, especially when the child is under a lot of stress. And
when you are considering situations that are stress-generating, a
child being placed in a locked psychiatric unit has to be at the
top of the charts. It did not matter that we were trying to create
an environment that was different from traditional models—

being hospitalized is stressful and scary to children. We needed to consider the presence of parents and families as an essential component in the creation of a nurturing and child-centered environment.

From a family-centered perspective, how could we state in good faith that we were trying to develop partnerships with parents when we had relegated them to secondary status in the lives of their children while they were here with us? "Visiting hours" was a term that packed a punch. If parents were our partners in caring for the children of the unit and we were serious about that, then we had to incorporate the principles of family-centered care (FCC) in all aspects of our program. FCC was a philosophy of care based on four principles that were simple in their description but more complicated in terms of implementation. FCC involved looking at many aspects of the care we provided in a different way.

The first principle was that "people must be treated with dignity and respect."[5] That did not seem like earth-shattering news. Yet in order to think seriously about the way we related with parents, we needed to take a closer look. Being respectful meant believing that a parent's time was as valuable as ours. On a concrete level, this meant that if we scheduled a meeting for 2 P.M., we had to consider whether that time worked for the parents, or if we picked it because three staff members on the child's treatment team were free at that time and we expected parents to alter their schedules to accommodate us. Did we start meetings on time, or did we make parents wait ten minutes while we strategized a plan for directing the meeting? That was not respectful.

The second principle of FCC was that health-care providers must communicate with and share complete and unbiased information with patients and families in ways that are affirming and useful.[6] This is what you would expect from any program that was purporting to have expertise in family treatment. What was more difficult to assess was something more subtle. Did we *think of* parents in ways that were affirming and useful? That could be challenging in some cases. One of the messages we learned as we were developing our expertise in collaborative problem solving helped us with this. We tried to remember that, in situations that lent themselves to a judgmental stance, "parents would do well if they could, too." So, if we were having difficulty with a parent and were not in agreement regarding our understanding of a child and what we felt the child needed, and this was in contrast to a different view held by a parent, we needed to step back and try to understand the parent's perspective and see if there were areas where we could agree and then build on that. We were not always successful. If we perceived that a parent was giving up on a child or stepping back from involvement with the child, it was hard for us to keep our perspective that the parent was trying as hard as it was possible for him or her. This proved to be an ongoing challenge. We usually had at least one child on the unit at any time whose parents' involvement was much less than we desired. It took work to resist the urge to want to "rescue" the child. Developing a rescue mentality hindered our work and did not help in building relationships. We needed to be watchful of this when working with vulnerable children to avoid the development of insidious repercussions. This mentality tended to grow and had the potential to infect our work, our objectivity, and our effectiveness.

The third principle was that individuals and families should be supported to build on their strengths and participate in experiences that enhanced their control and independence in the process of receiving care.[7] This was a perfect statement to support parents being able to spend as much time on the unit as possible. They would be able to see us in action and see how we intervened when a child became frustrated and upset. They would be more likely to ask questions, and we would have more opportunities to engage in a dialogue about being collaborative with children. Their increased presence would provide many opportunities to engage in discussions about our strategy to "pick our battles" about what areas we thought were important and indicated an area for teaching a child skills to better manage frustration. Our whole approach was about helping children learn the skills they would need to problem solve on their own. That was the essence of developing independence.

The fourth principle of FCC was that collaboration among patients, families, and providers should occur in policy and program development and professional education, as well as in the delivery of care.[8] How could we get to this level of parental involvement and inclusion without having parents with us all the time?

I began talking about what it would look like to have parents on the unit with us at any and all times. Some staff said that they really hadn't considered what it would be like. Other staff admitted to feeling uncomfortable with the idea. When asked to elaborate, they mentioned a number of possible concerns: We would have too many people on the unit; it would interfere with their getting their work done; it would feel self-conscious to be interacting with the kids while parents were present; and what if the parents were critical—how would they be expected to "handle it"; lastly, it would be chaotic.

I was glad we were talking about this and putting concerns on the table. In my heart, as well as in my head, I knew that the only way to go was to open up the unit to parents and significant persons in the child's life. It was putting our values to the test. We had been telling parents that we wanted to partner with them and that we were all about collaboration. Yet we still had an archaic visiting policy, with restrictions and limitations. We were like most other psych units—visiting times were determined to cause the least hassle for the staff and to avoid interference with unit routines for the children. If I was being honest, I would have to say that, in general, visiting hours were viewed as a necessary annoyance.

This was not in the least family-centered. Parents were dealing with the stress of a child having been psychiatrically hospitalized. That, in and of itself, was a huge event in the family's life. Many parents worked and had other children at home. And we expected them to juggle a job, other kids, and the stress of having a child hospitalized. To make matters even worse, we prescribed when they could "visit" their child, and the visiting hours were usually at the most inconvenient times. On our unit, that time was from 4:00 P.M. to 6:30 P.M. It interfered with a nine-to-five workday, and it ran into the dinner hour for families. This time frame may have worked for us, but it was not in the least bit convenient for parents. I also thought to myself, what right did we have to tell parents when they could see and not see their child? I knew that if it had been me and my young child, I would have been perceived as difficult, at best, in questioning this policy. I would have put up quite a fight about these restrictive hours. It was inconsistent with all that we were trying to do. We needed to have parents on the unit. More importantly, their children needed them here.

I talked with my administrative partner, Vic, and said we needed to do this and it was time. We needed to set a date and tell everyone that part of our change in culture meant we were partnering with parents and letting parents come whenever they could. He agreed. I broached the issue at one of our nursing staff meetings and set the official date for the next week. I was asked if this meant that parents could stay all day long. Yes, it did. I was asked if this meant that a parent could spend the night. Yes, it did. I was asked if this meant that more than one set of parents could be spending the night. Yes, it did. Opening up the unit to parents meant that parents could come whenever they wanted, for as long as they wanted.

Where would they sleep? I ordered some extra mattresses. We became highly creative. Most parents slept in the bedroom where their child was sleeping. We arranged rooms so that if a child whose parent was sleeping over was in a double room, then we would assign roommates so that the other child slept in the hall near staff and was not interested in sleeping in the bedroom. This was not unusual; we frequently had several children at any given time who preferred to sleep on a mattress in the hall in view of staff. There were occasions when we had two mothers sleeping over, and they shared a double room and slept in the room with their children together. The first time we had a parent who started the night on a mattress in the room and ended up in the bed with the child, a staff person reported the event as inappropriate. There was some inference of a sexual connotation. I and several of the other staff who were mothers met this criticism head-on, stating it was natural and normal for a parent to sleep with a child and comfort him or her. We compared it to parents having a sick child climb into bed with them.

We were often asked: What do you do if the parent has been abusive to the child? We never witnessed any parent being abusive to a child while sleeping over. The reality was that if a parent had been abusive to a child, that child was usually in the custody of the child protective services and was not residing with the parent. Children who were in state custody had parental contact determined by the social worker of the child protective agency, and those parents often had very limited visiting. Those parents were not sleeping over. We had a few situations where the parent wanted to spend time in a child's room privately, and we had to explain the nature of working together and our policy of checking on every child every five minutes, day in and day out, and being able to determine what they were doing and with whom.

This was our five-minute checks policy, and having the children on such close supervision really freed us up to be innovative, as we had backup documentation of where everyone was the entire time they were with us. It freed us from liability concerns.

In the few cases where a child made allegations of sexual miscon-duct about another child or a staff member, we had a document that showed where every child was for every five-minute interval, and I would be able to do an investigation and report that the alle-gation was not true based on the "check sheet." This showed that, at the time of the alleged incident, the child was in the day hall with four other children and not in a bathroom with the alleged "abuser."

We printed signage for the lobby and began our "Open Hours" program. Staff members who had some hesitancy and feared this change were relieved to find that the issue of the unit becoming chaotic never materialized. It was a non-issue, and in a matter of weeks, it was as if we had been doing this all along. What did become a challenge was dealing with our emotions over the children whose parents were not involved or rarely present. That proved to be the most difficult aspect for us. The staff became very creative in cases where a child had no parental involvement. A staff person would take the child off the unit when a lot of parents were present, and they would arrange special staff visits with a child when we had a number of parents present. They would bring in special items for the child who had no one coming to see him or her. Some children had social workers from the child protective agency who had followed a child for a number of years, and some of them were wonderful. They appreciated how devastating it was to be on an inpatient unit and feel like there was no one in your corner. Several of these people made sure that they visited on a regular basis, and they often brought gifts or clothing items for the child.

One of my most poignant memories of the rightness of parents sleeping over is depicted in the story of Antonio. He was a twelve-year-old boy who was admitted for "out-of-control behavior" at home and in school, and he also had a history of school truancy. He had an older brother who was in juvenile detention. His mom was overwhelmed as a single mom trying to raise two boys while dealing with her own diagnosis of having terminal-stage AIDS. Their home was chaotic, and we suspected that they may have been homeless or on the verge of homelessness.

We tried to engage Antonio's mom, but she was hard to reach, and often her cell phone was disconnected. She had given us several different phone numbers, but when we called, the person answering the phone would indicate that Antonio's mom did not live there, and the person had no idea where she was. Antonio had been explosive and angry at home and was not listening to his mom, and she was at a loss as to how to deal with his behavior. As we built a relationship with Antonio, we learned that his explosiveness and anger were tied to his frustration at knowing that his mother was dying. He was anxious and worried. She had not discussed this with him directly, but he had heard her talk with others on the phone and he was aware that her mental status had changed. In fact, when they were together, he acted parentified—cueing her and worrying about her responses to us. He was very protective of her. Part of our job would be helping them with services in the community, including housing—*if* we could facilitate Antonio's mom confiding in us about needing a place for them to live. We also wanted to learn what, if any, supports she had available and what other agencies or relatives could provide them with help.

A larger part of our work was helping her understand that Antonio's difficulties and out-of-control behavior were the only way he knew how to deal with his anxiety and grief over her terminal illness. We let her know how important she was in his life and how much he needed her to be present for him. The result was his asking her to stay and spend as many nights as she could with him. He wanted to sleep in the hall, and he asked if she could sleep at the end of the hall with him. We gave him two mattresses to set up at the end of the hall. They put the mattresses together, and he fell asleep with a smile on his face, cradled in her arms.

When I was asked by some staff if this was alright, my response was that it was more than alright. She was giving him the gift of warm memories that he could carry with him after she was gone.

We had one occasion when a father asked us if he could bring in his hospitalized son's two younger brothers for a "camp out" on a Friday evening so that they would know that their brother was okay. We arranged for the four of them to sleep in our family room for the night.

Usually we have only one or two parents sleeping over at a time. Our banner night occurred when we had five parents sleeping over. The nurse in charge that night had to borrow two additional mattresses from elsewhere in the hospital.

It was an adjustment for us to be more closely involved with parents and to be sharing the unit with them. Sam and his family were a case in point. Sam was a nine-year-old boy who was admitted with the usual reasons of "being out of control at school and assaulting his mother at home." These incidents had increased in frequency the three weeks leading up to his hospitalization with us. Sam's parents reported that he had been spiraling downward over the past year.

Sam's mother slept over the first night and was spending a lot of time on the unit. The staff had observed that Sam was having more frequent meltdowns when his mother was present on the unit, and these meltdowns usually occurred as she prepared to leave. When he began to get frustrated, his mother became increasingly anxious. Sam's mother was also very vigilant and appeared to hover nearby when staff were interacting with her son. We had observed that when Sam began to get frustrated and make demands on his mother, she was quick to grant his request, even when some of his requests seemed unreasonable to us. We suspected that she was probably in Basket C much of the time at home and, when overwhelmed, she would jump into Basket A, which would result in Sam's having a total meltdown. This was not unusual. When a child became increasingly difficult to manage and you feared his becoming angry, it was easy to decide that it was not worth the struggle and to just not bother to make it an issue. The problem was that the child would soon learn that this was the modus operandi, and he or she would make more and more unreasonable demands. At some point, the parent was pushed beyond his or her capacity to deal with the demands and would decide "enough" and would say "no." The result was predictable in most situations. The child would have a full-blown meltdown.

Our job was to determine why Sam was having such a difficult time and to develop an understanding of the pathways that led to his aggression (i.e., what thinking skill deficits were lacking, causing him to become frustrated and unable to problem solve, leading to a meltdown). Our assessment would involve:

- Determining if medication could help him so that he would be more able to function.

- Determining if his school placement was suitable in meeting his particular needs.

- Determining if there was a better approach in understanding Sam that we could share with his parents so that they, too, were better able to meet his needs.

In order to do this, we needed some time to see Sam interacting with us and with other kids on the unit. We needed to assess him in different situations to learn under what circumstances he became frustrated. We needed some time with him without his mother present. We needed for her to trust us enough that she could leave and not worry about our care of her son. We also wanted her to have some small opportunity to rest and take a break and restore herself. His mother was very worried that the hospitalization would, in and of itself, be a traumatic event in Sam's life and thus make him worse. This was a natural concern, and we needed to have her trust so that she could entrust her son to us.

Sam became the subject of our group supervision that week. One staff person piped up with: "Let's talk about Sam; he makes one hair-brained suggestion after another!" Ross asked us to give an example. Ashley came forward and said: "I can tell about my going to give him some meds. I said to Sam, 'I have your meds.' He said, 'I want my mom to give me my meds.' I said to him, 'That's okay with me, but I need to watch you take the meds.' Sam responded, 'I won't take them if you are watching; you need to turn around and walk down the hall to where the rug turns blue.'" Ashley asked how she could have approached this differently. Ross commended her on the "nice A" approach but said that a Basket B approach would have gone something like this:

"Here's your meds."

"I don't want to take them from you!"

"You don't want to take them from me."

"My mom can give me my meds."

"Let's see how we can do this. We need to find some way for your mom to give you the meds and for me to watch you take them. How could we do this?"

With Sam, we needed to keep in our consciousness what our goal was and how we could reach it. He needed us to be concrete about what the goal was. Ross shared another possible scenario:

"Hi Sam, I have your 4 o'clock meds."

"I want my mom to give the meds."

"You want your mom to give the meds. Your mom is not here and it is time for your 4 o'clock meds. Let's see what we can do about that. Do you have any ideas how we can work this out? Sam, what if I put the meds on the table and you take the meds?"

Our goal was to try and prevent Sam from getting into the mode where he was yelling, enraged, and inflexible. So we needed to find out how and why he got into that mode.

We needed to get his mom on board with us and with what we were trying to do. We needed to remember that she worried that if the hospitalization was not a positive experience, it would damage her son's emotional health further. As a parent, it is normal to be vigilant of people caring for your child. We had to allay her anxieties so that she could feel that Sam was safe here and that our approach would not hurt him. (Sometimes it helps to imagine that this was your own child and how you would feel; at other times this is an obstacle rather than an asset. If you have particular concerns or values and they are different from the values or concerns of another, then your imagining being in their place may take you further away from understanding their concerns, not bring you closer.)

We needed to talk to Sam's mother about this. We could approach it with: "Let's not waste the hospital stay. We need to see Sam with you, and we need to see him without you." We would need to share our goals with her so that she understood what we were trying to do. The goals we would share with Sam's mother would be:

1. We wanted to medically stabilize Sam so that he had a longer fuse.

2. We wanted to help him melt down more adaptively. (i.e., so that he did not get completely out of control. He was physically held a lot at school and we did not want to do that here— were there things we could say that would prevent him from totally melting down?)

3. We did not want him to waste meltdowns. (We wanted Sam's mother to be thinking: "I know what they are doing—they are trying to learn what caused the meltdown, what set him off, and what calms him down. Is he able to do any Basket B after he has become frustrated?)

4. We were trying to get Basket B going for Sam. His mother needed to understand our program. We needed to be honest that there might be a few extreme situations where a child could get held briefly here, and there were some things that we did not do in Basket C—that we would rather do in Basket B.

In the next supervision, Stuart suggested that we should acknowledge with his mom that Sam was anxious and that for a child his age, it was not uncommon to have difficulty with transitions and separations. We should acknowledge that we saw him having difficulty and becoming upset when she left but that we were able to distract him within a short time. At that point, he was able to put the anxiety out of his mind. Our job involved helping her when Sam began to act up and to help her learn when and how he was able to do well. We could do this by helping in the interactions between them and seeing if we could assist them in working things out without Sam having a full-blown meltdown. We also needed to acknowledge that many explosive kids were able to behave well in certain circumscribed situations, but at home they were explosive and their behavior was difficult to manage. This was due to the special role and importance that goes with the turf of being a parent.

In working with Sam's parents, we agreed with their request that Sam be discharged to our partial hospitalization program so that he could be present on the unit for programming during the day and be home at night. As this was important to his parents, we accepted this request despite having some reservations that Sam was ready for this step. He did well the first day, but on the second day of the partial hospitalization, he had a difficult time at home with several meltdowns and became assaultive with his mother in the car on the way to the hospital. At this point Sam's mother was able to say, "He needs to go back to inpatient," and she was no longer ambivalent about this. We set a goal and a time frame—one week that would include daily family therapy sessions.

How did we see Sam? We saw him as sad and depressed. He was inadvertently parentified. He had not chosen to act as the adult in the family. He was not enjoying the role of having the most authority at home, but he was habituated into it. We worked with his parents to help them see that Sam's overpowered role was exacerbating his anxiety and depression. They needed to step up and realign the family structure, and Sam's mother was going to need a lot of help from her husband.

Our job entailed helping Sam reclaim his childhood. Our work with the parents was helping them embrace their role as parents who were capable of managing the family. We were able to help both parents see that Sam was the reflector of the tension and anger between them. We were also able to help Sam's mom see a continuum where she was able to draw a line for herself when it was no longer feasible to give in to Sam's requests. We developed a stronger relationship of trust and were able to draw some parallels between trauma Sam's mother had experienced in her earlier life and her feeling traumatized by Sam's behavior and demands upon her. We worked to help her identify good decisions and receive our support for those decisions. We were able to draw her husband in to become more involved and to take a step back from his demanding job to provide more support to his wife. We helped Sam's mom redefine her definition of being a good mom for Sam and what that entailed. We depicted for her a continuum that looked like this:

Continuum

Giving to Sam	^	Taking care of self

We helped her find a balance.

Less you think that we were always successful in our collaborations with parents, I will tell you about Abraham. Here was a situation where we were *not* successful in working with a parent as a partner in caring for her child.

Abraham was a seven-year-old Haitian-American boy who was admitted to the unit for being "out of control at home and at school." He was very assaultive to his mother and, upon admission, we had to separate them as he repeatedly tried to hit, kick, and bite his mom. Her response was to scream at us to leave him alone and that we should not intervene. She did not want us to lay hands on him, even if it meant she would be continually assaulted. This was a case that tested our ideals about partnering with parents to the hilt! Initially, the staff held back as Abraham continued to assault his mom while she tried to embrace him so that he could not gain purchase to swing at her. The staff were shaken. Every single one reported to me the awful sense of futility in seeing Abraham in a meltdown, assaulting his mother while they stood helpless at her side.

It was easy for us to see Abraham's mother's love and devotion to her son. She would spend the night, she would insist on washing his clothes, she wanted to know every detail of how he spent his day. He was well-kept, had good hygiene and manners, and was well-nourished—all reflections of her care and values. She wanted to be the one to supervise him bathing; she wanted to bring in clean clothes for him daily. It took us a little longer to see the signs of his devotion and caring for her. Initially, we had a hard time seeing beyond his repeated attempts to yell at her and hit her when she did not accede to his demands immediately. We saw that he anxiously awaited her arrival after a phone call from her stating she was on her way and that he was to wait to eat until she arrived with his breakfast.

We thought we were establishing some rapport with her initially. Then we began to identify areas where we were not working together. We had to talk with her about her son's assaulting her and our responsibility to make sure everyone on the unit was safe— and that included her. We also let her know that her son was assaulting staff and other children when she was not present and that was not okay. Therefore, we would be intervening when we saw him attempt to assault anyone, and that included her. Her response was that she did not want the male staff to lay hands on him, and she requested that we "tie him down in a chair." We let her know that this was not an option. We talked of medication that might help him become less aggressive. She was adamantly opposed to medication, other than using Benadryl for his agitation.

Then we noticed that she was instructing Abraham not to eat any of the food the unit provided but to wait for her to arrive with food from home. She would approach me to complain of various staff members and report that they were harming her son. When I pressed for her to provide specific details, she would retort that I knew what she was talking about. In the first weeks of Abraham's hospitalization, his mother appeared to be developing a good rapport with Lily, the social work supervisor who had been assigned to her case, so we had great hopes of this relationship working to cement a partnership.

Then things began to spiral on a downward course. She would instruct Abraham not to shower unless she was present and not to wear any clothes except the ones she brought. She was only bringing in one outfit at a time, so we had no reserves from his personal clothing items. Sometimes she would not come for a day or two, and that placed Abraham in a bind, as she had told him not to eat, bathe, brush his teeth, or get dressed unless she was there providing the items he needed. We also observed that he was calmer and less agitated when she was not on the unit. When she was present, she whispered to him and put papers up to cover the window in his bedroom so that we could not see in. Her complaints about his being abused by staff continued. Her mental state appeared to be deteriorating. She refused to give us a phone number where she could be reached, and the number she gave the admissions department was not valid. She would not allow us to contact any other relative. She started coming to the unit in an agitated manner and would talk loudly in the hallways—sometimes to the point of ranting. Abraham was embarrassed and would become angry with his mother when she was in this state. She became upset that a hat of his had been washed by the staff of the unit. She insisted that the staff were performing voodoo upon his clothing and that he was not to wear any clothing that we had touched, especially hats.

She began to avoid scheduled meetings. Abraham had a younger sister at home, and sometimes his mother would come to the unit at 9 P.M. after he was asleep and demand that we wake him so that she could spend some time with him. His sister would fall asleep in the waiting room.

We discussed the case at length, as we were in a quandary. We believed in open hours for parents, but we were thinking of restricting her contact to reasonable hours and to limit the amount of time she would be on the unit, as her presence was upsetting to her son and to the other children when she was agitated. We arranged for a member of our outpatient Haitian team to come to our clinical meeting to advise us. His opinion was that this was beyond a simple case of clashing cultural values. He felt that her behavior was indicative of her own mental problems and not attributable to our lack of understanding of Haitian culture.

Next, I brought the case to the hospital Ethics Committee. The unanimous opinion of the committee was that we needed help and we should contact the child protective agency. We also needed to restrict her visitation. Committee members also felt that we should try and supervise the visits as much as possible. We had been in contact with the child protective agency, had expressed our concern, and had relayed specific instances where we were worried that Abraham's mother's ability to care for her son was compromised by her own mental illness.

Once we had filed a report with this child welfare agency, our already poor relationship with her deteriorated further. She felt we had betrayed her, and she saw Lily, myself, and others as having been influenced by the staff whom she thought were evil. She felt we had been brainwashed. The child protective agency went to court and ultimately took custody of Abraham. The result of this event was that his mother was no longer able to work with us in any semblance of cooperation. Abraham was discharged to a short-term residential treatment center, and we hoped that this program would have more success in building a relationship with his mother. It was our hope that she would agree to mental health services and work cooperatively with the protective child agency so that their family could be reunited.

Here were two cases in which we tried to partner with parents in a collaborative way. In one case we were successful, and in another we were not. Abraham's situation reflected the difficulty in collaboration when a parent's problems were as great as if not greater than those of her child. It also involved our having to notify a protective agency of our concerns about a parent's current ability to parent successfully. It jeopardized our tenuous hold on a working relationship. For Sam's parents, we were able to forge an alliance that worked and that benefited Sam's family as a whole.

Sam's parents were an example of parents who came to us with clear expectations and held us to our values and beliefs. Sam's mother was one of a few parents who had specifically chosen our unit because she had heard that we were not using mechanical restraints or seclusion and that we were open to parents. These parents were more informed and came with an agenda to be involved and to be seen as partners. They observed us and gave us feedback. They let us know what we were doing well and what they appreciated about us. They also let us know where we were weak. I received a phone call from a parent of a child who had been on the unit, and so did Ross. In both instances, we received much praise for our efforts. However, both parents commented that 95 percent of the staff appeared to be on board, but there were 5 percent of the staff who definitely were not on board, and what were we planning to do about that?

We shared this in the group supervision and put the question out to the group: What do you say to parents who observe the reality and they articulate it and give us their feedback? This generated discussion on the larger issue: What do we do with the people who are not on board yet? Something needed to happen—at this point it was time to move ahead with a unified approach.

We identified possible reasons why some staff were not yet on board. Some people continued to have misconceptions about what we were doing because they had not been attending the group supervision sessions. And others were lacking in understanding and skill development because they had missed the group supervision sessions and were not even reading the notes on the sessions. The question before us was that if they were bypassing the process the rest of us were engaged in because they did not agree, then what should we do about this?

The staff response was that we needed to be consistent in our approach and that it should not change shift by shift. Some staff responded that it was crazy for parents and kids—above and beyond being confusing for the staff. They went on to iterate that it was causing a lot of staff tension when they had to work a shift with staff members who were not on board with the changes. One staff person said it went further than that: "You dread a shift where you know there will be tension and where someone is continuing to work under the old ways and you worry you will be directed to do something—like set an unnecessary limit with a child—that you do not agree with and do not want to implement."

Staff members suggested that the leaders of the unit should sit down and talk one-on-one with the staff who did not appear to be on board. Another suggestion was that shifts end with a wrap-up where staff members would critique what went well and what did not go well. There could be an analysis or assessment to determine if the difficulties on a particular shift were caused by too much Basket A and if any situation could have been better handled in Basket B, etc. Someone suggested that we develop formal evaluations of staff for CPS skills, and that staff perform self-evaluations of CPS skills. Another suggestion was that we develop a mini task force to develop a CPS wrap-up sheet to fill out at the end of each shift. Two staff members volunteered to work on this last item.

I did follow up on a number of these suggestions. I had conversations with staff members who were not implementing CPS about our new values in their everyday practice. Some were counseled as part of the job performance evaluation process, and in those areas that were identified as "Needs Improvement," we developed action plans and follow-up sessions. For some, this was the start of a process for out-counseling. Some staff members caught up with the group by having shift mentors, who were assigned to assist them and provide more hands-on supervision. I developed a CPS competency that all staff on the unit were expected to perform and pass. This became one of our standard unit-based competencies. A CPS 1 competency was given to all staff working on the unit and was to be given to new employees after working on the unit for three months. Later I developed a CPS 2 competency that involved a more comprehensive understanding of CPS skills and pathways. This became a unit-based competency for all staff who had worked more than one year on the unit.

CHAPTER 6

THE END OF THE ASSAULT PROTOCOL

• Darrin •

"All progress is precarious, and the solution of one problem brings us face-to-face with another problem."

— *Martin Luther King, Jr.*

The next supervision time started with an incident that involved Pierre but that evolved into a much larger issue and pushed us another step further along our journey to change the way we provided care.

This supervision was started late, as Vic, the medical director, Ross, and I were at a meeting in Boston. We returned late to find that the unit had been somewhat paralyzed in determining what to do about an event that had occurred that morning. It was a classic example of a clash between our new thinking running head-first into the barriers of our old structure.

71

The children were involved in a physical group activity on the unit. We often had indoor physical activities when the weather was too cold or rainy, etc. The kids were playing dodgeball. Dodgeball was an amazing activity to me. When I first observed it, I thought it was insane to attempt a game such as this with a group of kids who were all explosive. The game involves someone throwing a ball at the players who are lined up and trying to move down the hall. The object of the game is to be the last person standing. You are eliminated by being hit with the ball. So it is a game where at one time or another all but one person will be hit by the ball and eliminated. I was amazed to observe that the kids loved this game.

Andy was running the group, and he reported that all was going well until a boy named Darrin was hit on the head with the ball by another child. Immediately following this, Darrin was hit on the shoulder by the ball when Pierre threw the ball at someone else and missed. Darrin grabbed the ball and then quickly went up to Pierre and hit him forcibly in the face with his fist. Earlier in the day, Darrin had been annoyed with Pierre's behavior and had remarked, "I'm going to punch that kid in the face." Because of this remark, some of the staff thought the later incident had been premeditated.

After the assault, two staff members walked Darrin to the Quiet Room, and he remained there for approximately three hours with the door open. He made no attempt to exit, and at one point when staff checked on him, he was sleeping. At another point, he was given a Gameboy to play, and he also requested and was given a book that he had been reading. None of the staff who interacted with him felt that he appeared in any way distressed. When his mother arrived on the unit, he began crying and told her he had been there for several hours.

The dilemma for the staff was that they felt a serious assault had occurred, and they were unclear how to handle the incident.

Under our old unit structure, there was a very clear and specific way to deal with assaults. It was called the assault protocol. Under this protocol, when a child assaulted another child, he or she was taken to the Quiet Room. When the child calmed down and could talk about the incident with staff, he or she was allowed to leave the room. If the child resisted staying in the room, the door was closed and the child would then be considered to be in locked-door seclusion. (If a child resisted going to the Quiet Room and continued to be assaultive, the child was often placed in four-point mechanical restraints on a bed in the Quiet Room.) The child was expected to apologize verbally or in writing at the next community meeting, which was held every day. The child was also put on a room schedule with alternating times in and out of his or her room for twenty-four hours. The child lost all privileges and had to re-earn them.

It was clear that this dinosaur of a procedure no longer worked for us. The staff were aware of this, but they had nothing in their tool kit that they thought could be used as an alternative. And since we had not specifically discussed what to do about the assault protocol, they were in a quandary. As a result, they left Darrin in the Quiet Room awaiting our return so that we could help them figure this out. Unfortunately, we were all off the unit when the event occurred.

The solution upon our return was simple. We discussed the assault protocol and its inconsistency with our perspective on managing children's aggression. We made a decision to eliminate this procedure, as it no longer made any sense. I spoke with Darrin's mother and apologized to him in front of her. He had not needed to be in the Quiet Room all that time. He was caught up in the unevenness of our process to change our structure.

If you looked at the elements of the assault protocol, most of them were well-intentioned and consistent with traditional consequence-based approaches for managing aggression.

The protocol was designed to remove the child from the conflict and give him or her a time to calm down. The mechanical restraint/seclusion response to assaults was an attached adjunct and not specifically listed in the protocol, and it had to do with continued assaultiveness. It had not been used in this situation. Once the child calmed down and was able to talk with staff about the event that occurred, he or she was free to return to his or her room.

The apology for transgressions was a controversial subject. Some staff thought it was very important to teach the child about social justice and life lessons. They felt that this moral teaching was a part and parcel of the job. It is not mentioned in any job description that I have seen for milieu or nursing positions. But wanting children to develop a social conscience is a laudable goal. What was hard for me to see was how you foster a social conscience when the method sometimes involves embarrassment and more than that. The expected response becomes rote rather than a genuinely felt emotional state.

During my first three months on the unit, I observed many of these apologies being made at community meetings. The more I watched, the more uncomfortable I became. First of all, if you were not able to agree to do this, then you could not attend the community meeting. (On some days, this was not a bad idea, for often the kids' idea of participatory democracy was wrapped up in a daily critique of the state of the bathrooms and who had left pee where!) I watched child after child get up and read his or her apology and I was struck by how many of them lacked any spontaneity or genuineness. I thought that the forced quality was really teaching children how to get along with the system rather than helping them with a real sense of understanding the impact of their behavior on others. Other kids were so ashamed and embarrassed that they resisted the apology for days. For those children, I thought the focus should be on helping them lighten up and not be so hard on themselves. Group apology was not the answer for them either.

The next consequence embedded in the assault protocol was that every time the unit had a quiet-time activity, the assault protocol dictated that you spend that time in your room by yourself. This occurred for one day. Not earth shattering, but I felt that there was a subtle degree of ostracizing here. And I thought that this was not the way to teach understanding, tolerance, or kindness. Nor did I feel that this was the role of a psychiatric hospitalization.

Lastly, you had to earn all your privileges back. This meant that if you were able to go off grounds and a field trip was scheduled for that Friday, you had to wait a week to be eligible for the field trip. That seemed a long time and extreme as a consequence.

The assault protocol no longer made sense to us and conflicted with the approach we were all trying to develop and master. It died a quick death that day.

The discussion of the assault protocol led us to another conundrum. When a child was becoming upset, the usual tendency was to pull his or her privileges—you held the child close because you were afraid that he or she would lose control—the reasoning being that the child needed to be contained. We were finding that just the opposite was true. When a child was upset, often the best way to calm things down was to get the child off the unit for awhile. A staff person would take a child for a walk and often a talk, and the potential meltdown became a non-issue. We were finding that taking a child out and off the unit was meeting with good results and was often effective in helping a child calm down.

The event with Darrin brought home some of the somewhat scary aspects of major change. While we were learning new ways of doing things and handling situations, we sometimes felt at a loss. Old tried and true interventions from the past did not seem compatible with what we were doing, but we were still beginners. We did not as yet have a large supply of new tools to replace the old ones that we did not want to use or had consciously discarded. This is probably a factor in why people often resist the thought of changing ways of doing things. On some level, we all know that it will not be easy. And old ways of doing things, even if they are problematic, are comfortable and predictable. Changing means being thrown into the unknown until the changeover becomes familiar.

SECTION TWO

Reaching a "Tipping Point"

CHAPTER 7

THE UNIT HEATS UP: MULTIPLE MELTDOWNS

*"The challenge of leadership is to be strong, but not rude;
be kind, but not weak; be bold, but not bully;
be thoughtful, but not lazy; be humble, but not timid;
be proud, but not arrogant; have humour,
but without folly."*

— John Rohn

We were now at the point where we viewed ourselves as having eased in to a new way of doing things. Slowly, we were beginning to develop some confidence in what we were doing. A number of the staff felt good about our new approach. There was another group of staff who were not yet convinced that this was the way to go. They weren't opposed; they were still reserving judgment and observing the staff who were giving it their all in trying to master the new approach.

The unit heated up. Most people who have worked on inpatient units know the phenomenon of having a "bad mix" and how that can wreak havoc on the milieu. In fact, it takes concerted work to keep on top of things to prevent the emergence of chaos. We now had such a mix. We had four children on the unit who were highly explosive and not yet stabilized. It was our job to assist them in becoming "workable." This meant that we needed to learn a lot about them quickly so that we could determine at which points they became frustrated and then explosive. On top of that, we had a mix of children who not only did not get along with one another; they were rubbing each other the wrong way. In plainer words, they were barely able to tolerate one another. The staff were stretched to capacity putting out brushfires on a day-in, day-out basis.

One of the biggest fears that staff on inpatient units will express is "the domino effect." This occurs when one patient "loses it," or, as we would say, has a meltdown, only to be followed by another patient having a meltdown, followed by another patient having a meltdown. When these events occur, there is a fear of losing control of the unit and chaos descending. Often you will hear that certain psychiatric units, although they have beds, are not accepting admissions because the unit is "too acute." This means that they have a number of patients who are not stable, and the staff are at the end of their resources in being able to care for the needs of all the patients on the unit at that time.

Our week started not only with a series of new admissions, but also with some challenges in the physical environment. There had been a power outage in Cambridge, and the unit lost power for almost six hours. This followed several days of rain and snow, leading to power lines going down. The power outage initially was viewed by the children as exciting. Something new had occurred from the daily routine.

We had a lot of extra people on the unit. The maintenance staff were there, and men were stringing up temporary lighting for the day hall and nurses' station—some of which were very bright. The bedrooms had the nightlights, but the overhead lights were not working. The implications were that we had to confine the children to a small area, and we were not able to separate the children into smaller groupings.

After four hours of this, it was no longer interesting to the children, and we began to see the effects of their stress. Several children became involved in verbal altercations, and two children began to hit one another. This event started our week, and it was a good barometer of the state of the unit in general.

By the end of this week, the staff felt the mix on the unit was highly volatile and reported that they felt they needed to be everywhere at once. They said that even with extreme diligence, they could not stay on top of the number of children arguing and fighting with one another. That weekend, the staff reported that they had actually kept a tally and had totaled fifteen meltdowns. This was exhausting, and there was some degree of trepidation. Would the situation deteriorate further? Could it deteriorate further?

Pablo was a large eleven-year-old boy who had been on the unit for more than a month and a half, and he had been having an increasingly difficult time. He was very strong and was intimidating when angered. He had learned since his arrival that he would not be returning to his old program, and this meant that he would be with us for an extended period while another program was identified and secured for him. Based on our experience with children awaiting placement, his stay might range from six weeks to months if there were stumbling blocks to a placement being located for him. The previous two weeks had been rocky for him, and we had seen an appreciable increase in his meltdowns. When he became explosive, he tended to strike out and would attempt to assault anyone in his path.

Ethan had been admitted recently, and although he had only been on the unit for less than two days, in that short time he had experienced a number of meltdowns in which he was agitated to the point of his face turning from red to purple while he screamed obscenities for up to forty-five minutes.

Carl was also new to us, and he had severe problems with social interactions. This resulted in the other children becoming enraged with him when he would say things that aggravated them to the point of their going after him. He tended to have melt-downs at bedtime, and his standard retort to the staff was, "I don't want to do it and you can't make me. I can get away with anything here."

Pierre was still with us, and he would become agitated when other children became aggressive. We had our hands full.

There were some staff members who had become increasingly vocal behind the scenes with comments that were negative and had escalated from skepticism to overt sabotage.

Other staff members would report to me that when I went home, there was one nurse who would tell the staff on her shift, "When she is here, you can do what she says, but while I'm in charge, we will be doing things my way—the old way!" The staff were somewhat discouraged by this and were confused. No one felt comfortable confronting her on her comments, and no one was likely to outright disagree with her. The staff were looking for direction and were waiting to see how this would play out.

I made a number of attempts to engage this nurse in conversation initially, and she paid me lip service and did not disagree with me directly. The majority of her remarks were made when I was not present. I learned that she was also making phone calls to staff at home to voice her disagreement with our new approach. I was apprehensive about this development. This nurse, who had appointed herself as leader of the opposition, had a long history with the unit; in fact, she was there when the unit opened. She had seen the unit go through many changes, and as she would say, she had withstood them all. She was a strong personality, and she spoke with conviction and authority. She was a formidable foe. I had felt from early on that we would eventually go head-to-head. I knew that I also was a strong personality with a strong sense of conviction and that the unit would be hard pressed to find equanimity with the two of us as adversaries. I did not believe that I would be able to bring her around to my way of thinking. I made some initial attempts, but I was met with placid acquiescence that did not seem genuine and that was in direct conflict with the reports I was receiving of things being said when I was not on the unit.

As to be expected, as the unit heated up, so did the negative voices regarding our approach in managing the children. One incident stands out for me as symbolic of the rising conflict that epitomized the clash in values between our old values and culture and our new ones. It was where I took a clear stand in a public venue. In my mind I thought of it as my "High Noon" moment.

We had a twelve-year-old girl on the unit, Jakira, who we had learned would not be returning home but would be staying with us until a residential placement was found. She had spent the previous week repeating over and over that she wanted to be home by her thirteenth birthday to celebrate it there. Unfortunately, that was not going to happen, and Jakira was told that she would be on the unit for her birthday.

The day arrived and Jakira's mother came in with a big tray of cupcakes for us to distribute at her daughter's birthday party, to be held later in the afternoon. Jakira had seen her mother drop off the cupcakes. Lunch arrived, and Jakira was in a very irritable mood. She opened her lunch tray and said, without mincing words, "I'm not eating this shit!" She went to the lunch counter and said, "I want one of my cupcakes." The nurse was there and said, "You have to eat all of your lunch first." Mind you, there was a big sign in the kitchen for just this type of situation. The sign read in big bold print: **"FOOD IS NEVER IN BASKET A."** Jakira said even more emphatically, "I want my g...d... cupcakes!" The nurse responded, "They are not your cupcakes. Your mother brought them in to the staff for your party later this afternoon. You can't have them now." Jakira was now enraged and slammed her lunch tray on the kitchen counter. "Give me one of my cupcakes!" she yelled. By now, everyone was paying attention to the interplay. The staff were poised around the dining room. The children had stopped talking at their tables.

My heart went out to Jakira. Here she was on an inpatient psychiatric unit for her thirteenth birthday. Her one wish had been to be home for this event. Not only was she *not* going home for her birthday, she was not going to be going home from our unit. She was going to a residential placement. And on her birthday, things were not going well.

I intervened. I walked up to the lunch counter and said, "I thought we had decided in group supervision that food was never in Basket A." The nurse responded, "We have to keep some semblance of good nutrition on the unit. And the cupcakes are for her party in a few hours." I said, "It's her birthday. Give her the damn cupcake!" The nurse was visibly upset and slammed down the cupcake tray on the counter. She said, "You want her to have the cupcake, then you give it to her!" And she left the area. I took a cupcake, placed it on a paper dish, said "Happy Birthday, Jakira," and gave her a hug and a kiss. The staff who had been observing the incident gave me silent support with a show of high-fives hand signals. This nurse continued to resist the changes we were trying to make and took her opposition to greater lengths in the coming months.

Why do I relate this incident? First, I think it was a defining moment. The battle lines were now clearly drawn and they were out in the open. And I felt that the conflict needed to be brought out into the open rather than remain behind closed doors, where it was much more elusive and more difficult to deal with. Second, it epitomized the old approach versus the new one. That nurse was viewing the situation from a need to reinforce group norms, and individual needs were to be subsumed to group norms. We were trying to create a culture where individual needs were considered over group norms. We were not trying to fit square pegs into round holes. We were trying to tailor the environment to assist in meeting the child's individual needs whenever possible.

On some level, I also felt that this was not really about the rules. It seemed to me that saying "no" and referring to rules was often the way staff in positions of authority asserted their power. And this felt like a power struggle that was totally unnecessary.

Last, but not least, I felt that the staff were holding back from a total buy-in until they were sure of the lay of the land. I felt that they were waiting to see if I had the strength to take on the opposition to our approach and our efforts to change the culture of the unit.

As Ronald Heifetz identifies in his book, *Leadership Without Easy Answers,* you have to know when to hold steady and when to hold back. In Heifetz's frame of reference, holding steady means that you stay the course, even in difficult times. You take a stand and do not relent. Holding back, on the other hand, is not speaking out—it means deciding that it is not the best time to make a stand. Holding back might mean letting someone else take the lead, or it might mean waiting for a better opportunity when the time was ripe.[9] In my heart, I felt that this was one of those hold-steady moments.

CHAPTER 8

OUR FIRST TEST WITH ONGOING AGGRESSION

• Pablo •

"You cannot acquire experience by making experiments.
You cannot create experience. You must undergo it."

— Albert Camus

Pablo had a visit from his Department of Social Services social worker. She brought him a picture of his mother with his other siblings, who were at home with her. Initially, he was glad to have the picture. But within twenty-four hours, the picture became a gnawing reminder of his being left out of the family picture—both literally and figuratively. There were no plans for him to return home. His mother had clearly stated that she felt incapable of caring for him and was afraid of his aggression. In fact, she lived at the other end of the state and had declined offers from the social worker for a ride to the hospital to visit him. Pablo was tracked within the state welfare system for long-term residential care. Within forty-eight hours of Pablo having received the picture, he had had fifteen explosive meltdowns. The staff reported that his behavior was "unnerving." And some admitted to feeling traumatized by Pablo's going after other children and then becoming assaultive with the staff members as they intervened. There was also some tension within the ranks. Some staff reported that they felt other staff were holding back and being slow to respond when assistance was needed. The question was raised, "Even though we are trying something new here, do you think this is one of these situations where we should be setting consequences for behavior?"

Knowing that the unit was in tenuous control, the medical director and I stayed late into the evening shift that day. I had been working on the floor with the staff to help deal with the situation. In fact, Miguel, the senior milieu counselor, and I had paired off to deal with Pablo's ongoing aggression, freeing up the staff to deal with the other children.

During Pablo's attempts to assault male staff the previous day, they had observed that he was specifically targeting the male staff and aiming to hit them in their genital area. His explosive episodes not only occurred when limits were set on his behavior, but also occurred seemingly unprovoked. One example was that Pablo was sitting quietly in a group, got up and left the room, and charged at a male milieu counselor in the hallway. He had assaulted several children earlier in the day. As a result, the other children were angry with him and frightened of him. This caused them to have difficulty, and although they were trying to avoid him, they were fighting with one another.

During the evening, Miguel and I stayed by Pablo's side. When he tried to assault us, we held him briefly on his bed. We stayed with him until he was ready to fall asleep. He had been given a number of "PRN" medications (medications given "as needed," determined by his highly agitated state) to help him calm down, but unfortunately, they appeared to have little effect until cumulatively they kicked in at the very end of the day.

The next morning, Miguel and I met with Pablo for what we called an "administrative meeting." We told Pablo that we knew he was having a very hard time, and that we wanted to help him in any way we could. We knew that he was upset that he could not be with his family and that he was angry at his life and his situation. We agreed that life had not been fair to him and that he had a lot to be angry about. We told him that the bottom line was, we would give him all the support he needed, all the one-to-one time he needed (in fact, when he was aggressive, he had two or three staff members with him)—but we would not allow him to terrorize the unit. We wanted to help him all we could, but we also had to make sure the other children were safe and well cared for. We told him that if he was having a hard time and was striking out at other people, then he would have to stay with us in his room, and we would not let him have the run of the unit to go after other children or staff.

We had also observed that during these episodes of rage, Pablo had a glazed look in his eyes and would make comments that had no bearing on the current situation. One such example was him stating, "I'm going to hurt you good like you have done to me." We thought that the stress brought on by the picture had stirred up old memories of his earlier life, and that in his rages he was dissociating and reliving some of these experiences. We had increased his antipsychotic medication to help him deal with these symptoms, but the medication was not yet working to any discernible degree.

The staff were reminded that, when Pablo was in a meltdown or was just beginning to calm down, he was not able to verbally process with them what had occurred. We needed to remember that our primary goal was for him to calm down and stay calm.

He was the topic of our group supervision for the next two sessions. These supervisions drew a big crowd. We were challenged and worried. This was our test. Could we pull this off? Part of our discussions centered on what to do now that we were not containing children with mechanical restraints or locked-door seclusion. Stuart felt that it would be helpful to talk with all the children and explain to them that we did not do restraints or seclusion here, and to share our approach with them. He suggested we tell them up front that we didn't want to hold kids down. Kids who had been in restraints or had come from programs where restraints were being done might think we were allowing them to get away with something rather than trying to tailor individual plans to help them.

The staff picked up on his comment and asked Stuart directly if he was implying that physical holds on kids were less than ideal and should only be used as a last resort, similar to the way we now viewed mechanical restraint and seclusion. He agreed that this is what he had meant—that holds on kids should only be used as a last resort to keep everyone safe. He explained that trying to build a trusting relationship with a child so that you will be able to answer the question, "What is this kid's deal?" is almost impossible if you have to hold the child down. As a result, it was better to avoid interventions that were coercive whenever possible. Almost all of the staff agreed with this sentiment. The unease was in imagining how to manage aggressive kids without holds as an option.

The group discussions focused on the events of the past three days, and various staff members shared their responses to the meltdowns that occurred as well as their perceptions and their concerns. The staff stated that talking openly about this was helpful. Everyone verbalized a feeling of satisfaction that we had weathered those difficult three days without using mechanical restraints or seclusion.

The next supervision focused on specific children and what we had learned and what interventions had helped.

Pierre was discussed first. Terry, a female milieu counselor, spoke of having difficulty in maintaining positive interactions with

Pierre due to his frequent hitting of her, for no apparent reason, as he moved past her. She also reported that he would begin to yell and make insulting comments to her whenever she tried to talk with him. We decided that we would minimize her interactions with Pierre. Other staff would deal with him, and Terry would be freed up to interact with the other children.

Stuart suggested that the two primary reasons why a child targets a particular staff member is usually because that staff member was most frequently in Basket A, or the child had an association of that staff member with someone else. It was suggested that a staff person who had a good relationship with Pierre should initiate a conversation with him about his difficulty with Terry. Another staff member recollected that Pierre's mother had indicated that a similar situation had occurred with a female staff person at Pierre's last program. She was also blond-haired and blue-eyed. We resolved to ask his mom about this to gather more information. We agreed that when Pierre was agitated, it was not helpful to have conversations with him to process an event or to present him with a need to make choices—he was not capable of this when he was agitated. Our job was to try and get him to calm down and to prevent him from provoking another child who might also be agitated.

We identified interventions that had helped: taking him to his room, staying with him and closing the door, and using distraction techniques to get him to calm down and stay calm. Miguel shared that he had helped Pierre calm down by helping him pick his clothes up off the floor and folding them and putting them in folded piles in his cubby. I had some success when I began to pick up small pieces of a game Pierre had thrown all over the room. Within minutes, he joined me in a race to see who could pick up the most pieces first.

We reviewed how the previous weekend had gone with Pablo. Staff reported that he had received a lot of one-on-one attention, and this had helped in keeping things calmer. It was the consensus of the group that Pablo would become overstimulated in groups, especially groups of more than two other children. His blowups had been instructive in that we were learning more about him and how he responded to different situations. We were now able to identify that Pablo was beginning to wind up when we saw him hovering in the day hall. We had learned that, even at that point, he was already beyond any capacity to verbally process how he was feeling. Distraction had been effective, and staff reported that taking him off the unit for a one-on-one walk had also been very effective in helping him calm down and in giving the unit a rest.

A discussion of Ethan led to one person observing that "he likes to play the victim." Another staff observed that "he misperceives things"—and gave the examples of Ethan believing that the other kids were laughing at him when he heard them laughing over something totally unrelated. In another situation, Ethan had thought he was being yelled at when a child was yelling at someone else. Here was another child who was becoming too overstimulated in group activities. The staff had reported that when Ethan's grandfather came to visit, he had made remarks to Ethan such as: "You are in trouble with the staff because they play favorites and you are not one of their favorites"; "The food here is poisonous—I know, I used to work here."

We needed to discern how much Ethan's misperceptions were influenced by remarks made by family members and how much were related to his early physical abuse. We had observed that he was hypervigilant. We had also observed that he was not globally impulsive—he was compliant with unit routines, he was polite, and he was not particularly irritable. He was a bright boy and was able to understand quickly what was happening in the milieu. He had the capacity to verbalize his impressions of what was occurring. His difficulties seemed to manifest themselves in social situations where he appeared to have a difficult time processing social information. His perceptions had a hostile bias. He appeared to be reacting to a perceived threat, and that was when he would strike out.

In other domains, he had the ability to be reflective. Our job was to be his lens and help him sort out social situations. Since his difficulty was with other kids, we needed to help him by explaining the situation when his bias was that the other kids were out to get him.

We felt we needed some psychological testing to help gain more information about this.

The question of the hour was, Can we make inroads with his grandfather? Can we have a conversation with him that might go something like this?

Ethan is a really great kid and he has all these strengths that we see everyday. But we have observed that where he gets into trouble is in social situations, and we know we all have to work really hard to correct this by the way we say things to him. We would like him to be able to become more trusting of others so that he can better manage social situations. It is really important for the adults in his life whom he trusts to share a benign view of social interactions—to share the belief that people want to interact with Ethan and that they do not have any ulterior motives to do him harm. Can you help us with this? He really looks up to you, and your words carry great weight with him.

Ethan had a difficult history, but he was making great strides in spite of this. Our job was to correct his cognitive bias. Could we teach him through intervening in his interactions with his peers by providing our assessment of those interactions? Our hope was to help him in correcting his misperceptions and to teach him the skills he would need to be able to handle frustration in social interactions and to become less frustrated as he adjusted some of his initial perceptions in social interactions with a more benign assessment of the situation.

CHAPTER 9

LEARNING TO DEAL WITH AGGRESSION

• Pablo •

"Nonviolence is the answer to the crucial political and moral questions of our time; the need for mankind to overcome oppression and violence without resorting to oppression and violence."

— Martin Luther King, Jr.

The concern that continued to be raised was: What should we do about children who were being assaultive? Everyone agreed that we needed a plan to manage this, and we all needed to feel that we were capable of dealing with it. First, we tried to understand what was happening in each situation by asking questions such as: When kids are assaultive, is it totally impulsive? Is it unprovoked? Out of the blue? Is it situational?

The staff response was that it was all the above. Using Pablo as an example, Lorraine reported: "He can be triggered by seeing

95

other kids laughing and he thinks they are talking about him and he has a meltdown. But he can also appear calm in his room, then suddenly charge out the door looking for someone—anyone—to bang into."

We decided that an important issue for us in considering each child was his or her propensity for violence. It would be a unit issue, and it would be important for us to determine this to our best ability for each new admission. It would be our first task. We talked about identifying the major factors in the unit crisis over the past two weeks, and everyone had identified Pablo's behavior as a major factor in the unit destabilization. Why was he repeatedly lashing out? It was the consensus that he was misperceiving things and that family issues played a major factor. He had been relatively calm on the unit until he received the picture of his family.

Was there a way for Pablo to be less aggressive? How could we help with this? Would being placed in a mechanical restraint teach him anything? Did we think that it would help him? These were some of the questions we asked ourselves. In thinking about using mechanical restraints, we realized we would have the same problem once he came out of the restraints. Restraints could not extinguish the anger he felt at his life situation. In fact, there was a danger that the restraints might increase his anger at his life events.

We looked at the interventions we had already attempted with him. A number of staff members responded by offering the different interventions that they had tried: taking Pablo off the unit to shoot hoops, taking him off the unit to do errands with them, bringing in some special items for him such as Spanish rice or "Spanish salad," buying little items for him such as pens and markers, and letting him help the teacher by correcting a younger peer's papers. The consensus was that these interventions were helpful.

Coworkers' observations were that Pablo had extreme difficulty when we had expectations that he attend groups with other kids. He had shown us that he was not yet able to handle this. He would become overstimulated, then he would become frustrated, then angry. Inevitably, a meltdown would ensue.

The larger issue here was: What do we do with kids who can't be part of the group? What were our options? We could insist that they go to the group, but it was highly likely that they would explode. Then we would have the choices of one-on-one time, time-out/room time, or, in a worst-case scenario, the options of restraint or seclusion. All of these options required one-on-one time and were staff-intensive compared to the options for the children who were able to partake of the group programming. We needed to look at getting rid of as many precipitants to meltdowns as it was possible for us to do. What were some of these precipitants?

A big precipitant was that of being with other kids. Often we had a number of children who at some point were not able to be in group situations successfully. So we decided to give this official status—we were going to remove these children from the mix multiple times daily. We decided to legitimize this option as part of our program and give it a name and fine-tune it. We developed an official non-group: the Explorers. They were our equivalent of the "Not Yet Ready for Prime-Time Players." These were the children we identified as "not yet workable." They were not able to meet the expectations of remaining calm in the presence of two or more other children with a focus on completing an activity. They were the kids we identified as currently "explosive" (defined by their behavior the day before or early that morning). The non-group would not be expected to attend focused groups for an hour at a time.

Our job was to help these kids become workable so that they would be able to interact and focus in the presence of two or more other kids. We wanted to help them so that they would be able to handle some degree of frustration without having a major meltdown. First, we needed to help them get a handle on their aggression. We added an additional column to our schedule board. This third column would identify "the Explorers."

The staff person assigned to this non-group was not expected to attempt group activities with them. In fact, it was contraindicated. The job was to help them select individual activities to do during that period of time, and we recognized that a child would more than likely make several changes in activity during the hour time period. The staff person was to observe and note where a child was having difficulty and to intervene early. The staff person also was to observe what each child liked to do and what the child was able to do well. For example, if the Explorer group was comprised of four kids on a given day, the staff assigned to them might have one playing Gameboy, one or two roller-blading in the halls, and one doing some homework or listening to music. As the children lost interest or became increasingly frustrated, the job was to move them into a new activity.

The challenge for the milieu counselors and nurses was to resist the impulse to make the non-group into a group and to expect them to interact. It would be tempting, because you only had to come up with one activity and all the children would be centered in one location. However, that would defeat the purpose of our creating this non-group. The purpose of separating out the Explorers was to create a less stimulating environment for them. We also did not want them to "mess up the milieu." We would view the Explorers as having more individualized needs and a lower threshold for interactions with other children. A general assumption was that they would not be able to concentrate for fifty minutes and focus on one task, as the children participating in the group program were doing. The difficulty would be mastering the coordination of the non-group, hour after hour, until it became second nature for us. The better we were able to work together and share the load, the higher the likelihood of success in doing a good job with each child.

We discussed that, although our group program looked great on paper and appeared very impressive to insurance companies and other outsiders, the more we thought about it, the more we questioned how realistic it was. The kids were kept going from morning until afternoon in one group after another with little downtime. We most often had a unit of kids who had difficulty getting along with other kids, and we had them all together for hours at a time. We thought about decreasing the number of groups and interspersing each focused group with some down-time—either some room time or a quiet activity. A child could play quietly with another child, but the idea was for them to have relaxed time and a time to play as part of the normal daily rhythm. We also realized that "divide and conquer" was a strategy we needed to put in the forefront of our thinking. Having a unit of children who were all potentially explosive meant that we needed to keep the groups small and be conscious of not creating environments that were overly stimulating or too challenging. The kids who were not yet "workable" were blowing out of the groups anyway, so we had nothing to lose by trying this.

We would allocate staffing so that the children in better behavioral control had less staffing, and the children who were the Explorers would have more staff available to them.

By far the most difficult challenge for us in helping kids become more workable was the issue of aggressive behavior. We talked of our concern regarding Pablo's baseline level of anger. We asked ourselves: Could we do anything about it? Is there a way, the next time, to avoid a situation like we had with Pablo? We had been, in the worst of times, allocating three staff members to be with him to keep him contained and away from the other kids. Were there ways to reduce his level of aggression? Some were fairly undesirable and were only temporary—the use of mechanical restraints and locked-door seclusion. What was our goal? We wanted to be able to stabilize children and help them become workable. Restraints, seclusion, and intensive staffing would not help a child stabilize. There was a medication issue here that we needed to look at closely.

If a child was aggressive, little work was getting done. When a child was being aggressive, we were not able to identify the underlying issues that needed our assistance. We were unable to see them because they were covered by the overlay of ongoing aggression. Our job was to assess, and we agreed that we were not able to do our job when the child was being aggressive. We needed to help get the aggression under control so that we would be able to see beneath it—be able to glimpse what was fueling it. In Pablo's case, we had identified his recent episodes of rage as being related to his family issues.

In frank terms, when we talked of medications stabilization, we were careful to identify that we were not looking to "snow" a child. This was not our intention. When people refer to "snowing," they often mean that you have used medication in sufficient quantities to sedate a person so that he or she is sleeping or unable to carry out purposeful activities. This is a highly charged concept that is even more so when the person is a child. It is done as a last resort when someone is repeatedly violent and out of control for extended periods of time. Your intention may be to not only end the violence, but to break the cycle and provide a break and some rest for the patient. In our case, we wanted to use medication judiciously. We did not want to turn aggressive children into zombies, but we did want to calm children sufficiently so that they were not being aggressive. We wanted children to be workable—so that they could do the work that needed to be done, with our help, and then be able to move on to the next place in a calmer, more manageable state.

Medication became an essential tool in our toolbox for managing aggressive behavior. Antipsychotic medications were most effective in this area. They were strong drugs and carried with them serious risks. But when we thought of a child on a locked psychiatric unit who had not been manageable in the community, we thought that the advantages outweighed the risks. We did not view using these medications to manage aggression as a lifelong prescription. We saw them as a temporary aid for a child. Our hope was that, as a child became more workable and was able to work on issues that led to frustration and rage, the meltdowns would become less frequent, the child would develop a higher level of frustration tolerance, and the child would have increased problem-solving skills with the help of our teaching. All these factors would influence the need for this medication. We viewed success as being able to have a child move on from our unit in a more controlled, manageable state to a less restrictive setting. Our hope was that, when the child was settled into the next place, the outpatient providers or the treaters at the next program could begin the task of decreasing this type of medication to as low a dose as possible while the child remained in good control. For children who did not have psychotic illnesses or severe mood disorders, many could reasonably be expected to come off this medication totally.

We discussed the role of PRN (as needed) medication and its place in helping a child become more workable. From a practical point of view, when you initially assess that a child is beginning to have a hard time, you may wait it out and see if he or she is able to ride through it—and maybe talk about the difficulty later. With children who were extremely aggressive, we needed to be astute observers to assess when the frustration was beginning to build, and we had a very small window of opportunity for intervention. PRN medication was useful here to "nip things in the bud" before they became total meltdowns. And if it was not offered early enough, then a child would be too far down the road to a meltdown and would not be reachable by using the medication to help him or her calm down before reaching the explosive stage. Here, the balance was between being preemptive with the offering of medication, viewing it as an easy solution, and being judicious, using your understanding and observations of a child to clinically assess that the child was in the early stages of escalation and, based on your observations and history of the child's behavior, that the escalation was likely to continue and result in aggression without intervention at the present time. But any way you cut it, PRN medication was reactive in nature. It was in response to warning signs we saw as indicators of a difficult time ahead. It was not proactive. It did become part of a proactive plan if the PRN medications were used as an indicator for increasing the dosage of the standing medications. They were useful tools for titration of standing medication regimes and for finding the most effective dose to reach a stabilization of the worse symptoms a child was experiencing. Our discussions in clinical rounds each day included reporting on the use of PRN medication and the context in which it was used. It was used as a yardstick for assessments and decision-making around titration of standing doses of medications. Our thinking was that if a child was on a therapeutic dose of medication then we would not need PRN medications for that child.

If a child was chronically aggressive over a day or two of evaluation, then our main job was to get him or her in workable shape as quickly as possible. This meant making a decision to be more aggressive with medication and prioritizing medication as a very important tool for helping children manage severe aggression.

We had learned during our most difficult times on the unit that failure to respond quickly to what we were observing could wreak havoc on the unit. On day one and day two of a child's admission, we should be assessing the child's impact on the unit. We learned that the unit was able to handle approximately forty-eight hours of aggressive behavior and then the whole milieu began to crumble. It couldn't and shouldn't be expected to deal with prolonged periods of aggressive behavior.

An important consideration was: What do you do with a child who was frequently aggressive? We could use mechanical restraints, resort to locked-door seclusion, or use medication to decrease the aggression. We opted for medication as less coercive in our assessment of interventions. We needed to be on top of this in the first forty-eight hours, and that meant having discussions with parents and guardians about our reasoning and our decisions not to use mechanical restraints or locked-door seclusion. Since our patients were minors, we did not give medication without the consent of the parents or guardians. We also gave medication orally. We did not like using medication by injection, as most children were afraid of needles, and giving medication by needle to a child who was already agitated seemed an unlikely way to build a sense of trust in us.

Giving antipsychotic medication without parental authority was considered a chemical restraint even if the child took the medication willingly. In the case of children who were in the protective custody of the child welfare agency, we had a thorny problem that had no quick fix. In those cases, the use of antipsychotic medication could only be given after a judge deemed it necessary. This meant that if a child in the custody of the state was hospitalized and not already on antipsychotic medication when admitted, we had a lengthy process to go through to obtain the court's permission to give the specific medication. In our state this was referred to as a Roger's Petition for medication.

The lesson we had learned from the past two weeks was that when you had four children who were at -30 (and melting down all the time), then you had a unit where no one could get any work done—not only the aggressors, but the other kids were prevented from getting work done, too.

When a child was admitted, we did not necessarily have all the information we needed. When the child had a major meltdown on the unit for the first time, the only option might be containment.

But once we had the information from the first meltdown, we needed to be proactive from that point on, to the best of our ability, and not continue with a reactive stance.

Our job with a new admission was to maintain constant vigilance—to learn as much as we could as fast as we could. A question we needed to ask ourselves was: Did we have enough data to know that the PRNs indicated that we needed to be proactive in meeting the medication issue head-on to assist the child in becoming workable?

Once again, this discussion of dealing with a child's ongoing aggression brought up an unresolved issue for some people. The question was raised, would we have anarchy without consequences? Carl's quote was given as an example: "You can do anything here and the staff will not do anything about it!" What should our response be to this comment? We could talk with Carl and with the group to explain that we *were* doing things about a child's aggression. We could do a little teaching and point out that the difficulty a particular child was having in his or her life may be affecting that child's behavior.

Ross urged us not to buy Carl's simplistic view of things. Carl's perception was wrong. We *were* doing something about aggression. We may not have been punishing a child, but we were still doing something. We had shut down the unit for several hours when we had four children experiencing meltdowns; we had instructed all the children to go to their rooms until the unit calmed down. We had removed a child from group situations. We had held emergency clinical meetings to look at interventions, and we had conducted long discussions to problem solve the issue of ongoing aggression, which included looking at our medication practices and especially the role of medication in helping a child become more workable.

Ross helped us look at our rationale for not having a consequence-based model. In some ways, a consequence-based model was ineffective. It did not reduce the likelihood of the aggression happening again. The child assessment unit (CAU) was an artificial environment for children—it was not the "real world." There was not an easy applicability between what happened on the CAU and what went on in the real world. The children who arrived on our doorstep for repeated aggression and violence had experienced consequence after consequence when they were in the community, with no success. As a result, they were here with us on a locked child psychiatric unit.

Our discussions evolved into a process of identifying the "work to be done" on the unit.

We defined the "work to be done on the CAU" as assessing, stabilizing, and getting a child ready for the next step (or what came next in his or her life).

This led us to our goals for each new admission to the unit. They were fourfold:

1. That a new admission not "mess up the milieu." (We had learned that when a child "messed up the milieu," no work got done.) We were looking at the unit as a whole and at the children already there, and how a new admission to the environment would impact all of us.

2. That we assist a child in becoming workable.

3. That we perform a thorough assessment (we would find out "what was this child's deal?").

4. That we make recommendations based on our assessment and formulation of the child and his or her needs, and that we pass on what we have learned to the next program or to the parents or guardians of the child.

In considering medication stabilization, we had to find a balance between *not* using medication as a chemical restraint and *using* medication as an important tool in helping a child stabilize and become less aggressive so that he or she would become workable. By so doing, we would be able to carry out our assessment. A child needed to be workable enough so that we could learn at which points and why the child was having difficulty, leading to frustration and meltdowns. Many of our children might need long-term therapy to deal with issues that were very complicated and had no immediate solution. Most frequently, the long-term work would take place from their home setting or the program to which they would be going. Our job was to assess, make recommendations, and pass on what we had learned. If a child was going to be with us for awhile, then an additional task was to start the long-term work until the child was able to move on.

We had learned from Pablo that, even though he had said after a series of meltdowns, "My mom and dad used to hit me with a belt," this was not an indication that he was ready to do therapy. He was giving us "historical debris" that was useful for us to know to understand him better, but he was not workable enough yet to go down that difficult road. He was still functioning on a primitive level.

We had extensive conversations about the role of medication for managing aggression, and we talked of the place of medication as a tool in our new culture. We developed a hierarchy of interventions, going from most restrictive to least restrictive. This was based on our unit set of values:

- Mechanical restraint.

- Locked-door seclusion.

- Chemical restraint.

- Brief physical hold.

- PRN medication.

When we talked about creating alternatives to a consequence-based milieu, it generated questions and unease. Some staff stated that they were confused. They asked if we were telling them that we "do not have a level system any more." Some staff expressed anxiety and stated that they feared that if we abandoned the old rules, we would "flounder."

At this point in time, no one was talking about doing away with the unit level system. The unit had a system that gave a child graduated steps toward more freedom. When you were admitted, you were designated to be on unit restricted (UR). You could not leave the unit. After a child had been on the unit for a few days, and if the child's behavior seemed to be in control, he or she was moved to hospital restricted (HR). You were entitled to go off the unit with staff to walk within the hospital or across the hospital entrance to the unit play space. After a child was on the unit about a week, and the behavior was not very problematic, the child was granted off grounds (OG) privileges. A child with OG was able to go off the hospital grounds with staff in a small group. OG opened the range of opportunities and experiences for a child. We took lots of trips off the unit to local parks and playgrounds and went to museums, movie theaters, etc.

We had discussed that at some future point the level system might just fade away as something we no longer needed or used. That time was not now—not when we were trying to master a new way of doing things and did not yet feel comfortable with the new tools we were using. One staff person volunteered that some staff were setting consequences by dropping a child to a lower level or back to UR and that it was a problem for the rest of the staff. We agreed that there had to be some thought to doing this and that before setting a limit, you needed to consider carefully the goal you were attempting to accomplish. The next shift did not need to be stuck with your Basket A intervention and be hamstrung regarding what options or choices they had available to them in managing the children.

There was general consensus that there should be some logic or rationale in decision making and in the giving of a consequence. An example was given of a child having received an early bedtime for being rude to a staff member earlier that morning. It was pointed out that there was no connection here between the behavior and the consequence. It was also based on the assumption that consequences are motivators for kids. And it was based on the belief that we needed consequences to prepare kids for the real world.

What we had observed was that goals were motivators for kids, and we did have goals for them. The reality was that this was an artificial environment, and nowhere outside looked like an inpatient locked unit. Therefore, our ability to prepare kids for the real world and to teach them "life lessons" was very limited by our mission and by the time we had to do our work.

The issue of brief physical holds again resurfaced. And the consensus was that holds might sometimes be necessary, but they were a genuinely last resort. Holding a child increased the wariness of a child and made it more difficult for him or her to feel comfortable enough to be able to "open up" with people who had been doing the forceable hold. We may have felt that we were doing it out of necessity, as we could find no available alternative at the time, but it complicated our work.

Another concern was broached. We put out on the table the issue of the night shift feeling a huge sense of internal pressure to keep things quiet so that everyone was able to sleep. This created a natural sense of apprehension when a child was up and agitated, as there was a fear of the child escalating and waking up the unit. The reality was that there were fewer staff members working on the night shift, and they worried that if more than one child was having difficulty, they would end up with a situation that was difficult to manage. Charles, who worked evening and night shifts, stated that the night-shift staff did not have access to the information that the rest of the staff had on the day and evening shifts. Those shifts spent most of their time with the children awake and had a sense of what worked and what did not. This was a good point and led us to think about how and where to document information regarding particular strategies that were successful with individual children. We needed to document things we had tried that worked, and things we had learned that would make a particular child become more upset or cause the child to have a meltdown.

We had a book on the unit called the "Pass On" book. It was here that we kept information regarding tests to be completed the next day. In it we conveyed important information between shifts, which children would be having a pass the next day, who was scheduled to be discharged, who was just admitted, and what paperwork needed to be completed. Another resource was a child's individual safety plan or tool. This was encouraged by the Massachusetts Department of Mental Health for all inpatient units. It was a plan that involved talking with a child and having staff members designate what interventions were calming in nature and what interventions were likely to trigger the child or make him or her more upset. On our unit, we called this the Child's Protection Plan (see Appendix 11).

What needed to be stated clearly was that *our job was to help children*. And that was a twenty-four-hour job. It was a goal for all the children to receive a good night's sleep. But that goal should not interfere with our providing for the individual child who was not asleep and needed our help. That being said, it was under-standable that the night-shift staff were anxious and trying their best to avoid meltdowns occurring at night. But the pressure needed to be taken off; if a child did have a meltdown at night and it affected the other children's ability to sleep, it would be unfor-tunate but not a significant event. The night shift needed to have the same set of skills the other shifts had; in fact, they needed to be masters at it, for there were fewer of them on duty at any given time. Helping a child before the child erupted and had a melt-down would be an essential skill for night staff. And if we were collaborating with the children throughout the other two shifts, any child had the right to expect that the night shift would be using the same approach. It was a matter of dealing with unmet expectations, and the night shift would also get style points for interacting with Basket B interventions.

Once again, the group supervision ended on a recurring theme. The question of consequences was raised but in a different way: Shouldn't the unit replicate the real world? The issue was phrased as: "In the real world there are consequences; why not here?" We reiterated that most of the children who were placed on our unit had many consequences set in the real world before land-ing here with us. Despite all those consequences, they were not able to control or manage their behavior. In fact, you could prob-ably go one step further; it would not be a far-fetched assumption to state that the setting of consequences in some cases played a part in their admission. Their aggressive behavior probably esca-lated after a consequence had been set. They probably "lost it" after being "consequenced." If you thought about it, almost all children knew right from wrong before ending up on our unit. On basic issues, they were told, over and over (regardless of their fam-ily situation), "you can't hit," "you can't swear," "you can't bite," etc. Even in situations where there was considerable swearing at home, or they witnessed their parents physically fighting or being hit—they still received the message at school that it was not okay to hit or swear. But *hearing* the message and *understanding* the message did not prevent them from hitting or swearing.

What actually happened when we tried to replicate the real world? When we operated with a consequence-based model on the unit, what did we see? We messed up the milieu—kids started blowing up as we set consequence after consequence. We didn't make the kids workable either. We upset them more and then dealt with them after the fact. We made it more difficult to assess them because we were not learning anything from a meltdown, and they were not learning anything when they were in that state. Lastly, if we were not making them workable, then we would not be able to get them ready for the next place.

Another related question was raised: What do we tell parents who tell us they "feel we are letting the kids get away with things" and who ask us to give consequences so that we will have an opportunity to see them "really stressed out and out of control like they were at home?" We discussed letting parents know that our job was to assess their child. We could elaborate further and state that we understood that their child did not become explosive overnight, and we couldn't "fix" it overnight. Our job was to observe, assess, and then make a formulation as to why the child was behaving in a certain way. On another level, an inpatient unit was not a car repair shop—kids were not here for tune-ups. Often, doing our job well involved connecting the family with a therapist who could continue the work we started and work with them over a much longer duration. One parent who was having difficulty reconciling our approach with what she had been taught by out-patient treaters stated, "No wonder our child loves it here—it's like Shangri-La." This was not said as a compliment; it was said derisively. But the more I thought about it, the more I thought she had hit the nail on the head. Why not strive for Shangri-La? In Shangri-La, people were friendly and there was no violence, hunger, or strife. Wouldn't we wish this for every child—even if only for a sojourn?

In our work with families, we had an opportunity to get our foot in the door, thus giving us an opportunity to convince them that their child was not a Basket A child. We could explain our belief that using a consequence-based approach would not be successful. Our job was to help parents see the importance of determining their priorities as a situation was occurring. We wanted them to be asking themselves—in the moment—when their child was behaving undesirably: "How can I help to change this behavior?" We wanted them to be thinking: "I do want to keep the behavior contained—so what is the first goal? It is to try and prevent a total meltdown." They would not want to be in the position of having their child mess up their milieu. This did not mean that we were asking them to placate a child at all costs; parents would still have the same expectations that they had before, but hopefully, the style in which they engaged with the child would be different. Leading with a style of collaboration was more likely to have parents' goals met.

In a traditional approach, if you see a child hit another child, you call the child on it and then set a consequence. In this approach, you observe the behavior and try to answer the question: Why did she hit? Your task is to identify the situations that elicit that response and then determine what skill deficits are lacking with that child in those situations. What does the behavior tell you? You are seeking to learn that information. You are looking at behavior in terms of cognitive distortions and skill deficits. The question you want to answer is: "What is going on in this child's head that I wish wasn't?" (cognitive distortion), or "What isn't going on in this child's head that I wish was?" (skill deficit).

Going back to Pablo as an example, you would ask: What skill(s) was he missing?

- He was missing a vocabulary to identify and express what he was feeling.

- He was missing impulse control.

- His irritable and sad mood affected his ability to problem solve.

You would also ask:

- What cognitive distortions were present? He misperceived situations—sometimes he thought people were purposely trying to "get him" when they were not doing that.

We wanted to use this information to help Pablo in his interactions and to promote prosocial behavior. We wanted to help him problem solve in situations in which he became involved. We wanted to help him put his feeling states into words. We would try to help by inserting a thought when we saw he was misperceiving a situation.

We wanted to do a thorough assessment and develop a formula that used more than the standard Axis I through VI diagnoses based on the DSMIV *Manual of Psychiatric Disorders.* The important discussions we needed to have with one another were about our observations so that sharing them would help us see patterns. We hoped to be able to make connections by sharing our observations at times when a particular child was becoming frustrated. These connections, we thought, would help us identify the situational factors that would lead us to understanding what *was* going on in a child's head that we wished *wasn't*, or what was *not* going on that we wished *was.*

Despite the unit being an artificial environment, it did provide opportunities for assessment. We still had many opportunities for observing a child who became frustrated, and our observations at these times would help us determine why a child was behaving in a certain way. We had expectations, mealtimes, bedtimes, and other routines—all of which would provide opportunities for observation and assessment.

CHAPTER 10

ADAPTING OUR STRUCTURE AND FINE-TUNING OUR LENS

• Pablo and Sally •

"To acquire knowledge, one must study;
but to acquire wisdom, one must observe."

— Marilyn vos Savant

At one group supervision session, Ross talked about the task of assessment by asking us to look at a child and think of four levels or boxes for our perspective. The child's current presentation (meaning the behavior we observed) was the first layer or box. This layer or box was located above the surface. Underneath this top layer was the next layer or box; this was where we looked to answer the two questions: "What *is* going on in the child's head that I wish *wasn't*?" and "What *isn't* going on in the child's head that I wish *was*?" The third layer or box beneath the first two was the child's life itself: the trauma, losses, moves,

115

etc.—all the significant events that had played a part in the child's life. Beneath this was the fourth layer or box, where the pathways to the child's frustration and aggression were located: executive functioning skills (deficits), emotion regulation skills, language processing skills (expressive or receptive language deficits), social skills, cognitive flexibility/adaptability skills, and sensory integration skills.

The bottom two layers were a result of the impact on a child's constitution by events and situations that had resulted in a hospitalization on our unit. They were areas that we could not change. We might be able to help the child with medication, but we could not change life events that had occurred, nor could we change the pathways leading to aggression. But we could identify them and then begin to teach specific thinking skills via our Basket B interactions so that the child would be able to work around or through the pathways and be able to problem solve. In order to do this, we had to focus on the second layer and answer those two questions, "What is going on in the child's head that I wish wasn't," and "What isn't going on in the child's head that I wish was?" This was where we would do our assessment.

While considering this, we thought of Pablo. We couldn't change his pathway. If his problem was mood regulation, we could try to help him with medication, but we were unable to change his bipolar disorder. We couldn't change his early life experiences, his trauma, or the abuse he suffered, or his foster placements, etc. To assist him, we needed to focus on answering our two questions. In response to the first question, we needed to determine how our observations could help us. For the second question, we could already answer:

• He did not trust adults.

• He was unable to delay gratification. (We had observed that on some occasions he wanted attention, then became angry when staff were not immediately available. As a result, he hit another child.)

Scenario:

Pablo comes up to Miguel (the senior milieu counselor) and waves a piece of paper in his face. What should Miguel's response be? Here is one possibility:

> "Pablo, it is not okay to get someone's attention by getting into his space and waving a paper in front of him. Why don't you go to your room for a few minutes to think about it and then apologize? As soon as you do that I will talk with you."

In this example, Miguel sets a limit and gives a consequence. Pablo may be able to comply with this, but it is more likely that this will frustrate him and he will swear, become angry, storm off, and probably hit any child in his path as he heads down the hall. We just lost an opportunity to learn more about what frustrates him and to assess him in relation to answering the two questions.

Another possible response that Miguel could give:

> Pablo waves the paper in Miguel's face. Miguel thinks quickly to himself—What is this about? What is not going on in Pablo's head I wish was? Pablo does not know how to let someone know that he likes them. He does not know how to approach them, how to start a conversation. He has difficulty delaying gratification. He likes me despite his belief that adults cannot be trusted. Miguel's response: "Pablo, my man! Good morning, I like you, too! Can you put down that paper so I can have a conversation with you?"

In this scenario, Miguel takes a benign approach that assumes that Pablo will do well if he can. He recognizes Pablo's thinking deficits and how they are impacting the current situation, then he enters into a friendly, in-the-moment, Basket B intervention. Here Miguel recognizes that part of our work involves helping Pablo with social interactions, helping him learn how to start a conversation, and then role modeling that in his interactions with Pablo. We could help Pablo learn how to let someone know he likes them. We could help him learn better ways to approach people. After Pablo has been able to do this with staff helping him, we can begin to help him with suggestions on how to approach the other kids.

What did we know about Pablo? We knew that he had a lower IQ, so there were cognitive deficits with which he had to contend and that made problem solving more difficult, especially in complex situations. Social interactions were by their very nature complex. He was unable to express his feelings verbally. He did not know how to start a conversation. He was impulsive, so he had difficulty waiting; he thought about something and wanted it to happen that very moment. He had an underlying deep distrust of adults based on his early life experiences.

What were we trying to teach him, and how were we going about doing that? Perhaps coaching Pablo would be helpful. We could provide him with scripts that he could use to start a conversation with someone. We had already made progress. And we could see that Pablo was building connections with some of the staff despite his tendency to be wary and distrustful. We witnessed an example of the progress he had already made when he stated in a case presentation interview (a training interview seminar for trainees and clinicians where a child is interviewed in a group teaching setting): "I have been able *not* to hit someone if they hit me; I can walk away sometimes."

We needed to always keep in mind that 99 percent of meltdowns were due to cognitive distortions and deficits.

In our family work with parents, it was just as important for us to also be thinking of the two questions: "What is in their heads I wish wasn't?" and "What is not in their heads that I wish was?" Here we were trying to assess the parents' understanding of their child and the child's difficulties.

The child's behavior was relevant in helping us answer the two questions and determine whether a particular child was able to handle the expectations of the group program, or whether the child needed to be an Explorer until he or she was more workable and better able to handle the expectations of the group program.

If a child had not met our expectations, we could set a consequence to deal with this situation. What would setting a consequence do?

- It would not alter the child's life situation.

- It would not alter the child's pathway to frustration and aggression.

- It would deal with the current presentation or behavior— either in a successful fashion or unsuccessfully, in which case the child's behavior would escalate.

- It would not help us answer the two questions.

Finding the answers to those two questions was the work we had to do—it was our assessment. What we learned about the answers to the two questions needed to be passed on to one another so that we would all be on the same page and working on the same things with the kids—otherwise we would be confusing them.

The discussion then shifted. Staff brought up a more generic and practical concern. How could we make our jobs easier, and how could we structure things to enhance our new knowledge? Group members started making suggestions:

1. Post key phrases and goals on the unit so that we are frequently reminded.

2. Develop a "cheat sheet" that lists the most common cognitive skill deficits so that we will have an easier time answering the two questions.

3. Put some signage in the lobby to the unit to let parents and visitors know "right off the bat" what we are trying to do.

4. Have a "Suggestion Box" into which staff can put their concerns, especially if someone is not comfortable identifying their concern openly.

In the next group supervision session, we had a long discussion about how difficult it was to change the way we were doing things and to think about our care and our jobs in a new way. We were in the midst of trying to implement a new model of care and trying to master the collaborative problem-solving approach in real-life situations. We recognized that making a paradigm shift was difficult and that it was normal for people to be having difficulty in expressing their concerns openly. There was a natural reticence in expressing our feelings about how difficult it was, and fearing the sensation of feeling exposed and then being fearful of criticism or ostracism.

Stuart stressed that this was taking a tremendous effort, and that just giving praise was not enough. We needed a place for everyone to be able to express their frustration and for us to talk through what we were going through with our frustrations. He also stressed that we needed to acknowledge the nursing staff (nurses, milieu counselors, activities coordinator, and teacher), as they were in the trenches dealing with meltdowns and trying to manage kids and the group program in a new way. We needed to recognize this and figure out a way to provide more support and build outlets into their routine. We would need some time and further thinking to come up with ideas to do this.

The issue was broached of how difficult it was to master answering the two questions. We decided to use examples to explore this.

Lorraine gave the example of Sally, a five-year-old girl who had been admitted in the past week. She had been very explosive at home and at school, hitting both her mother and the teacher on repeated occasions. The sudden worsening of her behavior, as well as some of the behaviors we had observed on the unit, led us to believe that she had somehow, somewhere, experienced sexual trauma. The example Lorraine gave was of Sally sitting in the day hall and then putting her legs in the air and making sexually inappropriate gestures. The question Lorraine asked was: "What am I supposed to do about that behavior?" The response was: "What should we be inferring about her behavior?" One way of thinking about it was, if we could put words to her behavior, we might infer that Sally was saying: "I need help; someone come talk to me." We needed to help Sally learn a better response than the one she was using. We would like her not to be exhibiting this inappropriate behavior, but we did not want to tell her simply not to do this and then set a limit—for then we would have lost the opportunity of her being able to feel like she could tell us what was going on with her.

So we might approach her and say, "Sally, come, let's take a walk. Do you want someone to talk to?" She may say in response, "Shut up." In our attempt at a Basket B intervention, we would respond with empathy. "You want me to shut up." But over time, it may penetrate in Sally's mind that people here can be trusted to talk with. By having her take a walk with us down the hall, we have removed her from the day hall, and we have distracted her from her behavior. Lastly, we are beginning to help her by imprinting on her brain that it is okay to talk here about what has happened to her.

Another example was given. Diego was a nine-year-old boy who had been admitted two days earlier. For the first two days, he had presented no problems. Then his behavior began to change. He appeared resistive. When staff requested that he go to the group for which he was scheduled, he would respond that he wanted to shoot hoops, and when asked to stop to do something else, he would ignore the staff person making the request and just continue to shoot hoops. What could we infer from this example? What was in his head that we wish wasn't, or what was not in his head that we wished was?

It appeared that he had a hard time shifting cognitive set. So we would expect transitions to be very hard for him. We needed to realize that when we asked someone to stop what he or she was doing, we were asking that person to make a shift in his or her mindset. This was a different way to look at behavior than viewing the behavior as an example of the "he wants to do what he wants to do" interpretive school of thought. Our job was to help Diego see that he had a hard time shifting gears.

Children who have a difficult time shifting cognitive set need preparation time. This meant that we needed to draw out the transition, and we needed to give warnings ahead of time. We would need to verbalize the transition and help the child shift gears. We would also need to gather information; for example, when did Diego have difficulty shifting gears, what was happening before we asked him to do something different, for how long, etc. *We needed to be situationally specific.* This was an area for our mastery. Often when we tried to do this, we ended up in the life layer, or the box with a big psychological explanation for the child's behavior. This was interesting, but it did not shed light on which cognitive skills we were observing, which skills were lacking, and which interventions we needed to develop to better teach the specific thinking skills a child needed to problem solve. We needed to be looking at the behavior, the situation, and the pathway box or layer (discussed earlier in this chapter). This was a big shift for us in our viewing behaviors and trying to understand them.

We realized that, in order for us to become adept at doing this, we needed to be collecting the right kind of information. Then we needed to be sharing that information back and forth with one another. This led us to another structural issue. Sharing information meant that we needed to look at shift reports, clinical rounds, and nursing notes in a different way. These vehicles were the standard unit means of sharing information about the children with one another.

The notes that would be the most helpful would be the nursing progress notes. These were written each shift and gave a synopsis of what had occurred with the child for that eight-hour block of time. They were narratives and often relayed information that was helpful. The notes documented when someone became upset during the shift and what the child did when he or she became upset. We needed to investigate these occurrences further, document them, and share them with each other so that we would be able to identify patterns by sharing stories about kids who had become upset. We needed to know what interactions were problematic, under what circumstances, with whom, when, where, and on what specific task or interaction. We needed to share these stories and then ask questions that would give more information about the incident. Then we needed to assess if we had enough information to answer the two questions.

So, when a child was having a hard time, we should be thinking:

- Under what circumstance did the child become upset?

- What time of day?

- With whom?

- Over what?

- During what activity?

- Does anyone have a similar story about the same child?

- Do we see a pattern?

All of our notes and discussions should be around determining, "What is this child's deal?" We would need to find time to collaborate in this way so that we could learn what we needed to know about each child.

This meant that in our clinical rounds each day, we needed to present information somewhat differently. We had the usual format of the charge nurse reading a report about a child's previous day on the unit, then the clinician discussing information gathered regarding the family situation, school, information obtained from outpatient providers, etc. Then a plan would be made for what needed to be done for the day, and often there was a discussion regarding the state of our assessment or formulation about why the child was having difficulty. *We needed to create space within this meeting to explore further the staff's observations of the child's interactions on the milieu and share the times of mastery and the times of difficulty so that we could identify the pathways and cognitive skills or lack of skills at play.* We had to integrate our traditional psychiatric formulations with our collaborative problem-solving approach.

Another implication of this approach was that it "takes two to tango." Before, we viewed behavior as occurring exclusively in the realm of the child. And we had no responsibility except to set limits and consequences. With CPS, it was the interaction between the adult and child that was important. Whether or not we ended up in Basket A or Basket B said as much about *our* style of approaching a child and interacting as it did about *the child's* behavior. In this sense, using CPS made us feel vulnerable. In relating our experiences in trying to use the baskets, we were exposing ourselves in a different way. If we were not able to figure out how to get to Basket B, and we used Basket A because it seemed easier and most natural, then we would have kids melting down, and we would be dealing with the aftermath. It was frustrating to deal with the aftermath, and it was frustrating to deal with kids melting down over interactions with each other before we even had a chance to use any basket! There was some self-consciousness knowing that our expertise was being judged by our ability to engage with kids in a collaborative style and enter into Basket B interactions. If the unit became unsettled and a staff member resorted to Basket A, that person's coworkers were now considering not just the children's behavior and assuming it was all them. Now we were all looking at the combination of factors—the children's escalation and the staff's intervention and the style and tone of the intervention. All were factors that deserved consideration.

After being with us for almost four months, Pablo finally moved on to a residential program in the part of the state where his biological family resided. His leaving was a milestone for us as much as it was for him. To him we owed a large debt. It was our experiences with him that helped us in the beginning stages of our shift toward mastering a new approach to managing aggression.

Here is the message we sent with our other materials to the staff of Pablo's new program.

What We Learned About Pablo

Pablo is a nine-year-old boy who appears older than his stated age. He has been on our unit for almost four months. He has attained many milestones during his stay here. This was due in large part to his ability to grow while on this unit, and in part to staff learning a lot abut Pablo's thinking processes and idiosyncrasies.

We are sharing some of our experiences in the hope that these interventions can be implemented in your program.

When Pablo arrived, he had many trust issues. During the first week on our unit, he honeymooned. We feel that he will probably do the same in your program. It would be very important during this first week to have one staff person ally with Pablo. This staff person could then act as a "buffer" or bridge between Pablo and staff. Pablo will then have an easier time and will be able to trust other staff over time. He feels overwhelmed and threatened when faced with having to deal with many personalities at once. This approach helped Pablo while he was here, as he did not have to feel thrown in the midst of having to trust everyone at once and all on the same plane.

Pablo responds well to one-on-one attention. He will seek this out from staff at times. At other times, we built it into a program that served as an incentive for him. Pablo has a lot of difficulty seeing other children receive attention from staff. We learned to be mindful of this. When other children were having a difficult time and required intensive staff attention, we designated a staff person to spend time with Pablo and distract him.

Pablo also responds positively to physical touch. He will ask for hugs. When he has difficulty, he can be distracted, and this will redirect his attention and help him become "unstuck" and able to move out of the rut he gets into when he has problems perceiving what is occurring or what is being said to him.

Staff on our unit have been implementing the collaborative problem-solving approach, and these techniques aided us in helping Pablo in his social interactions. We also found, in working with Pablo, that he could be distracted from escalating toward aggression by tickling him and by "squishing" him between two staff members. He referred to this as the "human sandwich." He immediately begins to giggle and is able to refocus. His moment of difficulty passes. Pablo likes to be chased by staff and prides himself on his speed. He would often challenge us to outrun him.

When Pablo begins to escalate, staff remind him to "stop and think." We then become his "thinking cap" and guide *him through alternative behaviors after discussing the outcome of the various alternatives.*

Pablo has a genuine caring side that was careful not to intentionally harm people when he had the opportunity.

Please feel free to contact us if you have any questions about Pablo. He is a very endearing child who has worked very hard to learn how to express his feelings and manage his anger. Please feel free to have Pablo check in with us if you feel it will assist his adjustment at your program or help him when he is having a difficult time.

—The staff of the CAU

CHAPTER 11

THE GOING GETS ROUGH

• Lawrence •

"Success seems to be largely a matter of hanging on after others have let go."

— William Feather

Three months had gone by since we had begun to change the way we were doing things. We already had a lot to be proud of. We were learning, and we had seen some real success in our first challenge with Pablo. Laura, one of the nurses, related that the day before Pablo left, he was anxious about leaving. He was irritable, sad, and scared.

Laura came upon Pablo, who was upset with another child. As Laura approached Pablo, she noticed that he had a sneaker in his hand and that his arm was raised; he was ready to throw the shoe at the other child. Laura said calmly but forcibly, "Pablo, look at what you are about to do." Pablo stopped, lowered his arm, and dropped the shoe. Helping him stop and short-circuit his impulse to strike had been effective. He had developed trust in us, and Laura's voice was able to get through to him and assist him in "stopping and thinking first." None of us would have predicted four months ago that this would be possible.

We had a lot to be proud of, and we should have been appreciating our accomplishments to date, yet that was not the case. When I raised this issue in our group supervision, it opened up a conversation about the emotional impact of trying to implement a new model of care, while already dealing with patients who were "very acute" (in hospital jargon, this means that the patients were difficult to manage and required a lot of care and intensive effort), coping with a volatile mix at times, and feeling frustrated about doing this work, day in and day out.

There was also a noticeable undercurrent in the atmosphere to which I had been paying particular attention. This was reflected in some comments in group supervision that were somewhat cryptic in their message. Tim said with conviction, "It is important only to speak for yourself and not try and speak for others. If I have something to say, I will choose to speak up and convey my concerns. I do not need anybody acting as my spokesperson." Sara chimed in that "the rumors going around are not an accurate portrayal of the staff, who are being depicted as dissatisfied, when the opposite is true. I am not dissatisfied, and the people I talk to say the same thing." Bob continued that "even though the going is rough right now, I am totally behind moving in this direction, and no one I talked with has any desire to return to the old ways of doing things."

I had been hearing in the past three weeks from staff who were telling me confidentially that when I was not present, a few of the seasoned nurses were making increasingly negative comments and expressing dissatisfaction with the changes—and with my competence in particular. I learned that one nurse was overt in her refusal to implement the changes we had agreed upon in our group supervision sessions and was using her position as charge nurse and her license liability as the reasons for her refusal. I assured the staff that I was supportive of their position and that I could be quoted as having instructed them to implement the changes. If any nurse had a problem with that, I would be more than willing to talk with her.

It was interesting that, among the group of people who were skeptical about what we were doing, some staff were not making any attempt to attend the group supervision sessions. This was the place where everyone had a voice and where we were working out the details. Here was the venue for disbelief, for failed attempts, and for questions and concerns, as well as for support regarding what *was* working well.

Our new model was empowering to the front-line staff, and that primarily meant the milieu counselors, who were out on the floor for the entire eight hours of their shift. Because this model was collaborative, it hinged on a trusting, respectful, and equal relationship among nurses and milieu counselors. Yet the traditional hierarchy was structured so that, on an organizational chart, the milieu counselors would fall under the direct supervision of the charge nurse. There was a genuine sense of a power inequity that made it difficult for the milieu counselors to disagree with the charge nurses, who were trying to undermine our work based on their disagreement with the changes. What was also true, though, was that everyone reported to me. So if it was going to be anyone's license on the line, it would be mine and those of my bosses. And if I gave the okay to a process that we had agreed upon in group supervision, then it was my decision in terms of where the responsibility would fall for the outcome of that change.

Two nurses had already resigned, stating that they had problems with the model. There was also one milieu counselor who did not agree with our new culture and values, nor with our CPS approach. He was more comfortable with the ways we had done things in the past. He genuinely saw his role as one of protector of other staff, primarily the female staff. He also did not agree with our unit mantra, "Kids do well if they can." He continued to see their behavior as intentional, and at times he would hover over a child who was in a meltdown—a response that was clearly not supportive. I talked with him about his difficulty in embracing what we were trying to do, and about his need to mentor under some of the counselors who were more adept and who could provide him with support and advice. He eventually took another job. A female milieu counselor also resigned after being assaulted by one of the children who had been very aggressive.

Change was hard, and not everyone was able to embrace it. And despite the difficulty of filling vacancies when staff members resigned, it was a necessary part of a successful changeover. Staff who were not on board began to realize that fact and had to deal with it by moving on. That was an important part of our progress toward our goal.

One of the difficult tasks in leading the changeover involved the strategy of dealing with the dissenters. First, I needed to provide opportunities for the staff who had reservations to *express* their reservations. Then I had to follow this with the provision of supervision and training, as well as support. However, once it was clear that someone was not able to move ahead in the direction that we were going, part of my job involved helping him or her see that this was not the place for this person to work any longer.

My personal view was that not everyone could be convinced given enough time. The model we were undertaking involved being able to let go of control to some extent. Collaborating meant letting the children have a greater say in decisions. It meant collaborating with families and being flexible. It meant respecting and trusting the milieu counselors and making decisions collaboratively based on their observations of a child beginning to become frustrated and needing immediate intervention. This was a very difficult transition for some of the nurses, and also for some clinicians.

I also had noticed that people who managed their stress and anxiety by exerting control had a much more difficult time with the approach we were implementing. Staff who derived a personal sense of satisfaction with the power or status that the job provided also had some difficulty with this collaborative style. This model was not for everybody. And people who have a difficult time with major change and who have been used to doing things a certain way for a long time are often too uncomfortable to give change a full and open try. That being said, I was aware that the cryptic comments being made reflected an increase in intensity of the resistance of some staff, and that things were heating up.

In this group supervision session, there was a discussion of how much better it felt to be dealing with out-of-control behavior by asking a child to go to his or her room to calm down rather than using the time-outs and chair times we had used previously. Everyone agreed that having a child sit in a chair in full view of his or her peers was humiliating and was also a setup. How did we expect an agitated child who was being disruptive and needed to leave the over-stimulation of the group to be able to sit quietly in a chair facing the wall, in full view of his or her peers? How was that teaching a child how to manage frustration and stress? The group as a whole felt that the chair times were punitive and humiliating.

This led to a very interesting and sensitive discussion. The question was raised whether or not there was something inherent in the restraint process that aided the staff in working through their own frustration with a child and his or her behavior. The behavior usually was extreme in some way—either refusal to cooperate with a request that escalated when limits were set in response to that behavior, behavior that frequently was "pushing your own buttons" to some degree, and behavior that was upsetting to watch or experience directly. Someone bravely speculated that when someone has been spitting on you and has been verbally abusive and kicking you, it was hard to imagine your anger not building.

In the past, continued out-of-control behavior resulted in restraint or seclusion. The act of deciding and moving ahead to do a restraint or seclude a child mitigated some of the anger, because the staff had a sense of being in charge by determining that restraint and/or seclusion were warranted. Feeling in control lessened the intensity of the anger. Additionally, when the restraint/seclusion was implemented, often the child cried. The child's crying also served to dilute the feelings of anger and helped enlist the staff's feelings of support, which resolved some of the angry feelings.

This conversation was difficult, as no one liked to imagine that restraint or seclusion helped staff feel less angry, even if it was easier to admit that prolonged abuse from a child did make you angry. It was not a topic that we were ready to explore in detail at this first raising of it as a potential issue.

A number of people commented that there was a sense of frustration now that was attributed to the acuity of the unit. There was a request for a plan. How could we deal with this? We needed to look for support from one another. We talked of giving each other permission to say, "This kid really pushes my buttons—can you deal with him and I'll deal with so and so?" Someone suggested that if you have spent a grueling hour providing a lot of one-on-one time with a particular child and are tired—you need to be relieved. We needed to build in a way to "space" one another. We needed to rotate the load. We should be able to say easily, "Hey, will you look after Pablo and I'll concentrate on Pierre?"

It was also okay for us to talk about how kids are sometimes scary. It didn't matter that they were kids—they had powerful rage, and they were able to hurt you and do damage to you. It was also okay to talk about the fact that some kids had limited cognitive abilities and did not understand why we did one thing with one child and not the same with another. It was frustrating to be called on that repeatedly. It was also frustrating to have to explain the same thing over and over to a child who had a hard time getting it, and an even harder time retaining it once she did get it. It was frustrating to have one or two kids escalate and know that with this mix it would most likely lead to having three or four other kids going-off and ending up in full-blown meltdowns. The problem would not be solved simply by suggesting that they go to their rooms to cool off, because it was likely that they wouldn't follow through. Then they would most likely end up revving up in the hall, which could lead to other kids falling apart.

We talked about the importance of the staff mix and how this affected the unit and the shift. Some staff may not be as experienced as others and may not yet have the skills to manage difficult behavior with confidence. The kids were able to pick up on this when the staff mix had more unseasoned staff than experienced staff. This sometimes made the shift more difficult. Everyone agreed that the kids also picked up on when staff did not agree about the approach to the kids. This meant that those who were not buying in to what we were doing and were continuing with the old ways of doing things were adding to the confusion. We agreed that it was difficult to get the chemistry right for the best staff combination with the mix of kids. But as one of the leaders of the unit, that was my responsibility.

Our unit had implemented staff scheduling, and the unit was doing that when I was hired. I felt that it was a staff benefit, and I agreed with it philosophically. Daniel did the scheduling for the milieu counselors based on the requests they submitted, and Laura did the same for the nurses' schedules. Staff scheduling involved staff members submitting requests for shifts they would like to work and shifts they would like off. A peer coordinated the requests and balanced the requests with the needs of the unit (required staffing pattern, mix of male and female staff, mix of experienced and less experienced staff, contractual issues, etc.), then posted a schedule for checking and changes. Staff were given two weeks to request changes, at which point the schedule was finalized and posted. Under a staff scheduling model, I was needed only to arbitrate conflicting requests that were not negotiated successfully. We learned that, during difficult times, I would have to micromanage the schedule with them to ensure that the mix was strong, especially on weekends, when we had less staff working on the unit.

We spoke of the importance in recognizing that staff can become worn down, and that this was likely to happen if someone was at the end of a long stretch of working many days in a row, or if they were working a double (two shifts back-to-back). Staff members were likely to be tired at the end of these stretches and may therefore become frustrated more easily. The reality was that people sometimes do have long stretches and do work doubles. We could try to take that into consideration and, at the end of the shift, have them do less stressful tasks, such as checks or reading a bedtime story to a child who was ready to settle in for the night.

Related to this, we also agreed that with staff scheduling, there came an added responsibility. If you were trying to schedule your shifts so that you could have a longer stretch off, then you had to use some degree of introspection and do a self-assessment. If working doubles or a series of shifts in a row made you irritable, or you became frustrated easily, then you had to be honest with yourself and take that into consideration when you were weighing the benefits of having a long stretch off with the liability of working for a long stretch and functioning at a less-than-optimal level.

We also had a responsibility to help the newer staff become more seasoned and comfortable with difficult situations. We decided that when an experienced staff member was dealing with a problem with one or more of the children, he or she should ask a newer staff member to come over and observe how the other staff person assisted a child who was escalating.

We also considered that we needed to recognize when the unit appeared to be revving up, at which point it was important to have a lot of staff bodies out on the floor. It sent a message, and just a presence of staff was often powerful in restoring order.

Several people stated that opening the dialogue on being frustrated was helpful, and it was supportive to see that others became frustrated also. We needed to encourage these discussions and not feel that there was always an answer, yet realize that talking about some things made them easier to deal with. Listening and feeling supported felt good. We learned that it was normal to feel frustrated at what looked like chaos at times. And we needed to recognize that it was normal to feel frustrated at this point in our learning and our implementation.

We did some brainstorming to see if we could make managing the Explorers an easier task. It was suggested that we have three or four activities in our minds as possibilities and create "stations" in the hall so that the Explorers could rotate from activity to activity every fifteen minutes or less, since as a non-group they had a problem concentrating for long periods of time on any one activity. We thought of basketball, rollerblading, Gameboys, and Mankala as examples of activities we could set up ahead of time for them to do. We explored having one or two of the activities take place in a room rather than in the hallway—Mankala and Gameboy would lend themselves to this. We discussed the idea of using "music as glue" for some of the Explorers. As a non-group, they had the least ability to process and use words to describe their emotions. Why not try to reach them with music? We thought this had some exciting possibilities—expression without words.

Among our new admissions were seven-year-old twins. Their mother had died, and their father, who suffered from psychiatric difficulties and substance abuse, tried to care for them but was unable to do so. They were quickly placed in foster care, and within a couple of months, they had already been in three foster homes. There was a plan to separate them from one another after their hospitalization with us. They would run up and down the hall frantically, and if one of them became upset or agitated, it triggered the other. They both appeared to be acutely traumatized, one more so than the other. We wondered if some songs that were bluesy or sad might help them get in touch with their feelings of sadness in a way that could free them up so that they would be less frantic.

It could be valuable to introduce music and dance each day for the Explorers. We could begin to develop a library of different types of music to have at our disposal. We had all witnessed Laura's success in turning the dinner hour into "Mozart's moments" when the behavior at dinnertime escalated. What had been loud, boisterous, and silly with belches and farting noises changed instantly with classical music to a more subdued atmosphere. We needed to be creative and use more interventions at our disposal as part of our toolbox of options for managing aggression and frustration without coercive measures. It would be trial and error finding interventions that were successful with the Explorers.

Ross had observed the unit for awhile, and his perception was that we had at this time an entire group of kids who were very poorly regulated. They were hyperactive and impulsive; even the children who were not acting up at a particular moment were capable of it. His suggestion was to keep the groupings small so that there was less opportunity for the kids to dysregulate one another. He also felt that putting any one of these children in a large group activity was placing greater demands on them that far exceeded their abilities. He also helped us see that when the unit was like this, it was very difficult to have Basket B interventions.

He felt that putting the Explorers in large groups together would result in our setting ourselves up to engage in Basket A interventions to maintain order and control of the milieu.

How could we help a child self-regulate? What could we do? Here were some ideas:

- Keep the groups small (three kids to one staff member). We even developed a system to have the children eat in smaller groupings. We would have the younger children picnic at the end of the long hallway, keep the older boys in the day hall, and have the older girls eat in the conference room.

- Help kids become workable—look at medication possibilities.

- Maintain expectations— we needed to remind ourselves that Basket B and Basket A had the same agenda—it was how we would deal with our expectations that was different.

- Rotate the Explorers—right now, this was a very large non-group (two-thirds of the kids on the unit)—from activity to activity in short bursts of time.

- Plan ahead of time for the weekend shifts.

- Make sure we communicated with one another so that we were passing information back and forth that would help us work with certain kids. This would help us learn as quickly as possible what interventions did work and what situations made things worse.

The weekend had proven difficult and had resulted in two children being physically held for less than five minutes after repeated attempts to provide interventions to de-escalate the unit and their continued assaultiveness. Despite our efforts, these children had continued to assault other children and the staff as they tried to intervene. In thinking of Goal #1 for the unit—not messing up the milieu—we needed to get the unit back in better control before we had any chance of successful Basket B interventions.

Monday evening also proved difficult, and staff reported that a number of children started melting down all at the same time. Some staff who had worked that night felt the situation was worsened by a couple of staff people who took a rigid approach. Although this might well have been our procedure in the past, we were working to do something different, and this return to the old approach now made things more confusing and chaotic for the staff. It was also very confusing for the children to have staff working on a shift with very different approaches to handling situations as they occurred.

The medical director and I had observed a nurse take out the restraint stretcher on that Monday evening because she perceived the situation as out of control and wanted to restore order by forcibly taking a child who was escalating to the Quiet Room. As I saw her take out the old orange restraint stretcher, my stomach sank, and I thought that I could not let this occur. I approached her and told her that I did not agree with her perception that things were not safe and would not agree to use of the stretcher. I volunteered to take over her shift as charge nurse if she felt that restraining was the only option. (This was her last shift; she had already given her resignation due to her disagreement with our changes.) She finished out the shift, and I stayed and helped until the unit was calm and the children were in their beds. There were no signs of disorder, and no child was restrained or held that evening.

In our supervision that week, I shared my observation of how Dick had really gone the extra mile in helping out during a period of difficulty. A twelve-year-old boy named Lawrence had just been admitted because he had become increasingly out of control and aggressive, and he had been assaulting his mother repeatedly at home. On Tuesday evening, Lawrence was agitated and in a major meltdown. He was in his room destroying his belongings and was so agitated that he was sweating and red in the face. He was breathing hard and was not able to engage in any verbal dialogue at all.

Lawrence came out on the unit, and several staff spent considerable time near his side to no avail. At one point, during his escalation as he was throwing his belongings around in his room, a staff person had called our security department to assist on the unit. We were at a stage now that, when security came, it was as a last resort and for a show of presence only. (In the past, security would come and often take over, with the likely result of our going down the path leading to mechanical restraints.) With our new approach, security did not like coming to the unit. We had a conflict in approaches—they felt that we gave kids too much time and that we should be more efficient in our decision-making. We, in turn, felt that their approach was too strong-armed and did not allow enough time for a child to turn things around and avoid a coercive intervention. Lawrence was still very angry and not responding to us. He attempted to bite and spit at staff who tried to approach him. He laid down on the floor and yelled to the other children, impelling them to go after the staff and ignore their direction.

Our agenda was to move Lawrence from the floor in front of the day hall to a more private area down the hall near the Quiet Room. We hoped he would agree to take some PRN medication to calm down, but we recognized that he was beyond the point of that being likely to happen. Ashley, the charge nurse, asked Dick if he would help her with Lawrence. Dick neared Lawrence, and Lawrence attempted to bite, scratch, and spit at Dick. Initially, Dick said, "I can't deal with him." Ashley responded, "Come on, Dick, I think if we just try to work with him for four minutes or so, we can get him to work with us."

Lawrence was given a number of opportunities to get up off the floor and walk to his room or down the hall. Finally, Dick took

Lawrence's feet, Ashley took his arms, and I rubbed Lawrence's back. Dick took a deep breath and then started talking to Lawrence softly in a genuinely supportive manner: "Come on, Lawrence. I know you can do it. You don't want to stay here on the floor in front of everybody. Let's get you out of here—get you some privacy. We don't want to hold you; we hate doing this. We know kids don't like it, and we don't blame them. We just want you to calm down and go somewhere private if you are upset."

Lawrence responded. He calmed down, and then he cried and asked if he could have some medicine to help him calm down some more. He said he was tired, and Dick offered to bring his mattress down to the end of the hall (near where he was lying on the floor but out of view of the living room and the other kids). Dick did this, and Lawrence built a fort in front of his mattress with cushions from the built-in benches in the hallway. Dinner was brought to him at his fort, and he remained calm and then went to sleep for the night.

I was so impressed watching Dick get a handle on his frustration, then overcome it, make a visible decision to work with Lawrence, and be supportive. He worked through his initial hesitancy and negative response and interacted in a caring and positive manner—all of which helped Lawrence turn it around and keep it turned around.

The larger picture was that, with Lawrence calm, the entire unit calmed down.

From a different perspective, we had another problem. We were beginning to get some recognition for what we were doing. Our rate of the use of mechanical restraint, locked-door seclusion, and chemical restraint was at zero and had been so for some months. The Department of Mental Health was watching closely and was referring other units to us to talk about what we were doing. But we had an internal image problem. For some reason, we were not giving ourselves the credit we deserved. We were not enjoying or celebrating our successes to date. They had been hard won, to be sure, but we were not feeling celebratory. I think, in retrospect, that this inability to enjoy our successes was due to two reasons: first, it was too fresh; we were still in the thick of things. We did not yet have the confidence to know that we were succeeding. I think we felt that we could lose our gains, and we did not yet have a sense of permanence. The second factor was that we had not yet reached what Malcolm Gladwell referred to as a "tipping point." We did not yet feel that we had reached the point where we had more supporters for what we were doing than we had deterrents. So celebration seemed premature. Yet, in order to continue, we needed to keep in our mind's eye the positive growth and development of the change we were undertaking.

We talked of developing some concrete interventions to foster a sense of recognition. We planned to have the staff meet off the unit and celebrate our achievements to date. We started a CPS journal and kept it in the staff lounge. This would be a book where any staff member would be able to write notes about his or her observations of another staff member doing something well and praising this person for it. It could also be used to convey an approach with a child that worked—a successful CPS moment. We could also use it to convey a question that we would like answered. The back half of the journal was for readers to be able to comment and give feedback.

We discussed putting up a big poster on the unit for the children. We would fill the boxes with stickers each time they were able to have a positive interaction or when they were collaborating with us and with each other, and also when a child was able to turn his or her behavior around and stop from having a full-blown meltdown. The poster would have 100 boxes, and when they were filled with the initials of the children who "had collaborated" or "turned things around," we would celebrate by having a party on the unit with pizza and other treats. This proved to be a great idea.

We explained it to the kids, and they joined in with complete enthusiasm. They worked very hard to collaborate with us and with one another, and we witnessed many acts of kindness and concern for one another. We made a big deal of the celebration and made sure that their strides and achievements were shared with their parents and guardians.

We thought it was important to recognize when a child had been able to pull it back together and when a staff person helped a child do this without resorting to restraint or seclusion. Along this same line of thought, we also wanted to talk more with the kids about this being a unit that did not do restraint or seclusion. We talked of not feeling defensive when a child taunted, "You can't do anything to me because this unit doesn't do restraint or seclusion." Ross urged us to see comments like that as an opportunity. He suggested that our response should be, "Yes, you are right; we do not do that here. You are lucky to be here. You could be at a place where those practices are still taking place. But that does not mean that we do not have expectations for you, and it does not mean that we are not in charge of the unit. It means that we are trying to manage your behavior in other ways and that it is in your best interest to try and work with us. Hopefully, you'll leave here having learned something about yourself and some skills for staying in control. Hopefully, you will not have upsetting memories of being here, unlike some other kids who tell people that they will never forget being restrained or secluded. So let's work together in a way that's good for you and good for the unit, too."

CHAPTER 12

OUR SECOND CHALLENGE

• *Ramon* •

"I respect faith, but doubt is what
gets you an education."

— *Wilson Mizner*

After two weekends of high stress with multiple meltdowns, the next weekend went well. In our supervision, we explored why this was so. Several reasons were given. First, a couple of the children had passes, so there were fewer kids around during the day on both Saturday and Sunday. Second, everyone used a divide-and-conquer strategy so that the groups were consistently kept small and more manageable. Third, the staff used humor with the kids, and it acted as a decelerator on building frustration. Lastly, distraction in the initial stages of building frustration was effective. We wanted to capitalize on what had worked, so we talked about

145

trying humor and distraction with more children when we observed that they were at -5 and beginning to become frustrated.

One of the children, Ramon, was presenting particular challenges to us, and we decided to spend some time discussing him in group supervision. He appeared to need much staff attention and generally was able to do well if there was a staff person with him or available to him. However, when other children were in need of the staff's time and attention, Ramon had difficulty. A couple of people reported that he appeared to have no understanding or ability to wait when the unit was revving up or another child was requiring an intensive effort by staff. We had observed this behavior a number of times. Stuart reminded us that, even if Ramon was able to wait on one or two occasions, we should not assume that, in general, he was able to do this consistently. We had to keep our expectations reasonable. Ramon might need to play this out 100 times before his ability to wait for staff time was consistent and predictable.

What did we know about Ramon? He was a twelve-year-old boy who had experienced early trauma and abandonment by his parents. They had been heavily involved in substance abuse and were not able to care for him adequately. He had been born HIV-positive. He had been in many placements, including failed foster home and residential placements. He was hopeless, and he was angry. He also was limited cognitively, and his medical condition, while stable, was slowly deteriorating over time. He had come to us from a residential placement where there had been an attempt to place him in a pre-adoptive home, but it was not successful. There were no plans at this point to find a permanent home for him. He was admitted on our unit because he had been having meltdowns at his residential placement and had been placed in restraints frequently in the past few weeks.

We had observed that Ramon was very impulsive and that he acted before thinking. He had a very poor attention span. We wondered if he had memory-storage and processing problems. We had to determine whether his inability to focus his attention and retain information was due to his having attention deficit disorder, or was if it was due to his having little working memory, both of which were part of an executive skills deficit. Or, was his disorganization due to his mental status being compromised from the interaction between his psychiatric and medical medications? We also needed to determine if Ramon's medical condition had reached the stage that it was compromising his mental status. Until we received more information from his past medical records and from past residential programs, we would have to simply recognize that Ramon had definite cognitive limitations, and we would have to keep things simple when interacting with him.

Stuart suggested that when we tried to engage Ramon in Basket B interventions, we should not expect him to be able to come up with many choices. We should expect that we may have to provide him with some simple choices and ask him to choose. Even with this, we would need to be careful, as Ramon might choose just for the sake of choosing or because he knew it was expected of him, but it might not be what he wanted.

Ramon had been telling us that "he wanted a visitor," as he was observing the other children with parents and relatives visiting them. How could we help him with this, especially now that we had learned that he would not be returning to his previous program? There was a suggestion to have a staff person, with whom he had a connection, be available to him at times when a lot of the other kids were involved with family members.

We had also observed that Ramon did want to make friends. We had seen some acts of kindness where he gave up the use of Playstation so that another child could use it. We had designed a plan for him that enabled him to use Playstation when he was agitated to help him calm. We could assist him by seeing if he could invite another child to play Playstation with him and see if he was able to build some friendships by playing with them as a first step. We could help by suggesting ways that he might engage other kids in a positive fashion.

We needed to assure Ramon that we would provide him with lots of staff attention, but we needed to avoid making promises that we could not keep. He was very sensitive to feeling betrayed and lied to, so we needed to assure him that when we committed to something, we were able to carry it out.

A hypothetical conversation might be: "Hey, Ramon, I would like to spend some time with you this shift. This is what the shift looks like, and this is what I have to do. When would you like to meet with me?" What should we do if the shift got busy at the time Ramon had picked? We need to anticipate this ahead of time.

We could further say: "Ramon, is there another time in this shift that we get together if that first time doesn't work out?" This would teach him several things: how to anticipate how things may go, how to plan, how to problem solve, and how to make accommodations and be flexible.

Another child we discussed was Nancy. When Nancy was initially admitted, she was very explosive and assaultive to both her mother and to the staff. For awhile, this behavior had diminished, but now that she was seeing other children leaving and she did not yet have a definite plan, her behavior was deteriorating. The challenge with Nancy was that she was bright, so it was very difficult not to expect more from her than from many of the other children, all of whom had some degree of cognitive limitations. Nancy also had involved adoptive parents, came from an affluent background, and had received many material things to which many of the other children of the unit had not been exposed. Nancy was easily frustrated and reacted with rude remarks if her requests were not met with immediate success. A number of staff admitted that her behavior "pushed their buttons."

Nancy was taking things from staff supplies and from other kids' rooms, and she had developed a complicated distribution network using other kids to pass things around from one another and to hiding places on the unit. During an outing with three children, Sara had noticed that eighty dollars of her money was missing from her pants pocket. Shortly after this incident, a Gameboy game cartridge was missing, and a second one that had been missing from the prior week suddenly reappeared in the day hall. Everyone suspected that the large suitcase Nancy kept in her bedroom was filled with numerous items from the unit and from other kids. We knew that taking things had been a long-standing problem for her—a problem that surfaced long before this hospital admission.

Confronting Nancy directly was not likely to be successful. That had been tried unsuccessfully by her parents, storekeepers, the police, etc. Nancy knew it was wrong to take things; that is why she took things surreptitiously. She did not want to get caught. So asking her directly to admit she had taken things would not be a successful strategy. We needed to be able to talk matter-of-factly about her having these things in her room. We decided that we would not be successful if we opened up any dialogue with her by asking her if she was sorry or asking her to admit to remorse. The issue at large was taking things that were not yours and taking things when you did not feel good. We observed that in supervision Stuart had intentionally labeled the behavior as "taking things that do not belong to you" rather than "stealing." Reframing would be helpful for creating opportunities for successful dialogues. It was also helpful to keep us from getting heated about the behavior and using terms that were associated with religious concepts, such as "sin." The reframing would also foster our being factually descriptive in neutral terms.

"Taking things that do not belong to you" was an issue for the whole unit at that point in time. We had a number of children on the unit who had taken things that did not belong to them. We talked of bringing this issue up in small groups and having discussions. We would try and relate "taking things without asking" as a behavior that reflected not showing respect for each other. A core unit value for us on the CAU was having respect for one another and for each other's belongings.

This supervision session ended abruptly as five children began having meltdowns and we were all needed on the unit. Stuart observed us in action, and we were pleased to hear from him that we "had done an awesome job of redirecting and distracting kids who were melting down and restoring coherence to the unit in less than fifteen minutes without any restraints, seclusion, or prolonged physical holds!"

We were now reaching the end of the fourth month of our change in care, and we spent the next group supervision session reviewing what we had learned:

- Using the Explorer category for children having a hard time and new children who were in the initial stages of being assessed for potential explosiveness.

- Using the information from our shared observations to determine who belonged in which groups.

- Keeping groups small (three to four children) and avoiding large gatherings of kids.

- Monitoring which children were receiving PRN medication due to agitation or explosiveness and how frequent were the PRNs.

- Using information about PRN usage to help determine what the standing dosage of medication should be.

- Making sure that we had a good staff mix on all shifts (a balance of new with seasoned staff and a balance of CPS devotees with the naysayers).

- Using humor and distraction as successful strategies for helping a child in the beginning stages of frustration.

- Decreasing the number of groups requiring focus and sustained attention.

- Interspersing focus-specific groups with room time or quiet play for downtime.

- Encouraging opportunities for play (opportunities for learning skills in social interactions).

- Recognizing the importance of communicating observations so that we were able to see patterns of behavior quickly and could determine where a child was having difficulty; and communicating quickly to all staff members the interventions that we found to work with particular children.

- Having realistic expectations for what a child was currently capable of doing as a way to prevent potential meltdowns.

- Recognizing that when we were having multiple meltdowns, we had messed up the milieu, and when we had messed up the milieu, no work got done.

We had implemented a CPS journal in the staff lounge, we had started the Kids' Collaboration Project Poster Contest, and we had set a date to meet outside of work to celebrate our successes to date. We had also developed and hung signage in the unit lobby informing parents and visitors of the changes we were undertaking. We had put up signs in strategic locations on the unit to remind us of our approach.

The next supervisions focused on Ramon—again. He was having an increasingly difficult time. One Monday, early in April, we were tested in a way that we had never been tested up to that point. Ramon woke up agitated and angry and was aggressive the entire day shift. He raised his fists as other kids walked by, attempted to chase them in the hallway, did a lot of cursing, and was not receptive to numerous staff attempts to engage him in conversation or an activity. He actually told us he was having a bad day and that it would continue, and that nothing we did would stop it.

The staff members working that shift were awesome in their attempts and strategies. A number of staff were assaulted in one way or another by a punch to the back, a slap on the arm, and attempts to spit. Some successful punches were registered as staff members were trying to talk with Ramon and determine how they could help. Eight of the twelve children on the unit were taken on an outing by several staff and kept off the unit for four hours to give Ramon time to calm down and to keep the children out of harm's way. The clinical staff were asked to come on the unit and help at those times when additional staff were needed.

Ramon was given a total of nine PRNs during the day with no discernible positive results. He remained agitated and angry. To add to this, Ramon had a very difficult shift the evening before, so that his behavior felt like a continuation. A number of staff reported that his almost continuous aggression had started on Sunday morning; therefore, this episode really was one of almost thirty-six hours in duration—not just the day shift on Monday. In the course of this prolonged episode, tempers were running high and feelings were strong. The tension was palpable and opinions were divergent; a rift developed among the staff. An emergency staff meeting was held that Tuesday, where differing points of view were expressed. The climate felt tense, and there was a sense of battle lines being drawn rather than one of cohesion from having been through a bad time together and feeling bonded with one another.

It was natural for people to want and need to express their feelings about what had occurred and to want immediate solutions. It was also to be expected that we would not all agree on the assessment of what constituted a "safe environment" and what was perceived as unsafe. What did appear out of whack was the sense of hostility that arose when we were disagreeing with one another. In plain terms, when we became stressed, we tended to take it out on one another to some degree. That was the part that was not wholesome and needed some addressing. When feelings ran strong, they would get reduced and personalized, creating a sense of divisiveness rather than a banding together in a cohesive way. The heat was generated by some staff members questioning the effectiveness of our new model and wondering if, when Ramon did not appear to be responding and the aggression was not abating, we should have returned to tried and true interventions such as restraint or seclusion.

One area we broached was the safety issue. It seemed more productive to talk of feeling scared rather than stating that the unit was unsafe. Everyone could identify and appreciate someone feeling scared, but there was no quantitative way to measure safety and unsafety. People's perceptions on this varied a great deal; there was no consensus. What one person perceived as unsafe did not even move a hair on the head of another. But almost everyone was able to appreciate a coworker expressing a feeling of being scared.

At our next group supervision that week, the atmosphere was less tense. A number of perspectives were expressed about the emergency staff meeting. Some people felt that it had felt good to talk about different alternatives. Others felt that this meeting was very uncomfortable because the feelings expressed toward Ramon seemed harsh and non-compassionate. And some milieu staff expressed feeling negative about the meeting on Tuesday, because they were hearing some of the clinical staff ask questions that seemed directed toward wanting to return to some of the old interventions—restraint, seclusion, and chemical restraints—in response to their being assaulted. The milieu staff who were present and worked on Monday thought that, although Monday had been extreme, they had dealt with their share of kicks and hits and spits daily, and they did not think that the response should be one of returning to restraints or seclusion. Some staff members reported that they had never even considered these alternatives on Monday when they were in the thick of things with Ramon. They expressed that they were glad to go home when their shift was over, but there was a sense of pride that they went home without having resorted to old alternatives when "the going got tough." There was some general talk about the importance of sharing feelings and being able to talk about upsetting events. Everyone agreed that having strong feelings after Monday was normal, but that we had to learn how to come together without the situation being so charged that it created a fissure.

We were able to diffuse some of the emotional heat that had been present on Monday by approaching the discussion with a hypothetical question: Are there ever any scenarios that might warrant the use of restraint or seclusion?

We explored this in a number of different forms. First, we considered the different types of restraint and seclusion and posed the question: Which of these do you feel is the least bad of bad alternatives? The consensus of the medical and nursing staff present was that a chemical restraint was the most appealing of bad alternatives. Most people present seemed to feel that any use of a restraint had the likelihood of destroying the alliance that had been built with Ramon. The issue then was: Under what conditions would you consider jeopardizing this relationship?

We speculated if there was a way to develop an algorithm to help make this decision. For example:

X hours of acting-out behavior

Y number of staff tied up dealing with the situation

Z number of PRN medications given with no favorable response

Then we asked ourselves: How would it feel to tie someone up again after months of not having done that? How would it feel to shut the door and seclude someone who you knew had HIV, knowing the implications of the social isolation that accompanied that illness? How would it feel to hold someone down and give an injection?

Everyone felt that four-point mechanical restraint would be the most devastating to Ramon's sense of trust in us. Some people felt that shutting the seclusion room door would have the same effect, and we could not predict that the behavior would stop once we opened the door. Almost everyone felt that we had the greatest likelihood of changing Ramon's behavior by using the chemical restraint, and there would be no reason to take on any coercive measure unless there was a likelihood of changing his behavior.

We agreed that we had come a long way to have gone through Monday without using any of these interventions. Everyone agreed that Monday felt terrible, and no one wanted to go through it again. We also verbalized that when we were in the midst of a bad time, it was difficult to have any perspective. No one who was present on Monday knew when Ramon's assaultiveness would end. No one was thinking it would go on forever, either. Everyone had hopes, each and every time a PRN medication was accepted and given, that the behavior would diminish.

We next discussed the pros and cons of having the clinical staff on the unit helping out. Using clinical staff provided us with extra bodies to manage the crisis. That did not mean that they had the confidence or skills that milieu staff had in managing aggressive behavior or in minimizing injury. It felt much scarier to clinical staff, who did not routinely and on a daily basis intervene with aggression, to be in the midst of the activity when children were being aggressive. It might not be appropriate to rely on clinical staff to break up fights, do physical holds, or make decision calls on what behaviors were truly dangerous—their training was in other areas. Some clinical staff had experience working on a milieu at some point in their past, but the comfort level in dealing with aggressive behavior decreased with lack of contact. Even staff who were currently working on the milieu differed in their comfort levels. We had strong combinations and weak combinations and we knew that weaker combinations on a particular shift were a factor in the outcome. The bottom line was that milieu work was messy at times, and staff members were in the mud trying to restore order. Some staff might not be comfortable with this. We speculated on how we would determine that we had reached the point of no return and needed to consider restraint and seclusion.

That brought us full circle to our question if there was an algorithm we could develop to guide us? We wondered further that, if we did develop and define an algorithm, would that lead us to using restraint and seclusion as we had in the past? Did we need to hide away old tools so that people developed the skills they needed for the new tools? If restraint and seclusion were available as alternatives, would they get used? Would some people who were less comfortable with the changes on the unit be more likely to use restraint or seclusion if those alternatives were available to them? How do we determine the point where, despite everyone's best efforts, we have not been able to get the situation under control with all the other interventions?

Developing an algorithm was not an easy task. How would we measure intensity, variety, and duration of interventions tried? If we specified that a restraint was warranted after adding x number of people to the unit with no results, this would still be a subjective decision, because it would be contingent on the ability of the added staff members to be able to restore order based on their skills and level of experience in managing aggression. If we said that restraint was warranted after y number of PRNs, this would still be affected by the dosage of the PRN (i.e., Seroquel 25 mg. versus Seroquel 100 mg.), the weight of the child, the child's metabolism, and the body's familiarity with a given medication—

these were all factors to be considered if we were trying to quantify decision-making.

How would we make these decisions and who would make them? The staff present were clear that *not* everyone should have an equal voice. It would be hard for some people to use measures such as restraint or seclusion if the people suggesting these measures were not the ones who would have to implement the strategy (that is, the actual placing of a child in restraints and being responsible for the child while in restraints).

We were not able to come up with answers; we just had a lot of questions. But what was different was that we had an open and frank conversation about sensitive topics in a manner that did not feel threatening or hostile.

We did a little reflecting on how far we had come. Pablo had challenged our skills and values in our work with his aggressive behavior. His episode of almost continuous aggression had lasted almost seventy-two hours. This time it was Ramon who challenged us and led us to question our approach and desire to do things differently. We were getting better. After thirty-six hours with Ramon, we had made major changes in his medication regime, and he had an administrative meeting within twenty-four hours. We told him we genuinely wanted to help him and decrease his distress, but we also wanted him to understand that we would not allow him to mess up the milieu. If he was having a difficult time, we would be there with him as long as it took, but we would be in his room, or we would take him on walks. He could not be out in the midst of the milieu assaulting kids and staff.

We still wanted to look at how we could shorten the time a child was being aggressive in a near-continuous state. We would need to look further into medication titration and conversion of PRN medications into standing dosages as one way of assisting a child who was not workable. The medical director took the lead and was very helpful in talking with the attending doctors on the unit and with the residents and fellows who were involved in the care of our children. In our clinical rounds meetings, the role of medication in thwarting aggressive states was frequently discussed with the development of plans for medication dosing, assessment, and reassessment.

We had moved beyond our second milestone. After this, things with Ramon calmed down. We attributed it to several factors: (1) we got the medications right, and this helped him become more workable; (2) Ramon began to trust us more, and even when he had angry days, he had become attached to us and cared about us and knew we cared about him; and (3) we developed more realistic expectations for him and took his cognitive deficits into account.

We began to teach Ramon skills for managing his frustration at a low level before it erupted into a full-blown rage. We accepted him for who he was and the level at which he was functioning. He began to show interest in joining younger kids when they dressed up and did a lot of pretend play. We observed that, at the end of the group, he was not retuning the gold lamé skirt he was wearing and often would keep it on for hours after the group. On other occasions, he would select the black witch's dress. On two occasions, he found the play lipstick and applied it to his lips. We wondered what this behavior meant and talked about it in our group supervision. He definitely seemed to be enjoying wearing the costumes. He also joined the girls' group one night and had his nails done there. There was some tradition on our unit of having groups in the evening that were purely for enjoyment or relaxation. We had a girls' and a boys' pampering group where everyone received foot soaks. We did not make a big deal of Ramon's dressing up. We wondered if it could be his way of expressing his sexual preference. Or, we mused, could he be seeking girl activities because he saw girls as having some advantages—i.e., easier access to hugs and affection? A few staff reported that they had heard him say, "I wish I was a girl!" when he had seen a girl receiving staff attention. Could he be comfortable enough here that he was working on very delayed developmental tasks that he never mastered before he moved on to other tasks? We agreed to stay neutral.

Ramon asked to go off the unit to the cafeteria while attired in the gold lamé skirt. What should our response be to this? We could matter-of-factly discuss the potential repercussions with him. "Ramon, not everybody outside this unit would be okay with seeing you in that outfit. Some people may not understand and may say things. But as long as you understand that and you will be okay and not upset, it is not a problem with us."

He did this for several weeks and then gave up the clothing. After four months on the unit, he was accepted for a state intermediate unit and left us for his new placement.

CHAPTER 13

KEEPING IT SIMPLE:
Replacing Unit Rules With Basic Unit Expectations

• *Bobeed* •

*"Out of intense complexities
intense simplicities emerge."*

— *Winston Churchill*

We began to take a closer look at defining our "A moments." When were we dealing with a situation in Basket A? How could we categorize them to better understand them? We knew that there would always be some Basket A on our unit. In fact, "soft A" was done a lot of the time and it was not a problem. It helped maintain order. But we needed to recognize that it did not help us deal with a child's problem or better understand the problem. "A" often felt very efficient, so people tended to gravitate to "A" to maintain order. But the danger was that "A" could distract you from getting to what was behind the behavior.

Rules are "A" statements. Our unit had a large white board in the day hall, and on this board were listed the unit rules. There were eight rules, and they all started with "No." The rules covered issues such as no hitting, cursing, taking things, telling secrets, etc. We discussed them in group supervision and decided that we thought there were two things about our rules that no longer seemed to fit with what we were trying to do. First, the rules were dealing with our agenda in a Basket A approach. Although most people, including children, like to know the lay of the land and what was important to the people you were with or who were supervising you, it seemed best done in a less negative manner. Second, although the rules were concrete and clear, they were too specific. We thought about what we were trying to convey. All these rules were about our values, and they could be distilled down to two basic premises: respect for yourself and respect for others (the other kids and the staff). So we came up with three basic expectations that seemed to cover it all:

1. Unit members will respect each other's private space, rooms, private property, and their right to physical and emotional well-being.

2. Unit members will respect staff's private space (staff office) and physical and emotional well-being.

3. Unit members will respect each person's culture, religion, and race.

We wanted to achieve these expectations for our unit by using Basket B interventions. Basket A did not provide us with an opportunity to teach, and although Basket C would not cause a meltdown, it ignored unmet expectations.

We came up with three categories of general Basket A moments:

1. Basket A as a reaction to what was happening.

2. Basket A as a reaction to a problem we did not understand.

3. Basket A as a reaction to a safety concern.

We wanted to save "A" for a minimum number of situations in dealing with our unmet expectations. So we developed a rule of thumb: When a child violated a rule, we would try to use Basket B to find out what was going on and learn more to understand the underlying issues beneath the behavior that violated the rule. We needed to figure out how to do Basket B when we were feeling challenged by a situation before us.

We had a new admission on the unit who was proving just such a challenge. Bobeed was an eight-year-old boy who had come to us for "out-of-control behavior at school." He had been restrained a number of times there. He had a traumatic early life that involved neglect and abuse, and it was suspected that his mother was using drugs during his pregnancy. He was taken out of his home at an early age (eighteen months), was placed with a relative, and then moved into a foster home. After this, he had been placed with his guardian and had been with her for years. She was the mom he remembered, and he was attached to her. His guardian mom and her adult daughter were committed to him. His mom was frequently present on the unit. He really looked forward to spending time with her and often was able to keep his explosive behavior in check when she was present.

How did the unit expectations apply to our challenges with Bobeed? He was having extreme difficulty being able to meet the unit expectations. He was frequently assaultive to other children and to staff. In fact, his meltdowns were so severe that the entire unit was affected. We spent many hours discussing how to better help Bobeed. We believed that his failure to follow our expectations was based on his inability to do so. He was not yet workable, and our job was to assist him in becoming more workable. A large part of this would involve finding a medication regime that would allow him to contain his aggression so that we would be able to identify his pathways for aggression and teach him the skills he needed to better handle his frustrations.

During a supervision session, we started with Laura giving the example of Bobeed refusing his medications. Was this a Basket A or a Basket B situation? What did we think he would say if we asked him, "What happens when you do not take your meds?"

Did we have answers to the two questions, what is going on in Bobeed's head we wish wasn't? and what is not going on in Bobeed's head that we wish was?

We had learned that when we asked him about taking his meds, he did not have any idea what the meds helped him with. We would need to spend some time on this and begin to teach him the connection between the meds and how they were expected to help him in his daily living and functioning.

What had we observed, and what did that tell us? We knew that he was often psychotic and had cognitive distortions and that he also had some cognitive deficiencies. We knew that these vulnerabilities were more evident when he was agitated. We also knew that he was not yet able to dialogue with us about many things. Ross has explained that to "do talk therapy," you needed to have basic linguistic anchors—you needed to have a rudimentary feeling-state vocabulary. You needed to be able to say, "I feel bad." So our first step was to help train a vocabulary so that Bobeed could communicate with us. "You look like you feel bad." "You have that expression on your face." We worked with him to help him make an association that taking his meds made him a little better. We wanted to work with him so that he would be able to say, "I feel bad; I feel sad." This would be a big leap forward for him. Helping him recognize that the meds helped him so that he wouldn't bite, hit, or scratch others would also be a big step. Our goal was to help him build a vocabulary that would allow him to tell us how he felt generally and what he felt like specifically when he was starting to become frustrated.

Debbie had found a way to communicate with Bobeed and to help train him by taking him to his mirror and having him look at his face in the mirror, then saying, "That looks like a mad face." He liked to make faces in the mirror, and when Debbie did this with him, he was able to tell her that "Corey hit me before." That information helped us understand a meltdown that he had experienced earlier that day. We decided to continue this approach so that we would build a common vocabulary with him. We needed to agree on some basic feeling states with which to start so that we would not confuse him with different people doing different things at the same time.

Bobeed was explosive and assaultive on a regular basis; he was also very impulsive and reactive. In our CPS framework, we identified his pathways as: mood dysregulation (anxiety, PTSD, severe); cognitive distortions (psychosis); language (expressive, and lacking a feeling state vocabulary); executive skills (impulsive, not able to see the connection between cause and effect, limited working memory, disorganization); and many sensory integration issues. He had the ability to make connections and relationships, and we were impressed with the ability of his relationship with his mother to hold him and ground him and prevent some of his short-circuiting.

In the months ahead, Bobeed was a frequent topic of conversation and planning. There were times when he had difficulty consistently for days at a time. During these periods of increased meltdowns, he would be impulsive and his behavior included biting, punching staff or kids, spitting, and screeching in a high-pitched voice for prolonged periods of time. This had resulted in a number of brief physical holds, and the staff reported that when they let him go, he would lunge at them to hit or kick them. We moved him to his room, but his screeching affected the other kids. He had been receiving frequent PRN medications, but they had not been particularly effective. In fact, they appeared to show little immediate effect at the time but would catch up with him a significant time later in the day or evening. He would finally fall asleep for a brief period but would awaken and immediately return to an agitated state.

We spent time developing strategies to help him. We had identified some staff to whom he responded better than others. This proved to be male staff members. He had been resentful of the female staff spending time with other kids. We had devised a system to assign staff to work exclusively with him. He was having a lot of difficulty getting along with other children. We had developed a series of cards for him to carry. We had laminated them and attached them to a key ring so that he could carry the cards around. The cards were of two types: feeling state cards (basic feeling states of happy, sad, and frustrated), and some cards of activities that he had identified as things that helped him calm down (playing Playstation, taking a bath, listening to music on the radio, being allowed to make his own rap songs). We were working to get him to use the cards as a first step toward being able to let us know in words what he needed at the moment to avoid a meltdown. Since Bobeed had the potential to be aggressive at any time and continued to have difficulty despite many medication trials to date, we continued to strategize interventions that would help us in managing his aggression.

Bobeed continued to be psychotic and unstable, and we had not yet found a combination of medications that were effective in stabilizing him. We explored at what times he became aggressive; often this happened after we had set a limit or when we were expecting him to shift cognitive set—i.e., at times of any transition. We agreed that he required a 100 percent containment effort so that we could ensure that he would not mess up the milieu. This effort involved our always being aware of where he was and who was in close proximity to him, and we needed to know what his state of mind appeared to be at any given point in time. We needed to make sure that the staff with whom he had a better response remained on the unit and would be available if he began to have a meltdown. That meant we had to tailor our activity schedule for the shift so that these staff were not given tasks of taking other children out of the unit. We knew that Bobeed had little ability to use words to tell us what was upsetting him, and we assumed that his early life and abuse played a significant factor in his cognitive distortions and in his own personal sense of safety or danger.

We identified four male staff (Miguel, Daniel, Tim, and Dick) who were more able to contain Bobeed when he was having a meltdown. These staff members needed to be available at any time they were working a shift. We had also observed that Bobeed was less likely to assault these four individuals, and two of them he had never assaulted. We hypothesized that their size and presence were reassuring to him and that he was most comfortable with them. We needed to spread their presence evenly throughout a week's schedule. We needed to designate key people on any shift who were responsible for assessing Bobeed's mental state and communicating that to all coworkers on a shift. We found that Playstation worked in helping Bobeed remain calm when he was beginning to escalate, and it distracted him from being out in the milieu and going after other children. We decided that it was an effective intervention and that staff should feel free to use this intervention.

One staff person stated that she felt that staff were traumatized by Bobeed's assaultiveness; another staff member responded that she felt "traumatized" was too strong a word and was not an accurate description. Everyone agreed that it was normal to feel anger when someone was trying to assault you. We agreed that we needed to support one another in this work. If a staff person was becoming angry or frustrated, it was okay to admit that to your coworkers. In supporting one another, this meant that we would build a way for a staff person to be relieved of having to deal with the child to whom he or she was becoming angry. We needed to help each other get the space someone needed when they needed it.

We also recognized that Bobeed was almost continually agitated despite our efforts in assessing, reviewing, and revising his medications and their dosages. He was in a perpetual -20 state. It was not surprising that only a little bit of frustration was needed to push him over the edge into a full-blown meltdown.

We decided to enlist the aid of his mother in helping us manage his meltdowns. We met with her and Bobeed together when she next visited. We discussed our plans to help him manage his aggression, and she was very supportive to us and stated that she wanted all of us working together. She also commented that it was important for her to know that he was trying his best to work with us to get a handle on his aggression. During the times she was present on the unit, Bobeed was more grounded and able to engage with her in eating lunch. He was respectful and very considerate of her and would make a point of waiting on her and trying to make sure she had everything she needed. It was amazing for us to see him be able to do this for brief periods of time with her. We had not yet succeeded in helping him become workable, but we were hopeful when we saw him able to contain himself and extend beyond himself to show concern and affection for his mother.

After eight months, Bobeed left us to go to a state continuing-care unit. We had learned much from him and from the experience of learning how to manage his aggressive behaviors. A number of the staff had become very attached to him. We were glad he was moving on and sad to see him go at the same time. He actually handled the goodbye better than we did. A few of us were crying as he left, and he reassured us that he would be okay and that he was glad to be moving on. Here is what we sent the next program.

What We Learned About Bobeed

Bobeed is a delightful eight-year-old African-American boy who has been on the CAU for more than eight months. He is someone who we found challenging as we worked to explore interventions that we hoped would be successful. He has been diagnosed with psychotic disorder NOS, and it is clear that he has been significantly impacted by his early life, which included severe abuse.

Bobeed has periods when he functions relatively well and his mood is stable. During these times, he is a little gentleman with exceptionally good manners, generous and considerate of his peers, and affectionate with the staff. He has episodes where he appears insightful and is able to carry on brief conversations and maintain focus.

Bobeed also has periods where he appears unstable, his mood is quickly changeable, and he becomes extremely impulsive and assaultive. At these times, he does better with designated male staff with whom he feels comfortable. We have found that when he is having a difficult time, we have needed to have a "100 percent containment plan" for him. This plan involves us always being aware where Bobeed is, with whom he is playing, and what staff are in his immediate vicinity. Even if he appeared to be in a "good space" at the moment and was hugging staff, they needed to be very aware of where their body was in proximity to his and to have the ability to disengage and move out of arm's length at a second's notice. We have identified two different categories of male staff that we allocate to work closely with him. The first category is male staff who are able to contain him when he begins to hit, scratch, or bite but whom he assaults even though they are comfortable containing him in his room with a few very brief holds until he calms. The second category of male staff is two male staff with whom he has the closest relationships and with whom he feels the most safe and comfortable. These two staff he does not assault, and often his meltdowns end more quickly when he is with them. We try and consider what males are scheduled on a shift and identify who is going to be allocated to be in close view of Bobeed and able and ready to intercede at a moment's notice.

Bobeed's meltdowns follow a pattern that we would like to share with you so that you can have the advantage of what we have learned. We have identified that about 70 percent of the time, Bobeed has a meltdown in response to a limit having been set on him. He does not like the limit, and he becomes immediately extremely impulsive and may strike out at staff who have set the limit, or he may strike out at the nearest available staff. For some male staff, he targets their genital area, and for some female staff, he targets their breasts. About 20 percent of the time, Bobeed appears to suddenly melt down if a staff member who he likes is unavailable immediately to him and is spending time with another child. The remaining 10 percent appears to be targeted at staff who are in the way or first available after he becomes upset and impulsive. Sometimes we are able to intervene and contain him, and after one hold of a few minutes in duration he can be redirected. At other times, his meltdowns are quite severe and progress to a prolonged dissociated state where he screams a heart-wrenching cry for thirty to forty-five minutes and is unable to connect with the staff there to assist him.

Interventions that have worked with Bobeed to prevent a meltdown are distraction and redirection at the very beginning of his becoming agitated. We also use frequent PRN medication to avoid an impending meltdown. Bobeed does give us warning signs that he is about to become agitated, which is a precipitant to a meltdown. He begins to rap and curse, and this is a clear cue that he is "revving up." When he has entered the meltdown phase, he is much more likely to accept PRN medication from the nurse if a staff person he trusts is in the room. We have found that putting the medication close by him and stepping back are more successful than getting too close and possibly ending up wearing the medication and the glass of water.

When Bobeed's mom is present, he is grounded and able to stay in amazing control. They have great lunches together in the day hall, and he is able to focus with her for long periods of time (up to 1½ hours). She is a positive influence on him, and we have learned to involve her in our administrative meetings with Bobeed. We would suggest as much involvement from her as is possible in the first weeks, before he has built a trusting relationship with any of the staff. When new staff have arrived on our unit, it has been somewhat upsetting to him, and we have found that it is better to keep them at a distance for a few days until he becomes acclimated to their presence.

When Bobeed is doing well, we have worked with him to identify activities that will help him calm down. He likes to play Playstation, and often this can calm him when nothing else works. He also likes Gameboy and to rollerblade. He enjoys one-on-one activities off the unit with staff. We have developed a laminated series of cards on a key ring for him to use when he is upset, as he is unable to verbalize at these times. He is encouraged to point to the activity card that he thinks will help him at that given time.

We have found that Bobeed is not able to engage in verbal processing about what is happening to him or within him. Despite the fact that it has been quite a challenge to "help him become workable," we never saw his meltdowns as requiring more restrictive measures of containment than brief physical holds. We have never stopped our quest to try and answer the questions: "What is going on in his head that we wish wasn't?" and "What is not going on in his head that we wish was?" That speaks to what a wonderful boy he is and our never losing sight of trying to find ways that would make life easier for him. We genuinely feel that when he is impulsive and aggressive, he knows no other options at those moments, and that he has a compromised ability to tell us in words what is going on with him. He is not yet able to label his feelings, and we have tried basic approaches to help him develop a basic vocabulary of feeling states. One approach has been to stand with him at a mirror and say, "That looks like a mad face." We have tried to work on identifying only three basic emotions at this point that might impact his behavior: mad, sad, and frustrated.

Bobeed often arises early, and we have tried to establish a morning routine where he showers followed by a staff person helping him put cream on his skin. Then he dresses and is allowed to play Playstation quietly. This routine has helped him start the day in a peaceful manner and has allowed the other kids to sleep and not be awakened by his having a meltdown.

We hope this information is helpful, and we are more than willing to be contacted if you have questions or want to share ideas on helping Bobeed adjust to his new placement.

—The Staff of the CAU

Bobeed spent nearly a year in a state hospital continuing-care unit and then moved to a residential program. He called us recently and sounded wonderful. He said he was doing great and was happy at his new program. He hoped to finish that program and then return home with his mom.

CHAPTER 14

THE TIPPING POINT:
Staff Consensus

"People seldom see the halting and painful steps by which the most insignificant success is achieved."

— Anne Sullivan

Malcolm Gladwell describes the "tipping point" as having reached the critical mass or boiling point of a social change. He likens the spread of ideas that generate a social change to the spread of a viral epidemic. He reasons that all epidemics have tipping points, and that social change follows the rules of epidemics. The first principle is the contagion effect, the second is that little changes bring big effects, and the third is the possibility of sudden change.[10] He believes that when an epidemic tips, the equilibrium shifts or is jolted, and a sudden change in one or more areas occurs.[11] He also states that "what must underlie social epidemics, in the end, is a bedrock belief that change is possible, that people can radically transform their behavior or beliefs in the face of the right kind of impetus."[12]

We had already had our contagion effect. We were working hard to master skills and were role modeling after one another. A few key staff members had embraced what we were trying to do and began implementing these ideas. And those key people led the march. They generated a larger response from other staff who looked up to them and saw them as key players. We were seeing positive effects in our interactions with the children, and that was spurning us on to try harder, which led to more frequent attempts at Basket B interactions. I perceived that my "High Noon" moment over the cupcakes (in which I allowed a girl to eat her birthday cupcakes when she wanted, rather than waiting for the designated time) was an illustration of the second principle of how little changes bring big effects. I had taken a stand openly on a small issue that we had been working on, but it became symbolic of something much larger—it epitomized our working to change our culture to a more child-centered, nurturing environment. This small gesture had some larger meaning to the staff, and there was a swell in support following this event. There was less skepticism, and it was a time of larger buy-in by a number of staff. The third principle stating the possibility of sudden change jolting the equilibrium took place in the event that followed.

A number of staff were informing me that two particular staff members were making it clear that they did not agree with the changes we were making and were trying to do something about it. Their dissatisfaction was not voiced at our weekly meetings; in fact, they were noticeably absent from most of the group supervision sessions. They did not seek me out to voice their complaints either. But they were making their voices known to the staff with whom they worked, and the staff were coming to me to express their displeasure with the remarks they were making.

Things reached a head when I received notification from one of the nurses involved informing me that they had made complaints to the Board of Registration in Nursing (BORN) and to the Massachusetts Department of Mental Health (DMH). They had two main concerns. The first was that they did not agree with what we were doing, and they perceived the changes in our culture and model of care as making the unit unsafe. They felt that it was only a matter of time until someone was injured. The second point was that, as nurses who frequently functioned as charge nurses when working, they felt that the changes in our management of the children put them in a position of liability, and they felt that their nursing licenses were at stake. The BORN responded that the issues they raised were not ones in which they would become involved. The scope of the BORN was narrow, and it was likely to investigate reports of a nurse diverting drugs or of a nurse involved in inappropriate conduct with a patient, but it was not looking at nursing liability in relation to philosophical approaches to the care of patients.

The DMH was interested in what we were doing. It had been watching closely as we made changes, and I was open in sharing what we were doing as we moved along. The DMH was very invested in all units within the state that were altering their practice in any efforts to reduce and/or eliminate restraint and seclusion. We were out in front with some other units that were developing strategies to provide care in a more humane and trauma-sensitive way.

The DMH wanted us to succeed. It also wanted to be sure that the changes we were making had the support of the staff. The letter it had received indicated that many of the staff were not in support of the direction the unit was moving. The DMH asked what would be our strategy to handle this situation.

I discussed this with my mentor, Maryanne, and we planned to hold a large staff meeting asking everyone to come and share their thoughts, concerns, and doubts about what we were doing. The meeting would be chaired by Colleen (the CNO or her designee) and Maryanne. We would provide the opportunity for dissent and questioning in a forum where the staff working on the unit could express their displeasure directly to the nursing leadership of the organization.

The date was changed once because one of the nurses who had written the letters would not be available. After notifying everyone of the second date (which was based on a date that both nurses were scheduled to work), they both declined to come for other reasons, and one of the nurses stated that no matter what date was arranged, she probably would choose not to attend. I was initially in a quandary as to what to do, but a number of the staff came forward and asked that we go ahead with the meeting. They wanted to have a public venue to discuss this issue, and they wanted the administrators to be available and to hear them out.

The meeting was held three weeks later. I was amazed to see the turnout. We had a large representation and everyone spoke up. It was genuinely moving, and it was our tipping point. Even the most shy, quiet employees spoke proudly about what we were accomplishing. Every staff member spoke up and talked of the changes we were making and how positive they felt about what we were doing. They discussed their individual journeys from initial skepticism to some beginning successes to a feeling of pride and accomplishment. They wanted the administration of the hospital to know that they were wholly involved in this effort; they supported it and embraced it as their own achievement. They spoke of being unable to imagine going back to the way things were done before. They related the satisfaction they now felt when helping children in a non-consequence-based model, and they spoke of the freedom of being released from the roles of rule enforcers. They talked of their increased feelings of job satisfaction. They also shared their personal sense of reward at being able to help a child and being able to show affection and not worry about the old preoccupation with boundaries.

They also voiced a discontent with the two naysayers, and they were there in force to prove that it was only *two* naysayers. They wanted Colleen and Maryanne to know that these two people were the problem to be dealt with on the unit. Their negativism was disheartening, and the other staff members resented the false statements being made by the two nurses both privately and in public to outside bodies.

The administrators were impressed by the outpouring of support and were touched by the genuineness of each individual's personal comments and assessments. I sent an e-mail to the DMH staff, with whom I had developed a positive relationship and to whom we reported. They were pleased at the results of the meeting and indicated that no further action would be taken.

Things moved quickly from that point. We were no longer in a convincing phase or a "give it a try" phase. We were continuing to move forward, and we no longer referred to our efforts as a pilot program. This was the real deal, and we were all in it together.

A group cohesion had formed. The resistance and the notifying of outside agencies had pushed us over the hump. There was a sense of going full-steam ahead and of having weathered a difficult time together. I was conscious then, as I had been at other points before and after, of having a sense of gratitude for the very special and talented people with whom I worked. This was their achievement.

From this point on we would still have challenges, and there would still be times when we were stressed and when problems developed. But we were past the point of the problem being attributed to what we were doing or how we were doing it.

The two nurses who had stayed up to that point and resisted our efforts left within a matter of months after this event. Unfortunately for them, their resignations passed quietly with no big send-offs. It should come as no surprise that one of the nurses was the same nurse who had taken a stand over the birthday cupcakes. Her resignation was accepted in a New York minute. We were hiring new staff and recruiting new employees who were taking the job knowing what we were trying to do and wanting to be a part of it.

CHAPTER 15

THE END OF THE LEVEL SYSTEM

• Erica •

"The only way to make sense out of change is to plunge into it, move with it, and join the dance."

— Alan Watts

The next supervision after the special staff meeting started with a review of the meeting, and people voiced being glad for the opportunity to stand up and be counted. A few people stated that, in anticipation of the meeting, they had reviewed the past months in their minds. One staff person followed with: "You know, I really feel that I am getting it, and I feel confident when I say that we do CPS here. I feel like it is a part of me, and it is hard to remember at times what it felt like to do things differently."

179

Dick said that he thought this was a good time to bring up something he had been thinking about, and it was something that he had talked about with some other staff. He wanted to discuss the level system. If we looked at how we were operating now, we would see blank point cards for the kids. We had not been tallying up points for weeks. In fact, for the past two months, the only thing we saw on the point cards for the kids was a number of stars they had earned for good decisions, performing difficult procedures—the rewards we gave in recognition of a child having done something we thought was positive.

We had learned that going off the unit was not just a reward, but an essential part of our culture now. Taking a child off the unit often prevented a child from messing with the milieu. It was often a tool used by staff to help a child who was having a meltdown or about to have a meltdown—getting some fresh air, getting away from what was frustrating him or her, and having an opportunity to calm down. It was an effective intervention, and we were relying on this intervention with increasing frequency.

Dick pointed out that Ross had told us months ago that the time would come when we would realize that we no longer needed a level system. He felt that that time had come. We talked about how we were using the levels currently, and it turned out that they were used primarily as an administrative system.

We used Unit Restricted (UR) the initial twenty-four hours after a child was admitted to have a chance to get to know the child to some degree and for the child to get to know us and how the unit operated. Hospital Restricted (HR) was basically a trial phase off the unit. A child's first trip off the unit was usually with one staff on a one-to-one walk around the hospital or the grounds. It basically was used to see if the child was able to follow directions and stay close to staff. If that went okay, we had no reservations about moving a child to Off Grounds (OG) so that he or she could go out with the group. Based on this, we made a decision that the basic default for the unit was OG. And that each child would have the opportunity to reach OG in forty-eight hours of admission.

Our new administrative system looked like this: UR × 24 hours, then, HR × 24 hours, then OG. We had this incorporated into part of our standing admission orders for all children.

Ross stated that he was always glad when level systems rusted away on their own, but he reminded us that we wanted to make sure we did not eliminate rewards for the kids when we were doing away with a consequence-based system. We were not worried about that, as we had a star system for rewards and the staff used it liberally to reward at any opportunity—a child's attempt to collaborate with a peer or with staff, for acts of kindness a child undertook, and for a child handling a difficult situation such as psychological testing, blood draws, a teaching conference interview, etc. We would tally up the number of stars a child was given, and the child was able to redeem the stars at the Stars Cabinet. It was a capitalistic enterprise that was very successful. Within the first day or two of an admission, a child was taken to see the Star Cabinet. It was stocked full of toys and games with varying star values. The items ranged from very cheap (1,000 stars) to pricey (25,000) for a remote-control car. There were items that appealed to every age and sex. Debbie kept it replenished, and the kids loved cashing in their stars for items. Usually, there were one or two children who were able to resist immediate cash-ins to save for a more expensive item. These items were also likely to be earned by the children who were on our unit for months awaiting a placement in a residential program of one of the state agencies.

Our teacher also ran a weekly awards ceremony. On each Friday, there would be a brief celebration complete with the beating of drums, where each child was recognized and given a certificate for some admirable quality. Amelia was very creative and thoughtful in personalizing these certificates with a little speech about each child that included giving examples of each one's behavior that warranted the certificate for outstanding performance. Some of the awards celebrated academics, and some celebrated positive traits such as helping a younger child, most improved in a subject area, or most improved in behavior. The children enjoyed this ritual.

In our supervision, we discussed the importance of letting kids know at the point of admission what we were doing. We wanted to let them know that we did not put kids in mechanical restraints or seclude them. We wanted them to work with us and take advantage of the unit working to be restraint-free. We also admitted that one of the scariest things we encountered was a new child being out of control. We knew less about the children when they first arrived, and we did not yet have a relationship with them to help us in our interactions. It would be proactive to let children know how we worked and to go over this in our formal orientation to the unit as a child was being admitted. We speculated that there would be less likelihood of a new admission becoming out of control if the child had some understanding of what we were trying to do. We were hoping to capitalize on a window of opportunity to get to know the children, and they would have the same opportunity to get to know us before they became frustrated and agitated.

I had rewritten our parent handbook to cover our new approach and to provide information in basic fashion about CPS and our values on the unit. We had also put signage in the lobby that highlighted our open hours and our approach with the children. I rewrote our child's handbook to include how we were trying to work with the children admitted to the unit, as well as providing basic information.

In discussions about our doing away with a level system that was consequence-based, the issue grew beyond this. The issue was about our admission process and the need to explain what we were about. This led into a dialogue about the need to go further back than that point in time. It had to do with our front door. Our front door was our Psychiatric Emergency Service. Our psychiatric services were so large that our health system had its own Psychiatric Emergency Department. The staff employed there were the first people at our hospital to work with the children and families who would be admitted to our unit.

We needed to talk with them about what we were doing so that they could begin to talk about this with some understanding of our priorities and manner of operating. Some of the issues that needed to be broached in the admission process were:

- Working toward a restraint-free and trauma-free environment.

- Our use of medication as a tool to manage aggression and its help in our assessment of what was underlying the aggression.

- The need to have parents present and to attend family meetings several times a week to facilitate our assessment and treatment.

- Our unit level of aggression at any point in time (if we had four children who were very aggressive and not yet workable, we would be limited in our capacity to take on another extremely aggressive child to add to the mix—until we had been able to help one or more of the children decrease their level of aggression).

- The need to know at the point of admission if a child would become stuck on the unit due to not having an available program or home situation to which he or she could return.

We identified an even more global need for interactions with other psychiatric facilities for children. Wouldn't it be better for all of us if we had collaborative relationships where we helped each other out and where we shared equally the stuck kids within the state so that no one unit would have half of their population being stuck kids? Wouldn't it be better for all of us to be able to coordinate the children who were extremely aggressive so that no one unit was inundated with a high mix of very aggressive kids at the same time? There was no such system at this time, but it was a goal worth working toward. Even better would be a system of care where there was no such phenomenon as stuck kids!

In our session at that time, there was a discussion about a girl named Erica. She had been admitted within the last three days because she was not listening to her mother, was putting herself in dangerous situations, was not attending school, and was hanging out with much older people (men in their late teens and early twenties). She was twelve years of age but looked and acted much older. She was also beautiful. We discussed the information we knew about her and then talked of our goals for her admission. We thought it would be helpful for her to be able to identify other attributes that she had besides her physical beauty in which to feel good about herself. In her interactions, we had observed that she used her beauty as the center point of her style of interacting and was letting her unrecognized attributes be thrown to the wind. We believed that if we could help her to grow down to be a twelve-year-old, we would be helping her in her present-day functioning and in her future. Our task was to identify things she did well and to help her build on them. We would comment on our observations of her interactions with other kids and would give her positive feedback when she acted as a leader in a group activity and when she showed her caring, gentler side. We would consciously avoid comments praising her for her looks and her beauty.

Over the next week, staff members made observations of Erica in different situations. Several female staff had meaningful conversations with her using these observations in their discussions with her. They had learned that Erica based much of her self-esteem on her beauty. She had admitted that it was a positive attribute but that at times she resented that many people gravitated to her due to her beauty. So she felt both good and bad about her looks. The male staff reported that some of her behaviors were so out there as to make them uncomfortable. They related her licking a popsicle in a sexual manner, and the staff agreed that there were things like this that she only did when male staff were present and female staff were out of eyesight.

Erica had created quite a stir on the unit with the boys, and there was much competition to be her "boyfriend." She also became involved competitively with another girl of the unit over the boyfriend issue. Amelia was able to have a productive Basket B intervention with Erica and the other girl in which they both decided that it was more important to be friends together than to compete over who was getting Donny's attention.

The group supervision session the next week ended up with a milieu plan to help Erica with her interactions. Female staff would talk with her about her interactive style with the male milieu counselors in a matter-of-fact manner. They would identify that the male staff had perceived her manner of interacting with them as flirtatious and at times having a sexual undertone. They were uncomfortable and did not feel that it was appropriate for her to relate in this manner with older men. The female staff members would share that their own perception was that Erica often ignored them and preferred to interact with the male staff.

The discussion took place with two female staff members and Erica. She was able to state that a part of her would like to change her behavior, but she had acted this way for awhile and it would be hard to change. She would be staying on our unit until a group home was found for her, and she agreed that she would like to work on this while she was here. We developed a plan where male staff would direct her to female staff when she approached them. And female staff would be available and would encourage her to spend time with them. If she displayed interactions that seemed flirtatious or sexual in tone, the female staff would bring this to her attention in a matter-of-fact way and use these observations as opportunities for learning and not to shame or embarrass her. We discussed with her that we appreciated that much of her style was automatic at this point and that she may not be consciously aware when she was behaving in this manner.

Erica stayed with us for about two and a half months. We found that she was very creative. She enjoyed styling the other girls' hair and providing them with manicures. Her manicure designs were complex, and she could design patterns of any flag on the nails she was polishing. She was a knitter, and we encouraged her to pursue this activity. She enjoyed the girls' grooming group and developed a relationship with two female staff while she was with us.

We heard that she had done well in her group program and then returned home to live with her mother and older sister. We also learned that she had been hospitalized a year later on our adolescent unit.

Moving Ahead
and
Lessons Learned

CHAPTER 16

FINE-TUNING AND RECURRING THEMES

• *Jennifer* •

*"We need four hugs a day for survival.
We need eight hugs a day for maintenance.
We need twelve hugs a day for growth."*

— *Virginia Satir*

We were now ten months into our change in the way we were providing care to the children. We had developed confidence in our skills. We were past our tipping point; we had consensus. The excitement of creating change had abated; the change was now our routine. The heady, early days were history. We had moved into a different phase. We were gaining recognition for what we had achieved, and that was very satisfying. The Massachusetts Department of Mental Health was referring people to us and to a few other programs for dialogue about the strides we were making in decreasing restraint and seclusion. These referred programs were in the beginning stages of questioning how to better provide care to children while working on initiatives to reduce restraint and seclusion. We enjoyed the opportunity to talk about what we were doing, and we encouraged people to visit us and spend the day to observe us in action. Since our health-care network was a teaching facility, we were used to staff rotating through the unit as part of their education. The children were also accustomed to parents and relatives being present and to staff rotating through the unit; having visitors who were observing our staff interactions was not a disruption in our routine. The unit was a learning lab for adults as well as for children, so we encouraged visitors.

Maintaining progress and change was more difficult than creating progress. It involved finding challenges and excitement in tasks that had become routine. It involved being aware of and resisting slippage as a natural force to be countered against. It also involved remembering that, when stressed, almost everybody inadvertently resorted to old, comfortable ways of behaving. Therefore, maintaining progress meant being vigilant and open to problem solving and to fine-tuning the processes that we had developed.

It also meant fighting complacency. It meant not getting overly confident. It meant working to avoid smugness and arrogance. It meant staying humble. It meant being open to new ideas and suggestions. It meant avoiding becoming entrenched. And it meant continuing to find joy and meaning in our work. Most importantly, it meant not taking ourselves too seriously.

In working to maintain our gains and to improve further, we were finding that we needed to step up our level of sophistication in our use of CPS. We needed to use the vocabulary more frequently; we needed to incorporate our formulations of pathways to aggression with particular children along with our biopsychosocial formulations. The clinicians needed to be incorporating more of the CPS concepts and skill building into the family meetings that they were having with the parents. If we had a shared CPS formulation, it would be easier to talk with families about their children and what they needed from their parents. This would teach parents the skills they would need to be successful in helping their children. It would also be easier to engage the parents and have them work with us if we approached them from the standpoint of our formulation of the child's needs using a CPS framework. The message would be easier to hear, and parents were more likely to accept what we were trying to say. CPS language was less blaming and therefore was more likely to generate cooperation rather than resistance.

In developing our formulations, we needed to start with a look at what behaviors brought the child into the hospital. We then needed to add to that our observations of a child's behavior on the unit. We needed to assess how far apart those behaviors were from what was developmentally appropriate—how far from the norm the behaviors were and which ones were the furthest out from the norm. What did the behaviors tell us in trying to answer: What is this kid's deal? Once we were able to figure out a particular child's deal, then we could begin to identify pathways. And once the pathways were identified, we would be able to tailor our interventions to specific skill deficits. We would know what skills we needed to teach.

We needed to develop an infrastructure to ensure that the changes in care that we had initiated would last beyond the individuals who were currently working on the unit.

Part of developing this infrastructure meant developing policies and procedures that spelled out what we were doing. The first policy that I developed was a CAU Nursing Standard of Care for the child with aggressive behavior. That was followed by a CAU CPS Nursing Care Plan template. These were followed by CPS competencies: CPS Competency I and CPS II.

Staff members requested a vocabulary list to help them in their documentation for nursing progress notes of the medical record. They wanted to translate their observations of a child's behavior and their interactions in Basket B in a way that indicated that we were providing teaching and skill building and to describe the behavior accurately. I developed a vocabulary sheet that had old terms we were avoiding and new terms we were encouraging. We wanted staff to be able to describe a child's behavior and interactions accurately and for the description to be specific and non-judgmental. Many words of the old psych jargon were judgmental in tone (i.e., gamey, provocative, attention-seeking, manipulative, intentional, secondary gains, etc.). They were more an indication of the observer's take on the child's behavior than an accurate description of what had occurred. A number of staff also asked if they could have a more extensive explanation of some of the definitions or descriptions of thinking skills involved in specific pathways. Based on Ross's advanced training seminar material, I developed a handout of descriptions of thinking skill deficits under specific pathways to aggression for the staff. It became part of our orientation packet for new staff.

Two areas that caused a frequent return to old approaches and needed clarification and discussion regularly were the issues of food never being in Basket A, and settling at night not being in Basket A either. We would discuss the issue when it arose in regard to a particular child, we would agree, and then it would resurface a few months later. There was something about basics like food and going to bed that generated Basket A responses when our expectations were not met. And it spoke to how ingrained some basic beliefs were to us that they resurfaced regularly and we had to think them through all over again.

We discussed making sure that there was a sign in clear view in the kitchen that stated: "FOOD IS NEVER IN BASKET A." The issue was one of weight gain. For a number of the children, the large increase in weight that they developed was closely related to their having been put on antipsychotic medication, which causes a large increase in appetite. This increase in appetite was at least partially tied to the reality that the kids were hungry and craving food. Restricting their food intake would not curb their hunger. For specific children, if we had concerns about weight gain and their health, we would discuss it and determine that food for a particular child would be a Basket B issue. For some kids, our concern was to curb their aggression or stabilize their mood, and food was not the major issue on the horizon. For those kids, we would discuss the issue and determine that for that child, at that particular point in time, food was in Basket C. The unit would have no set basket determination for food except that it was never in Basket A. We could also help with this by tailoring the environment. We closed the gated metal panel above the kitchen counter so that the sight of food was not tempting the children at all times. We worked with the dietary department about the food items selected for the unit. We came up with a number of changes.

We wanted to stress healthier eating habits and to provide healthier choices. We also wanted to do this in a child-centered way. Developing a menu based on adult healthy choices was not the answer and would also lead to frequent struggles with the children. We thought about what foods the children liked and which were the most popular items we served, then tried to work with those foods. The kids loved apple juice and consumed quarts of it every day. When I learned that apple juice was full of sugar and had no real nutritional value, our unit and the pediatric medical unit both made requests to the dietary department to eliminate the use of apple juice for our patients. The American Academy of Pediatrics had recommended substituting white grape juice, so we requested that we receive several quarts of white grape juice a day. We also received cranberry juice and orange juice so that we could make special drinks using diet gingerale, cranberry, and orange juice. This was popular. We served chocolate milk made with skim milk instead of whole milk. In fact, we substituted skim milk for whole milk for the unit and only received whole milk for the children who were undernourished whom we were trying to help gain weight. Instead of steamed vegetables, which came up with the lunch or dinner trays and went uneaten, we requested that several times a week we receive a large tray with raw vegetables such as celery, carrots, tomatoes, peppers, or zucchini. They were served with low-fat ranch dressing and the kids loved them. What was not eaten for a meal was refrigerated and served for snacks. The children's favorite meal was barbequed chicken wings. We served them baked instead of fried and the kids never knew the difference. We served cold-cut platters twice a week and the kids liked making their own subs. We supplied pretzels with peanut butter for snacks instead of potato chips.

The kitchen staff became engaged in their own customer service program, and they would bring up new food items and have the kids become involved in taste tests. They would listen to the kids' feedback about foods that were viewed as appealing.

We ordered more fresh fruit as part of our daily supplies for the unit. We found that some children liked fruit and had no hesitation in choosing fruit as a snack, but many passed it up for less nutritious items. Terry found that, when she took the fruit from the fruit basket and cut it up and made a fresh fruit salad in a big bowl, the kids loved it. It took more work, but it was an activity in which we could involve the children, and it proved to be useful.

We found that kids liked special drinks, so we developed a CAU juice bar. We purchased an industrial blender and made fruit smoothies for snacks. The kids loved them, and they loved getting to the front of the line and picking what fruit and what juice or yogurt they wanted for their own individualized smoothie. The smoothies were also useful for the children who had chronic problems with constipation due the medication they were prescribed.

We would add prune juice to the smoothie mix, and no one knew the better, as the taste was camouflaged with the other ingredients. We deleted French fries from the menu for all but one offering a week. We added rice. We substituted the beef hot dog for a turkey dog. We substituted sherbet and juice pops for ice cream. We added sugar-free popsicles as an option for unlimited snacks.

We found that it was not easy to moderate the quantity of food that some children were consuming, but it was much easier to moderate the quality of the choices they were making.

Our group supervision session at this time focused on a girl named Jennifer who was proving difficult for us to manage. She was eleven years of age and had moderate mental retardation. She had been admitted for "out-of-control behavior" at a previous placement. We were warned that she required frequent restraints. Recently, a placement with an adoptive family had fallen through. This had been her second failed adoptive placement. And she had been through five placements prior to this last one.

We were challenged by her aggressive behavior on the unit and were still attempting to determine to what extent we could involve her in Basket B interactions. Over the past two and a half weeks, her meltdowns had increased, and she was a big girl, capable of hurting other kids when she was assaultive and also capable of hurting staff. In supervision sessions, staff members admitted to feeling at a loss in trying to implement collaborative interventions with Jennifer, and the issue raised the question: "Does CPS work with kids who have mental retardation?"

We spent some time discussing Jennifer. Despite her cognitive limitations, she was an astute observer of relationships. She was aware of each child on the unit and whether or not they received visitors, and at what times their visitors arrived. She knew how frequently particular children had family present on the unit. It was easy for us to surmise that relationship issues and loss of relationships were likely to cause her difficulty. We needed to look more specifically at when, where, with whom, and under what circumstances meltdowns were occurring. We also needed to identify what coping strategies she had developed and what interventions had helped her through difficult times. She had been able to tell us, when she saw parents coming and leaving the unit, "I want to be loved, and I want two parents." We had also observed that distraction and diversion had worked the best with her. These tactics were often successful with young children who were pre-verbal and had not yet developed good language skills.

We set our goal as helping her to be able to participate in some linguistic give-and-take with us, and to help her access some language in the midst of frustration. We hoped to be able to teach her to tell us before she slipped into a meltdown that "I am angry" or "this is making me mad." If we could help her identify her emotional state prior to a full meltdown, we could offer some suggestions from which she could choose. Tim indicated that Jennifer had shown some ability to do this until recently. He identified a meeting with her guardian ad litem (the attorney appointed to look out for her interests) and the attorney for the state child protective agency as a turning point for Jennifer. Tim reported that Jennifer's meltdowns had become more frequent since the meeting, and we were also having less success in diverting her attention from the cause of her frustration. Laura chimed in that she thought Jennifer was feeling hopeless and had reached a point where she believed she had nothing to lose.

Stuart suggested that we break our interventions down into micro steps. The first step would be to help Jennifer with the question: What am I feeling? To answer that, Jennifer would have to know what she was feeling, she would need to categorize it or classify it, and then she would need to articulate this to another person. These were the tasks involved in problem identification. The second step involved answering the question: What can I do about it? She would need our help to develop some creative solutions to help with the problem. Stuart recognized that staff members had been very creative in coming up with solutions to date: We had developed a visitor list for Jennifer and hung it in the nurses' station. When we knew that there were going to be a number of family members on the unit spending time with their children, we put these times up on Jennifer's visitors list, and staff signed up to spend exclusive time with her when she would be the most vulnerable. Jason had been signed up to visit Jennifer this past Sunday at 5:30 P.M. At noon, Jason told her he would be visiting with her at 5:30 P.M. She was able to eat her dinner, go to her room for room time, and wait patiently until 5:30 for her visit. They went for a walk, and she did beautifully during what would have been a difficult time for her.

At bedtime, she became agitated. We identified that she thought about her family at bedtime, and it was a difficult time for her. She stormed to the nurses' station, actually climbed through the window, and stood in the staff area and pointed to the medical charts. She pointed from chart to chart and said, "He gets a visitor, she gets a visitor, he gets a visitor..." and she began flinging rubber bands. She was clearly in acute distress, and the staff present chose to deal with the situation in Basket C by just waiting her out. It was a tense thirty minutes, but then she calmed down and allowed staff to read her a bedtime story on her mattress. She then fell asleep.

We were not able to give her what she wanted: a set of parents. But we could give her caring, attention, and love for the time she was with us. We could also acknowledge how upsetting it was to have no available family that can raise you.

In going over the rubber-band issue and Jennifer's being in the nurses' station, we had chosen to let it go—to Basket C it. She was feeling heartbroken at the time. She would not have been able to discuss things with us right then, so a Basket B intervention would not have worked. And making her behavior a Basket A issue would have been a rules-driven approach and not one of understanding and appreciation for her legitimate distress.

Our job was to be proactive and identify times of difficulty before they occurred so that we could prevent meltdowns. In looking over the previous two weeks of events, we did see some patterns emerge. Jennifer had exhibited meltdowns almost every day at 4 P.M. and at 10 P.M. One suggestion was to explore whether some medication at 3 P.M. and at bedtime would help her. When she was roaming the unit, becoming upset as she looked for who was having visitors, we needed to remember that she was identifying who had families and was looking for reminders. We further developed her visitor list and we added to it so that some staff who were not working would call in and talk with her during times when families were present on the unit. Laura made a practice of doing this every Sunday afternoon. In fact, on the Sundays when Laura was working on the unit, she would go into the staff lounge and call Jennifer from there and have an extensive conversation with her about her week and what had occurred.

In our work with Jennifer, we advocated for more involvement of her grandparents. They were not able to care for her, but they cared *about* her. We encouraged them to visit on the unit, and we advocated that whatever residential program that was located for her be within visiting distance of her grandparents. Jennifer was on our unit for seven months. When she left us for a residential program, this is the write-up we sent to the program. Here are some excerpts from that letter:

What We Have Learned About Jennifer

1. *When Jennifer is having a hard time, she often goes to the unit door and bangs on it and states she wants to "Go home!" We have been able to talk out loud with her at*

these times about how hard it is for her over "x" issue and what can we do to help her through a difficult time. Then we make suggestions for what might help her. Often she will agree with one of the suggestions and we will be able to avoid a meltdown.

2. *Jennifer is very sensitive and has a difficult time when another child is being held or escorted to his or her room or to the Quiet Room. Initially, she would become aggressive to the staff and would shout, "Stop hurting him or her." Over time, she has been able to see that the staff are trying to help another child, not hurt him or her, and she no longer involves herself in the situation. An intermediate intervention we used was to allocate a specific staff member to distract her when another child was having a hard time. This was very successful and was well worth the effort, as it prevented her from "melting down" and also was proactive in preventing a domino effect on the unit, where a number of children become escalated at once in response to one or two children becoming aggressive.*

3. *Jennifer is very caring and was a good friend to several children on the unit. She was socially aware and was able to pick up cues from staff and would help other children who were beginning to have a hard time. She would share with them what had worked with her and would offer to play with them or to help them ignore a child who might have been teasing them.*

4. *Jennifer has a difficult time with her personal hygiene, and she responds to a supportive approach with some reward for fulfilling the tasks expected within a certain time frame. For example, to get her ready on time in the morning, a staff person would ask her to help with a task*

off the unit, but she would need to be dressed and ready to be out in public in order to help her with her morning hygiene. She appreciated the opportunity to have some special time with a staff person in the morning and liked being a staff helper. The tasks were not daunting; sometimes it was walking with a staff member to his or her car in the garage to get something out of it; at other times it was accompanying a staff member to a local coffee shop to purchase coffee for the staff.

5. *Jennifer sometimes wants to stay in her room, and we found that the times she sought to stay in her room were when she was feeling sad, when she felt scared, and when she felt she was not able to handle the milieu. We worked with her at these times around our understanding what she was feeling and how we could help her cope with that feeling. She is able to problem solve when she is feeling trusting of the staff, and if the staff are able to collaborate with her rather than laying down ultimatums. She does not respond well to imposing one's will rather than trying to work things out together.*

6. *We hope that you grow to care for Jennifer as we have and that she thrives in your program. With the involvement of Jennifer's biological grandparents and uncle, you have a wonderful asset in her cooperation in your program. Being able to link your program with easier access to "her family" is a very potent aspect that will work toward Jennifer's success. We would suggest that by involving them in frequent contact, the result will be seen in her adjusting and adapting to her new surroundings more easily.*

CHAPTER 17

SOME MORE STORIES

• Arturo, Debbie, Melanie, John •

"The parents exist to teach the child, but also they must
learn what the child has to teach them; and the child
has a very great deal to teach them."

— Arnold Bennett

We learned a lot from the children who came to us for help with
their problems. Different children helped us learn lessons about
what interventions worked best with them, and some of the time
we were able to see that the things that worked for them were
working for many of the children, regardless of their diagnosis or
their particular pathways to aggression. In some cases we were successful. In other cases, despite our best efforts, we were not able to
convince others of our approach. Here are a few additional stories
of some of the children who were most memorable.

ARTURO

Arturo was on our unit for approximately three months, and during that time he helped us fine-tune our ability to engage in Basket B interventions and to keep the dialogue going.

Arturo was a nine-year-old boy who lived with his mother, father, and twelve-year-old sister. His grandmother and uncle had also lived in the home.

He was admitted for "out-of-control behavior" at home, where he was verbally abusive to his mother and father and was assaultive to his mother. He was also having a difficult time in school and was seen as being a management problem there. He had disclosed having witnessed the sexual abuse of his sister by his uncle in the home. His parents did not believe him, and he reported that his father hit him every time he brought this topic up. During his emergency evaluation, he disclosed for the first time that his uncle had also sexually abused him. He related that the abuse with his sister was ongoing, and he had told his parents about the abuse several months prior to his admission to our unit. He also reported that his grandmother had witnessed some of the abuse, despite her denial of this.

After Arturo's parents finally came to believe him, his grandmother and uncle moved out of the home at the parents' request. His parents did go to the child protective agency to report the abuse, and they obtained a restraining order to protect their children from further damage by the uncle. The uncle was thought to be out of state at the time of Arturo's admission. In fairness to Arturo's parents, their hesitancy in believing Arturo's horrid story was tied to his history of telling tales that were not true and they had, over time, developed a skeptical attitude when he came to them with a story.

Our observations of Arturo after a number of days on the unit were the following: He appeared sad and was irritable most of the time, he exhibited poor concentration skills, he was hyperactive, he had difficulty sticking to any one task for any discernible period of time (he had difficulty maintaining cognitive set), and he was also unable to shift cognitive set when the environment demanded it. He had a low level of frustration tolerance but was able to concentrate on Playstation, Gameboy, and TV for extended periods of time. In his attempts to make friends, he told fantastic stories to his peers that were not believable, and as a result, he was teased and was considered by them to be a braggart. Based on this information, we began to categorize our observations of his behavior into a number of pathways to aggression:

Executive Skills Deficits

Difficulty maintaining focus

Difficulty maintaining cognitive set

Difficulty shifting cognitive set

Difficulty seeing the connection between cause and effect

Difficulty comprehending the impact of his behavior on others

Difficulty with working memory

Language Skills Deficit

Does not appear to hear what you said when interacting with him

We questioned if he had a receptive language deficit

We questioned if he had a central auditory processing difficulty

Mood Dysregulation

Irritability

Sad effect

Anxious mood

Depressed mood

Bland effect

Sense of franticness about him

Hypervigilance

History of extremely traumatic events/PTSD

Social Skills Deficit

Socially inept interactions

Difficulty making and retaining friendships

Difficulty conversing with other peers

Unless he feels he is controlling the activity, he believes he has been totally excluded

Telling fantastic stories to his peers

Tries to control verbal interactions with constant negotiations

Cognitive Inflexibility

Perseveration in verbal interactions

Difficulty with linguistic give-and-take

Rigid style of interacting

Black-and-white thinking

Difficulty adjusting his agenda based on circumstances

We were shocked to see that we had listed difficulties that fell into almost every pathway to aggression. It was no wonder he was having such a hard time. We also looked at the list to see what tools we would need to help Arturo. We identified that medication could be very helpful in the areas of executive skills and mood dysregulation. Neuropsychological testing could help us overall in clearly identifying areas of thinking deficits and mood and give us more information about his perceptions. It could also help us determine if he had language-processing deficits and if he had a non-verbal learning disability that might explain the rigidity in his interactions. Our CPS approach could help us understand his escalations and allow us to intervene early to minimize his meltdowns. CPS would also help us devise Basket B interventions to help him increase his repertoire of social responses.

When we considered the questions of "what was in his head we wished wasn't, or what was not in his head that we wished was?" we had several speculations. Arturo exhibited some hoarding behaviors, and items on the unit would disappear and show up in his room. At mealtimes he had a routine of asking for specific food items in large quantities at once, and he would begin to have a meltdown if he perceived his requests as being thwarted. His negotiations with staff left us speculating that his cognitive misperceptions were fearing that we would not look out for his needs and needing to fend for himself. Because he did not trust us, he was always vigilant in anticipating being deprived of what he wanted. As a result, he negotiated early, often, and unceasingly for what he perceived he needed. Lastly, he kept up this style of interaction even when it was not remotely necessary—i.e., he was stuck. He was habituated to this style of interacting.

Several staff members began to discuss how difficult it was to engage with Arturo in a Basket B interaction. Attempts at doing this were described as feeling that you were "being bogged down in interactions with a used-car dealer!" Everything was an endless negotiation. Every time you thought you had a workable collaboration, Arturo upped the ante and wanted something different. Staff reported that engaging with him verbally was exhausting. Daniel went on to say that every interaction was a request, and when that request was met, it was on to the next request before you had a chance to take a breath. It was so unrelenting that as staff became exhausted, they were passing him off from one to another in order to have some time to relax and recoup.

Arturo was extremely perseverative. He was only very briefly content. If he won a game with a peer, his eyes would light up for a brief minute, and then it was on to the next negotiation.

Ross suggested that we find a metaphor to use in working with Arturo so that he would have a better chance of listening to or hearing us. We were able to identify two things that he liked that we could use to set up a metaphor: cars and soccer. Examples of how we thought of playing this out were the following:

Soccer: "Arturo, you have a powerful right foot. But in order for you to do really well in soccer, you will need more than that. You will need to run fast, which you can do. But more than that, you will need a better all-around game—being able to dribble, being able to maneuver yourself and the ball into better positions, being able to coordinate plays with your teammates, etc."

Cars: The car metaphor involved using car sounds as a way of identifying that the car was operating to its fullest potential. In order to race the car well, he would have to be able to hear the sounds of the engine and know what they meant. Paying attention to these sounds and what they signified would be important for a successful car racer. These analogies would then be applied to a specific situation that had occurred. It was hoped that by setting up a learning interaction and using the above analogies, he might be better able to make the connection between the behavior we were discussing and the need to look beyond his immediate concern for the bigger picture.

On a more concrete, practical level, we could help Arturo by having him repeat back what we had just said to him. If he negotiated by putting his request out there and then was thinking what to say next or ask for next, he might not even be hearing us to be able to register our statements to him. He might not have in his working memory what was important to us as well as what he wanted from the interaction. His working memory might only be registering what he wanted, and by attempting to have him repeat back what we had just said may help him register our end of the collaboration.

Ross also suggested that, based on our speculations of Arturo's cognitive misperceptions, we would need to get our empathy out there right away or he would not be able to hear our alternatives, and we would not be invited into the process of collaborating with him.

We needed to check ourselves to make sure we were doing this consistently.

"You want to play Playstation **now.**"

"Let's see what we can do about that."

"You want to play Playstation now and someone else is using it."

"How are we going to work this out?"

"We want to work with you so that you have a chance to play Playstation."

If Arturo was rigidly wired as we suspected, then we would have to interject our comments and state the empathy upfront, or he would likely only hear what we were saying as Basket A alternatives. If we moved too fast with the alternatives and didn't spend enough time ensuring that this was a collaboration between us, then we might in fact be giving him choices that did not feel mutually agreed upon.

Tim asked, "What are we supposed to do if he asks for a pass with his parents and we know that at the present time he can't have passes with his parents?" Here is a possible scenario.

"Arturo, you want to go on pass."

"I just want to go on pass like the other kids."

"Let's work on this."

What choices could we come up with that felt like a pass? Could Arturo go with his parents to the cafeteria? Could he and his parents go for a walk around the hospital or out on the grounds of the hospital? Can they go for a picnic on the hospital green? We could be creative and offer some choices that seemed like a pass, yet he and his parents would still be within the grounds of the hospital, and we would be available to help if the visit went awry. We needed to think outside of the box and be creative.

Laura asked, "What about his threatening other kids?" We discussed the possibility that Arturo did not have the vocabulary to identify his feelings when he was upset, so we might need to teach him this. Instead of saying, "I am going to punch him in the face!" we would work with him so that he would be able to say, "I am mad at him!" Amelia indicated that she had witnessed some success with this when she had Arturo in the classroom. She went on to say, "But, what do I do when he starts at the very beginning of group time with an announcement that this is stupid?" We explored why Arturo might say this: Was it a reflection of his hyperactivity, of his difficulty changing cognitive set, or was it a reflection of his being ashamed or scared? We needed to have a discussion about what group would look like. We needed to share with him the structure of the group, and we needed to see if we could make him more comfortable with the idea of participating in a group. That being said, we needed to keep it simple. If Arturo was having a hard time finding words to describe what he was feeling, we could suggest a few choices: "I'm frustrated," "I'm bored," or "I'm getting fidgety." We needed to remember the distinct possibility that he associated school and groups with failure.

We learned that he had repeated the first grade twice, and there was an indication in his record that he had also repeated the second grade.

If Arturo was a rigid, concrete thinker, then we would need to coach him through another style of conversation. Here was an example:

"Dr. M, can I have off-grounds privileges (OG)?"

"Arturo, do you know that other kids start a conversation with me in a different way? They say, 'Hello Dr. M, how are you?'"

"Dr. M, can I have OG?"

"I'll start again. Hey, Arturo, it's good to see you this morning! How are you doing?"

"Hi Dr. M; can I have OG?"

"Arturo, that was a nice greeting. You started by saying hello to me and that made me feel good, and it made me want to have more of a conversation with you. So you want OG?"

"Yes, I want OG; I want to be able to go on the outings with the other kids."

"You want to be able to go on the outings. Do you see any problems with going OG?"

"I want OG like the other kids. What's the problem with that?"

"I think being able to go OG is great. Kids that are on OG have to be able to listen to staff and follow directions when they are off the unit. Do you think you can do that?"

"I will listen. Can I have a pass to go out with my parents?"

"Arturo, I hear that you really want OG and that it is important to you. I will talk about this in rounds this morning, and I'll get back to you right after rounds. I think it would be good to start with one thing at a time, so why don't I talk with all the staff about your trying OG. I'll let them know that you said you will listen to staff and that you will follow directions."

Another idea that was put forward was to start the day involving Arturo in a conversation to work on different things. "What could happen today that could make you happy? Let's make a list of possibilities." Right now, the consensus was that Arturo couldn't identify what would make him happy. He did not know what was doable.

Trying these interventions could help him define what "happy" meant to him. And we would be able to reinforce it. "I just heard that you got OG! You must be so happy. This is something that you really wanted. It is a good feeling to get something that you really wanted."

In exploring his concrete, black-and-white cognitive style, we planned out a way to "gray him up a little." And we attempted to do this out of the moment to prevent a meltdown. The place we started was with his breakfast routine. We talked with him about a minor change in his routine. His ritual each morning was to get his breakfast tray, then come to the kitchen and ask for Raisin Bran cereal with four packets of sugar. Then, when he was given the cereal, he would ask for two pieces of toast with maple syrup on top, and when he received those two pieces of toast, he would ask for an additional two pieces of toast with maple syrup. He did eat all of this and he was quite thin. Other meals he was less interested in, and he would pass up many food choices based on his likes and dislikes. Our intervention to alter his routine was to see if he was able to adjust to receiving three packets of sugar with his cereal. If he was able to handle this, then we would see if he was able to adjust to three pieces of toast with maple syrup.

When we looked at the big picture, we were able to identify that when we did a Basket B intervention in the moment, it had the steps of empathy and then invitation. We were working with a child who was becoming upset due to frustration, and we were trying to avoid a meltdown. When we did a Basket B intervention out of the moment, we were noticing something about a child, or staff members were passing on observations that were made about a particular child and his or her behavior. We were using an opportunity to work with a child out of the moment to teach a skill. The steps here were *observation* and *invitation*.

DEBBIE

Debbie was a thirteen-year-old girl with a genetic cardiac syndrome and cognitive deficits. In addition, she had been diagnosed with a mood disorder. She was raised for most of her life by her aunt, who was also her guardian. She had frequent contact with her grandmother, and sometimes when visiting her grandmother, Debbie would see and have contact with her biological mother. Her mother gave birth to her early in her teens but had never raised Debbie. Their relationship was more like one of older cousin to younger cousin. In her early years, Debbie was described as having feeding problems and developmental delays. When Debbie was about ten years of age, she was molested by a distant male relative. More recently, her aunt had separated from her husband and Debbie's contact with him was very limited following their separation.

Debbie was in special education classes from early on in her schooling and had been doing well until the previous year. As she neared adolescence, her problems at home and in school increased markedly. She was placed in a temporary foster home for three months and was hospitalized for three months at another child psychiatric unit. She was discharged from this hospital to a specialized foster home and then was hospitalized again on an adolescent unit one week later. Debbie was transferred to us three weeks later. It was felt that, due to her developmental status and her cognitive delays, she would be better served on a child unit versus an adolescent unit. Her aunt indicated that, due to Debbie's behavior over the past year, she did not feel that she would be able to manage her at home. We therefore understood that Debbie would be with us until a residential program had been located and funding secured.

This case was very challenging for us, as we had extreme difficulty in our relationship with Debbie's aunt. We had different perspectives on Debbie's abilities and functioning, different values regarding the management of children, and different expectations for behavior. Debbie's aunt felt that we needed to have higher expectations for her child and that we needed to give Debbie clear, predictable consequences. Our perception, on the other hand, was that Debbie's aunt appeared somewhat harsh in her interactions with her child and also rigid in her approach at times.

An example of this difference of opinion was that of the phone plan. Debbie's aunt had requested that we limit Debbie's phone calls to one call each shift (two calls a day—one on the day shift and one on the evening shift). Her belief was that Debbie needed to develop a more constructive way to deal with her anxiety than by calling her aunt when she was upset. She felt that limiting the calls would force Debbie to develop alternative coping mechanisms and turn to others (the staff) for support. Our perception was that Debbie had significant loss issues. She had recently been told that she would not be going home from our unit and instead to a residential placement. We felt that it was important for Debbie to feel an ongoing connection with her aunt, and we were trying to help her adjust to this news without major feelings of abandonment. Also, in general, we did not restrict children's phone calls. We allowed children to call family for support when they were feeling badly, and we did not view this as a deficit in problem solving.

Our becoming involved in a struggle with Debbie's aunt would not help her view her child's behavior with a different lens. It would not help our relationship with her aunt, nor would it help Debbie's ability to learn to trust us so that we could collaborate together in the care of her child. Our strategy was to agree with her whenever we could and to use some of our terminology in the process to move her a little—10 percent from where she was at that point in time.

- We agreed that it was reasonable to think that there were consequences for behavior.

- We agreed that we would like to have a plan that would generate positive change for Debbie.

- We agreed that it was good to have clear expectations.

- We agreed that there were times we needed to set limits.

- We agreed that when we set a limit and there was no compliance, there was usually a consequence.

- We agreed that the phone plan was not working.

We stated that we liked to work on the areas of limit-setting in Basket B. We believed that consequences were important and that the consequences we meant were natural ones as opposed to formal ones. For example, a problem becoming solved was a natural consequence. Debbie's aunt was setting a limit when a problem needed to be solved. Here the problem was defined as Debbie calling too much. The problem indicated that Debbie was not handling her anxiety well. Our approach was that there was more than one way to solve this problem. Setting a limit was one way of solving the problem of Debbie's calling too much. Debbie was aware that when her aunt set a limit on her, her aunt was not happy with her behavior. That was a clear consequence. Debbie's aunt felt upset that she and Debbie were not getting along and Debbie also felt badly about this.

We wanted to solve this problem, but we wanted to invite the child (Debbie) into the problem solving. We believed that even children with cognitive deficits were able to engage in problem solving, and we believed that involving them in this process helped them build skills they would need to navigate in society some day. This was the long-term goal or the big picture. We hoped that rehearsing this discussion would prepare us to talk with parents when initially we were not on the same page regarding how to work with children whose behaviors presented problems. We role-played this scenario, and the family worker rehearsed this, with Ross acting the part of the family worker and the family worker playing the part of the aunt.

The summary of our points here were:

- We agreed on the definition of the problem.

- Debbie was not able to manage her anxiety without calling her aunt.

- We agreed that this was a problem to be worked on.

- We wanted to fix it in a slightly different way than by setting a limit.

- We wanted to involve Debbie in the solution—we believed that if she bought into the solution, it was more likely to be successful in solving the problem.

We were able to come to an agreement and work out a solution that involved Debbie and did reduce phone calls. Unfortunately, this was one of many issues where our perspectives were different, and by the time Debbie did leave us for a residential program six months later, we were not able to hold on to a positive alliance with her aunt. Our beliefs regarding Debbie's abilities and about strategies to collaborate with children to find mutually agreeable solutions to problems were not compatible with her aunt's view of managing children's behavior, nor did we agree with her perceptions of the extent of her child's problems and functioning.

Melanie

Melanie was a twelve-year-old girl who stayed with us for almost five months and celebrated her thirteenth birthday on our unit. She came to us as a special transfer from another hospital where she was being mechanically restrained daily for weeks on end. We were asked to assess her and to see if we could find a way to manage her challenging behaviors without resorting to mechanical or chemical restraints. Melanie had spent the prior eighteen months in psychiatric hospitals and in a juvenile justice facility. She had a severe trauma history and had been sexually abused by a male relative. She desperately wanted to be placed at home with relatives, but this was not realistic at this point in time and she was placed with us, awaiting an intermediate-care facility within the state system (a state adolescent long-term hospital unit).

One of Melanie's proud achievements while she stayed with us was learning to read. Witnessing her conquer this belated milestone was memorable and brought tears to our eyes when she proudly read to us from a Dr. Seuss book she had mastered.

Melanie presented us with a number of challenges. The most difficult one was her "institutionalized behavior." She came to us expecting to be restrained and she would spout off psycho-jargon claiming that she needed the staff to contain her as she was not able to contain herself. She did have prolonged meltdowns that were very aggressive; she would also become self-destructive and was vulnerable to having a meltdown whenever another child was having a hard time. Her meltdowns often lasted for protracted periods of time. They would involve throwing of furniture, trying to rush out the doors of the unit, shrieking at and hitting anyone who approached her, lying down in the hallway, and refusing to get up and walk on her own. We learned over time to identify a staff person to distract her and keep her occupied whenever another child was having difficulty and to take her off the unit for a walk with a staff person when the unit was acute. We learned to prevent having to hold her by moving the other children off the unit out of the way. On occasion, three or more staff members were designated to work with her to help her when she was having a meltdown. Finding ways to collaborate with Melanie and to involve her in problem solving when she was frustrated was a test of our mastery of CPS and of our providing a nurturing environment.

When she left us to move to a state hospital unit, this is the note we sent the staff. It details some of the strategies we had learned to better manage her aggressive behavior.

What We Have Learned About Melanie

Melanie is an appealing thirteen-year-old girl who has been on our unit for five months. She had a long history of hospitalizations prior to her admission on our unit. She had extreme difficulty in her previous two hospitalizations, the end result having been numerous physical holds and mechanical and chemical restraints. She has had a very difficult life, and this is reflected in her difficulties trying to manage her intense emotional states. We have formulated her difficulties as stemming from mood dysregulation (anxiety and depression stemming from post-traumatic stress and a resulting atypical mood disorder). She also has extensive learning disabilities that have impacted her academics.

Melanie did surprisingly well on our unit for the first six weeks and was able to work with us around meeting her needs and her meeting us halfway so that we could do this. Initially, she let us know that we would be restraining her and that she knew what to do to make this happen. We told her that we were trying to find other ways to help her manage difficult times and that we tried to avoid those interventions at all costs.

In recent weeks, Melanie has had increasing difficulty, and we suspect that this is due to a number of important factors:

1. *Her initial hope was to convince us that she was able to go home to her biological parents; more recently, she has become aware that this was not an option for her at this time or the foreseeable future.*

2. *The unit was comprised entirely of boys until the past month. There are now a number of pre-adolescent girls on the unit, and Melanie has been trying to form peer relationships using old strategies that she utilized in the past.*

3. *Melanie had an increasing awareness that other kids on the unit were going home or moving on to other programs or had programs in sight, and she realized there was no specific plan for her as yet. She became hopeless, and this affected her ability to work with us. We suspect that she was angry and disappointed that we had not been able to give her what she wanted—to reunite with her family.*

4. *She recently had more contact with her stepfather, had one visit with her siblings, and surreptitiously managed to have phone contact with her mother.*

5. *Lastly, she recently disclosed alleged past sexual abuse by an important male relative.*

We were successful in avoiding mechanical restraints and seclusion with Melanie by keeping at the forefront of our minds that our overall agenda was to keep the milieu calm. We could best do that by collaborating with her whenever possible to find acceptable solutions for her frustrations. We also learned that we could avoid physical holds, although this required close observation, team coordination, and quick reallocation of staff resources in difficult times.

In the morning, we willingly worked on slowly reminding Melanie that it was time to arise, and we allowed her to sleep in for awhile and eat her breakfast before she performed her morning ADLs.

We encouraged her to go to groups when we saw that she was in a good emotional space, but we did not force her to go to group if she was very irritable or angry or very sad. At these times, we did not introduce additional stress but proceeded with a low-key approach for the day. We were able to help her with grooming by providing lots of positive feedback when she was showered and her hair was combed. She allowed a number of the female staff to style her hair, and that helped her with keeping her hair shampooed and clean.

We provided lots of opportunity for Melanie to have quality time from staff and arranged many one-on-one walks off the unit with her. We tried to intersperse a few short walks each day, as this really aided her in managing her restlessness. When she was irritable and cranky, we would try to see if we could joke or cajole her, and we also provided lots of hugs. A huge strength for Melanie was her capacity to continue to seek out affection and caring from adults despite her past confusing experience. This desire for affectionate, caring relationships with caretakers was a motivating factor in the progress she has made here. It would be important for the next program to capitalize on this and find ways to bestow a clear sense of caring for her. This would provide a base in building a trusting relationship in which she can tackle the difficult emotional issues before her.

Melanie became quite disorganized and dissociated when she was upset, and we tried to be observant of warning signs that this may be occurring. She had a distinct smile she wore on her face that told us we needed to work fast to bring her around to working with us as opposed to spiraling into aggressive episodes. We also observed that her restlessness was quickly followed by a brief period of silliness, followed by aggression. She would begin to jump on a couch with a smile on her face or pick up a kitchen chair. She has worked with us to be able, in many situations, to simply turn over the chair rather than throw it.

We also worked with her on a plan to go to her room at the first signs of upset and have her thrash with a large stuffed animal that we placed in her room for this purpose. We worked with her to be able to tell us that she did not feel good or felt agitated right away so that we could offer a PRN medication to help her contain her agitation before it became aggressive. When she was very upset and in a full meltdown, she usually appeared very dissociated with a glazed look in her eyes and a plastered smile on her face. She was very hard to reach in this state. Afterward, she would be sad and would apologize for the upset she may have caused. She was able to tell us that the precipitant was memories or flashbacks of sexual abuse she had suffered in the past. When she had a bad couple of days, she frequently mixed up present time with the past, and recently she talked of being held each day when, in fact, she had not, but had mixed up time in her mind.

We noticed that Melanie was much more vulnerable to becoming agitated when there were other girls on the unit who were close in age. Her wanting to be friends with them and her resentment at the same time for not having as much as she perceived they had led to her having meltdowns and trying to engage peers in her meltdowns. She was very vulnerable to being set up to become agitated by a peer who was more organized and was able to suggest to her that she misbehave. The person instigating would then fade into her bedroom, leaving Melanie upset and unable to calm down quickly.

Melanie often complained about having to go to school, but she did quite well in our schoolroom. Most days she gave a full-hearted effort to finish her work and complete it correctly.

When Melanie was having a difficult time, we moved the other kids out of the way quickly to avoid them becoming agitated. We concentrated several staff with her for periods lasting thirty minutes or more. This was a staff-intensive effort, but we felt it was worth it to avoid using restraints or seclusion.

Melanie will need some help in her next placement in continuing to work on managing intense feelings and memories of her horrific past experiences. In fairness to Melanie, she will have to unlearn what the mental health system has unwittingly taught her: that she needs restraints/seclusion/holds—outside intervention—to assist her rather than learning skills to manage her feelings by building internal control. Thus, we bear some responsibility in the skill deficits that she currently exhibits.

Melanie was physically held seven times in the month of November. The holds lasted from ten seconds to four minutes and fifty seconds. Most of the holds lasted less than sixty seconds. She was not held in the month of December, and we learned to avoid this by providing better assessment of beginning signs of agitation and by using a staff-intensive approach when she was having difficulty. On some occasions this meant that three staff members were assigned to her for periods up to thirty minutes.

> *We hope that staff at your program will continue the work we have started to help Melanie reclaim control of herself and ultimately her destiny. Please feel free to call us with any questions.*
>
> *—The staff of the CAU*

JOHN

John was a tall eleven-year-old boy admitted to our unit after he became very aggressive and assaultive at home when his parents tried to get him to leave the house to attend school. He became increasingly anxious over the past one and one-half years. In the three weeks prior to admission, his obsessive compulsive behaviors (OCD) had become more pronounced to the point that he had become incapacitated and unable to complete the simplest of tasks. John was a bright boy who was socially shy, and he arrived on our unit very fearful and distraught. He was extremely frightened of germs and kept his hands gloved. Despite his compulsion to avoid germs, his personal hygiene had deteriorated and his hair was greasy upon admission. His parents were very involved in his care, and he had received extensive outpatient treatment from some of the child experts in the area who specialized in the treatment of OCD.

John was nervous and very frightened of us upon admission and in the days thereafter. He became distraught when we asked him to participate in the most minor of activities, such as taking the pills out of the medicine cup and swallowing them with a cup of water. He vacillated back and forth in moving his gloved hand forward toward the med cup and then back again. He perspired and stated over and over again, "I can't do it; I just can't do it." The simplest decision seemed of monumental importance, and it was as if his life or death depended upon the outcome. His consternation was excruciating to observe. Initially, he stood immobile in the hallway and it took him hours to move down the corridor to his bedroom. His terror was so pronounced that his parents stayed in his room with him for the first two to three days. He felt unable to come out of the room and would not use the bathrooms on the unit initially. Because she knew that this would prove to be a serious impediment, Megan was creative and collaborated with John to clean a bathroom in his presence wearing gloves. After the cleaning, she agreed to restrict this bathroom for only his use.

Tim brought John's situation up in our supervision with Ross. John had been on the unit for four days and was holed up in his room with the covers over his head and only arose to go to the bathroom and to take his medication. Should we be expecting that he get up and go to groups? How should we approach this? Ross reminded us that we did have the expectation that kids go to group. The question once again was what were we going to do with our unmet expectation? Ross encouraged us to have different staff members make attempts to engage John and build a relationship. We also spoke with John's parents, and they agreed to spend increasingly more time off the unit so that we would have more opportunities to engage him in activities with us.

We assigned one staff member per shift to be designated to make frequent trips into John's room to try to engage him in conversation, activities, games, etc. We wanted to start building a relationship with him that would give us more leverage in working with him, and hopefully for him to be able to increase his participation on the unit. It was our hope that by finding one, two, or three people on the unit to whom he could respond, we could get things going in this direction. The more John was willing to engage with us, the greater the opportunity to observe the times when he was having difficulty. Concurrent with these interventions, the doctor was reevaluating John's medication regime and determining what changes needed to be made for more successful functioning.

After one week on the unit, John was engaging in conversation with about three different milieu counselors, and he was talking with the nurses when they brought him medication. He was able to describe his reactions to his medications, and he became more relaxed about the need to wipe down surfaces as he neared them. On day eight, we saw John get out of bed and move to the doorway to his room. He spent several hours there, observing what was occurring in the hallway. On day nine, he actually came out into the hallway. He began to eat the food on the unit and no longer insisted that his parents bring in his food. By day twelve, he was eating in the day hall with the other kids, although he sat at a table by himself and covered the table with paper napkins so that he would not touch the wooden surface. He was slowly but steadily improving. By day thirteen, he attended the school group, and by day fourteen he actually hung out in the hallway talking with staff for protracted periods of time. To our amazement, he was not wearing gloves and he took the med cup from the med nurse in his bare hands and did not flinch at contact with her hand. At the end of three weeks he was discharged and was looking like a different person from the one who had been admitted.

We learned from John to take things in small steps and to begin by meeting him where he was rather than forcing our expectations upon him before he was able to meet them. We did not rush things at a level that he was not able to tolerate. We allowed him to initially hibernate in his room, and we joined him in his space for a number of days while trying to establish the beginnings of a relationship. Our efforts paid off, and John was slowly able to trust us and believe that we were not going to harm him or make him ill.

CHAPTER 18

WRAP-UP:
Lessons Learned and a Plea

"Hope is a state of mind, not of the world. Hope, in this deep and powerful sense, is not the same as joy that things are going well, or willingness to invest in enterprises that are obviously heading for success, but rather an ability to work for something because it is good."

— Vaclav Havel

THE CHALLENGE OF MAINTAINING CHANGE

The excitement and passion of creating change fueled the energy that was needed to reach a momentum, and it helped move things along and off the status quo. The fear and excitement that accompany doing something different and unorthodox at times felt like an adrenalin rush. Seeing things fall into place and beginning to

225

get good results on a day-to-day basis was satisfying and enforc-
ing. Taking on the challenge of staff who appeared less willing to
move ahead and finding ways to dialogue with them was also satisfying, but at other times it was also hard work and exhausting.
Listening to the voices of dissent was sometimes scary and frustrating, but listening was paramount in achieving success.
Listening to and sifting through the objections of others helped
me to find the important points of ideas that may not have been
explained adequately and that may have contributed to a lack of
clarity. Listening enabled me to hear about great ideas that I had
not thought about myself. Pinpointing areas of general reservation
and attempting to identify underlying fears about the change that
was being proposed and its aftermath helped lead to the building
of a coherent plan of action and allowed us to focus the rationale
behind that plan. Listening to objections also helped in identifying opposing values and beliefs that were interfering with acceptance of the changes being proposed.

Malcolm Gladwell, in the *Tipping Point,* states that what
underlies the success of major societal change is the belief that
people are capable of "radically transforming their behavior in the
face of the right kind of impetus"[12]. He believes not only that
people can change but that, despite a resistance to change, human
beings by their very nature are drawn to change. He attributes our
"volativity" and "inexplicableness" as by-products of our ability to
be powerfully influenced by "our surroundings, our immediate
context, and the personalities of those around us"[13]. These qualities predispose us to be receptive to change, despite our resistance
to do things differently than what has been familiar. Thank good-
ness for these innate human attributes, for without them we would
never have evolved and progressed.

Maintaining change is hard work. It is easy to become complacent and to test the formulas we have developed. It is hard to
resist the impulse to do things an easier way and to forget that the

way we have developed is, in fact, the easier way, borne out of try-ing other alternatives that were found lacking in some basic or intrinsic manner.

We discovered themes that came up over and over again. There was a persistent pull to try and make the Explorers, the non-group, into a bona-fide group. It seemed easier to watch them as a group, despite having attempted that over and over again and learning that the not-yet-workable kids were set up for failure when we put them in groups. They would easily become frustrat-ed and then begin to curse at and bop one another when put together in a group for any length of time. Repeatedly, we had to learn that divide and conquer was an effective strategy that worked better than any other approach.

Staff would become complacent and attempt to create a large group out of one or two smaller groups of three or four kids. There was the draw of wanting adult companionship of a coworker on an outing, and this draw would win over the lessons we had learned. And on occasion, this attempt would work, but only with a particular mix. It did not hold true in general. I would hear of attempts to take a big group out with several staff to a playground and would also hear of difficulties that occurred with one or more children becoming agitated or several children fighting with one another.

Getting into struggles over food was a recurring theme. It seemed that we needed to discuss this among ourselves in group supervision or in our nursing staff meetings several times a year in the first two years. We again needed to work through our ration-ale and strategy for dealing with food in Basket B discussions and interventions.

One way to keep ourselves on our toes was to continue to be mentors and teachers to others who were interested in what we were doing. Orienting new employees and assigning them men-tors helped staff remember the reasons behind why we did things the way we did. Inviting staff from other programs to visit us and observe us in action also kept us fresh and provided opportunities to teach other interested people the lessons we had learned.

TRAUMA-SENSITIVE CARE

We decided that we were not going to engage in mechanical or chemical restraints or in locked-door seclusion. We were successful in this endeavor. Being successful changed the way we viewed other aspects of care that we provided. We began to use words that we did not use initially. We began to talk of our care as being humane, and we began to view our previous interventions of restraint and seclusion as being *in*humane.

As we took pride in avoiding these interventions, we came face-to-face with the realization that some of the things we had done in the past may have hurt children. We had to deal with very uncomfortable feelings about our having restrained and secluded kids. We became aware that our endless limit-setting in the past often was a source of provocation—not de-escalation—for a child. In a number of group supervision sessions, people verbalized feeling "terrible," "ashamed," and "guilty" about their previous participation in these interventions. We had to talk with each other and reaffirm that no one had intentionally tried to hurt the children for whom they were caring. We were the product of our experience and training. We had been trained that these were interventions to be used for children who lacked inner controls, and that they needed us to supply external controls for them in these situations. We discussed that we needed to forgive ourselves for our lack of understanding so that we could continue the good work that we were now doing.

We became sensitive to other protocols and procedures that had potential for being traumatizing or re-traumatizing in nature.

We had always been sympathetic to children who were fearful at bedtime. Now we were even more so. Children could choose to sleep in the hall for days at a time, and there was no expectation that we work with them to get them to be able to sleep in their room. We gave them more time to overcome their fears and were able to meet them where they were at this point in their lives. We developed a number of different interventions to help children who were having difficulty falling asleep at night.

We took a collective stand that we did not want to hold children down for blood draws, and we developed a protocol to deal with this. Included in the protocol was developing standing orders on all new admissions for anesthetic cream to be applied topically to both arms thirty minutes prior to blood-draw attempts. We allowed children to try the blood draw and to refuse if they felt unable to go through with the process. The next attempt would be preceded by application of the topical cream and some medication to decrease anxiety about the procedure. Again, a child was allowed to refuse if he or she was afraid. We allowed a child to watch another child complete the process who was not fearful. Children were allowed to bring in a staff member, a relative, or another child who they felt would provide them with support. The bottom line was that we would not hold children down against their will for blood drawing. In a few cases, blood work was never completed during the inpatient stay. It was determined in clinical rounds that recent outpatient blood work was sufficient for that particular child. In a few cases where it was determined to be clinically necessary to obtain the blood draw, parents volunteered to hold their child for the procedure as they did for outpatient procedures.

The child's feelings and fears were taken into account, and we made extensive efforts to collaborate with the child to come up with solutions to problems as they arose.

We saw our move to provide positive physical contact to children by giving hugs and pats, and carrying kids piggyback on our shoulders, as being tied to our desire to provide care that was trauma-sensitive. Being trauma-sensitive became a positive value that was considered an essential component of the care we were providing. We began sharing this perspective with parents of the children on our unit, and we shared our perspective with them when they asked questions of us. We would stress the potential for trauma or of triggering a traumatic response in a child when parents directed us to hold down their child, because they felt that holding their child down was preferable to giving their child medication to manage aggression.

THE RIGHTS OF CHILDREN

Another aspect of our care that evolved over time was our belief in children having inherent rights and our need to build that consideration into our practices, policies, and procedures. I had learned of the United Nations Convention on the Rights of the Child and felt that this document belonged in plain view on our unit. It was a reminder of the need to treat children as equals, despite their age, and to not presume that adults had the answers to all things pertaining to children. Teaching children skills to assist them in problem solving was part and parcel of what we did, day in and day out. We also needed to teach them that they had rights and that with any right there also was a responsibility. Empowering children by educating them about their rights would also help them feel strong and elevate their self-esteem. Many, if not all, of our children were vulnerable and had been victimized in some way. Helping them understand that they had rights was a way to allow them to gain an inner sense of control over their lives, even if it could not change their circumstances. The List of the Rights of Children, as set by the United Nations Convention on the Rights of the Child, was posted in our living room for all to see.

Developing a Definition of Child-Centered Care

Our work with children and our ongoing work to improve the care we provided led me to think about the need for a clear definition of child-centered care. Based on our values, a definition that worked for me was the following:

> Child-centered care recognizes the inherent rights of every child, is respectful, and believes that care should be nurturing. It is aimed at teaching and providing choices that are based on a child's individual needs. Decisions about care are collaborative and involve the child in the decision-making to the greatest extent possible based on age and developmental ability. Child-centered care recognizes that honesty and openness are prerequisites to the development of a trusting relationship where collaboration and decision-making can take place.

Use of Brief Physical Holds

Our collaboration with children to find mutually agreeable solutions to problems seemed to be humane and child-centered. We also believed that this approach helped children develop the skills they needed to problem solve.

This resolve was tested a number of times in the past few years. We had some difficult situations in which a child was out of control for prolonged periods of time. We were challenged to find successful interventions to help a child calm down and end the episode of out-of-control behavior. At times, professional colleagues who we respected questioned if this was one of those times when a child needed to be held, restrained, or given medication against his or her will. The staff each and every time said "no" resoundingly. We have now reached a point in our development that when we do resort to a brief physical hold, we view it as a failure in treatment. We now treat such holds as emergency interventions and consider them physical restraints. We follow the Center for Medicare and Medicaid Services (CMS) guidelines, and we require extensive attempts at alternative interventions prior to the hold, during the hold, and following the hold.

The most important procedure after the hold has occurred is apologizing to the child for our inability to find an acceptable intervention and resorting to a hold. We share with the child our view that the hold is seen as a failure in our treatment. We were at a loss to find any other intervention that might have worked to alleviate the aggression. We now recognize the potential for trauma with the intervention of a brief physical hold, and we recognize the breach of trust that must be overcome as a result of the intervention. We tell the child that we are sorry for the breach in trust and that we will work hard to restore that trust.

In 2003, we undertook a quality-improvement initiative to understand the times when we resorted to a physical hold of a child and to use that knowledge to reduce physical holds. I began to collect data on physical holds in three ways: (1) I reviewed the records on the children who had been briefly held; (2) I developed a staff survey to obtain the staff's perspective on how we could reduce holds; and (3) I met with a group of children on the unit who had been held during their admission.

The information was very helpful, and I shared it with the staff. I found that all staff members had the desire to avoid a hold if any other alternatives were available to stop a child from being assaultive. They worried most about coworkers and other children being assaulted. All staff felt more pressured in preventing an assault on others than in preventing assaults on themselves. Most of the staff felt that it would be possible to decrease the number of holds that took place, but the majority also felt that it would be unlikely to reduce physical holds to zero. They reported that a child was most likely to be acutely assaultive in the first forty-eight hours after admission. This they attributed to the child not yet having developed a relationship with us, the child's fear and defensiveness around being admitted to the unit, and our lack of knowledge about the child and the child's behavior.

The record review showed that children were held after they had been assaultive to another peer or staff member and were unable to desist when staff intervened to stop the assault. The observations from staff during the holds were that the child often perceived him or herself to be in danger while being held. A number of children seemed to be re-traumatized by the hold, as evidenced by their appearing to be dissociated. They would also make comments that seemed to refer to earlier abuse: "Get off of me; stop hurting me . . ." —when, in fact, staff members were not on top of them and were exerting minimal pressure.

In my focus group with five children aged eight to thirteen, I was struck by a few observations. All but one child reported that they did not feel the hold helped them, even though they realized they had been hitting someone. None of the children had been held in the past five weeks, so the hold they experienced had occurred—at a minimum—more than a month before. For two children, the hold had taken place a number of months prior to the meeting of the focus group. When the children talked about their previous experience with a hold, they became upset all over again. And their anger grew as they recollected the experience. Describing their experience brought to the surface the feelings of anger they felt at the time of the hold. They were sophisticated in their ability to sort out complex feelings and emotions. They talked of the affection they had for the staff and of how angry they felt being held down for even a short time. They were also able to state that they liked "Joe" and were mad at "Joe" at the same time. What was even more striking was their distorted perception of time during the hold. Their perceptions were that they were held from five minutes to fifty minutes. In reality, the holds lasted from ten seconds to four minutes and thirty seconds. The children all perceived themselves as being in grave danger and were afraid that they would be seriously hurt. All but one child felt that the hold was a "bad thing to do."

The one child who had positive responses when discussing the hold had been in psychiatric hospitals and residential programs for most of the previous two years. Her responses saddened me, as they were filled with psych jargon she had learned from staff at these institutions and she had internalized them. She reported that "the hold was necessary to control me, as I cannot control myself." And, "The hold was done for my own good. Sometimes people just need to be restrained."

I shared my information with the staff, and they were saddened to learn of the children's perceptions about the holds. They expressed collectively their support for our decreasing the frequency and duration of physical holds as a quality-improvement effort for the unit.

We began tracking physical holds in February 2003. In February, we had more than 100 brief holds. By December 2003, we had decreased holds to fewer than ten a month. By the end of 2004, we had decreased holds to less than four a month, and for a number of months we had no holds at all. In 2005, our holds never exceeded three a month, and for many months the count was zero.

We also decreased the length of time a child was kept in a hold. We developed a protocol specifying that a child was not to be kept in a hold one second longer than necessary and that the maximum time of holding before an attempt at breaking the hold was thirty seconds. At the present time, we are still working to bring holds down to zero, and although we have neared that goal, we are not there yet.

STAFFING

Our change in care was not costly. Our staffing pattern was only increased by a .8 of a full-time milieu counselor position. We used the same staff as we switched over to our model for managing children's challenging behaviors. We found that we were most vulnerable on weekends, when we had fewer staff members available and less programming. Therefore, we added a fourth milieu counselor to the day and evening shifts on Saturdays and Sundays. At times when we have not had enough staff available, we have used a swing staff position so that a staff member works a 10 A.M. to 6 P.M. shift—these are the busiest hours of the day. This swing person has worked well as an alternative to two staff members working (one on the day shift and one on the evening shift). During weekdays, we have two RNs (one for charge and one for meds) on day and evening shifts. We have three MCs on day and evening shifts. We also have a swing MC from 10 A.M. to 6 P.M. We have an activities coordinator and a special education teacher. On nights we have one RN and two MCs. Monday through Friday we have a variety of clinical staff: two thirty-hour attending psychiatrists, one social work supervisor (full-time) and one social worker (full-time), and a psychologist (thirty-two hours).

THE IMPORTANCE OF A COHERENT
THOUGHT PROCESS AND FRAMEWORK

Anyone embarking on major change needs to prepare for this venture. It is my belief that you need a vision and a coherent thought process upon which to design and structure your initiative. That does not mean that you know ahead of time exactly what you will do or what the change will look like. You do need a framework under which to operate. Our model is not the only model. There are many different approaches that have the potential to be successful. This one worked for us, for our values, and for our beliefs and our personalities.

Our framework grew and encompassed a larger theoretical base as we moved ahead. Planning and thinking about what we were striving to achieve led to envisioning what we needed to do, and these became our first steps.

For us, the underlying model of care was Ross Greene's collaborative problem-solving (CPS) approach. It rang true as a model that was a good fit with the children we were serving, and its perspective on children's behavior seemed to match up with our observations of the children we cared for. In addition, the approach's psycho-educational focus seemed less blaming and less judgmental than traditional psychiatric models.

It was helpful to me to gain some understanding of change theory and leadership and to step back and see our process in that context. The works of Malcolm Gladwell and Ronald Heifetz were great assets to me in understanding our process and in depersonalizing it. I also felt that our approach to care would be a good fit with any number of nursing theories. An easy consideration for a good fit would be that of Hildegard Peplau's "nursing relationship" theory. CPS is based on developing a relationship with the child so that you can work together to problem solve. It is the relationship between the staff and the patient that provides the ground for problem solving together to increase the child's functioning and independence. Peplau believed that "the aim of professional nursing practice was to assist patients to become aware of and to solve their problems that interfere with constructive living."[14] She also believed that "the nurse-patient relationship was dependent largely upon the conceptual knowledge which each nurse has about the patient's presenting data and the phenomena in the domain of nursing. This knowledge is in the nurse's head, available for recall and application during the interaction. It is this kind of intellectual work by nurses that can transform nurse-patient interactions into a learning event for patients."[15]

Whatever theory or model of care you embrace, the challenge is to provide a coherent framework around which staff can organize their learning and their interventions. It is possible to incorporate principles from more than one theory or approach. What is less viable is to pick and choose ideas and beliefs from a wide variety of theories and structures. Without a coherent, tied-together approach, it is difficult for staff members to wrap their minds around a basic belief system that will provide the structure for the changes in culture and care that lie ahead. Lastly, it is also more difficult to facilitate change when the outcomes become the structure. Outcomes such as the elimination of restraints and seclusion were not our driving force; they were the by-products of our efforts, our interventions, our culture, and our approach to care that we implemented.

THE NEED FOR SPREADING THE CHANGE

What has become clearly apparent is that one unit making a change in its care of children is insufficient. For change to be lasting and productive, the change must occur in a variety of places within society.

We saw dramatic success in the functioning of a child who was admitted to the unit, and then we were hit with the realization that the child would be returning to a program with values that were in opposition to the ones upon which we based our care. In CPS language, we made great strides with a child who came to us described as "very explosive and frequently in need of restraints." While with us, the child was not restrained. Our assessment process identified the areas in which the child became frustrated, and we worked with him or her to problem solve without the child having a major meltdown. We did this by engaging in Basket B interventions when the child became frustrated. And we were successful.

But the child was returning to Program My Way or The Highway—a program that relied heavily on Basket A interventions and on consequences to manage behavior. This was a setup for failure. Should we then prepare the child for his or her return by acting like *that* program? We felt that was a shortsighted answer. We continued our work, and we hoped that we had given the child some skills to deal with adults who did not know how to collaborate or did not value collaboration. In worse-case scenarios, we did let our reservations be known to the funding agency, and we questioned if this was the right program for that particular child. This happened to a lesser degree with children who were returning home and were going back to the same school where they were having difficulty. Many schools are bastions of Basket A approaches. They focus on group norms and on the "average" child who needs an education, not necessarily on the few children for whom that approach does not work. In some cases, we would advocate for the child's needs by recommending a smaller classroom, a therapeutic classroom, an emergency evaluation to amend the Individualized Educational Plan, etc. The more programs and services for children that will consider the child's needs, the child's rights, and the child's proclivities, the greater the opportunity for all children to succeed—not just the mainstream kids. And a more collaborative approach will also benefit the mainstream children.

A PLEA

As we have changed the way in which we interact with children, it has felt increasingly "right" over time. We have been able to watch guarded, highly defended, and aggressive children warm up, relax, and open up. We have seen them respond to hugs, positive touch, and positive remarks pointing out the wonderful qualities we observe in them. We have seen white children initially fearful of black staff respond to the affection that was bestowed upon them, and children have been able to let go of stereotypes. They have actually sought out and gravitated to that special staff person. We have seen black children, initially wary and restrained in the close presence of white staff, lose their reservations and delight in the wraparound hugs and praise from nurturing staff. We have witnessed latency-age children, who believed they were too old for hugs and expected little, come around and run up to staff with their arms open wide. We have unabashedly opened our arms wide to embrace the children we serve, and we have seen the results in the delighted smiles of the children who have come to us discouraged, defeated, and scared. They frequently leave a little more hopeful, a little stronger, and hopefully at least beginning to heal. In our program submission to the American Psychiatric Association for the Psychiatric Services Excellence Award (which we received in 2003), we referred to our program as "The Open Arms Program," and over time, it has proven to be an apt description and analogy for our work with children and families.

I firmly believe that clinicians and caretaking staff working with children would benefit from re-examining their beliefs and theories around the issue of "boundaries." It is assumed that staff vetting should be a rigorous process to protect children from harm, but it isn't child-centered to establish policies that are so liability conscious that they deprive children of essentials that they need in order to grow and develop into healthy, whole adults.

There needs to be continuum-of-care approach for children. The successes a child achieves in one program should be preserved and built upon at the next step. Continuums of care should be sensitive to the needs of children as the primary driving force in policies and relationships between programs. Programs need to be evaluated based on their interactions with children. Evaluations should include observations of actual practice to see if policies are implemented in a real sense on a day-to-day basis.

I believe it is time to reevaluate the heavy reliance on consequence-based approaches to managing the difficult behavior of children. Rarely is the cause of a child's explosiveness due to having been "spoiled" or to a lack of knowledge about expectations. The children who are served on inpatient psychiatric units and in child welfare and mental health residential programs have legitimate vulnerabilities—often multiple ones. Children want to be happy; they want to please adults. If they are angry and defiant, it is a clue that something is seriously wrong. Helping a child manage frustration and control his or her emotions is more easily done by an approach that first tries to understand what underlies the behavior, then teaches new skills for coping with frustration in a nurturing, problem-solving collaboration. Helping children develop the inner strengths to cope with their often difficult realities is best achieved by engaging them respectfully, with obvious caring, and teaching them the steps to master successful, individualized techniques for managing their emotions, behavior, and thinking. None of this is possible without building relationships with children and giving them some time to check out that this adult is potentially trustworthy of the child's engaging with them in a relationship.

The current thinking is that hospitalization is a last-resort intervention and should be avoided if at all possible. While it is preferable to provide services at the community level and to work to avoid hospitalization, it does not mean that inpatient hospitalizations cannot serve a purpose in aiding troubled children. Hospitalization should be more than quick medication stabilization. Providing good care involves more than tweaking medication regimes. Often it means peeling off layers of medication and reassessing and determining the roots of a child's difficulty, making a formulation, and then intervening to bring relief and better functioning. It involves a thorough assessment and understanding a child well enough so that it is possible to make specific recommendations to the child's caretakers and outpatient team or to the next program.

Good use of hospitalization involves allowing time for assessment and for initial treatments. Children are less likely to require repeated bouts of intensive services, such as admission to inpatient or acute residential units, if the initial hospitalizations perform thorough assessments and make detailed formulations that are complex and consider all the domains of a child's life—his or her biological vulnerabilities, the impact of the child's environment on the child's developing sense of self, as well as the contribution of the child's social context and the support that is needed to create a safety net so that the child can grow and develop to his or her potential.

Parents should feel empowered to try new approaches if the traditional ones that may have worked with their other children are not working with this child. Parents should question consequence-based approaches if they have not proven successful. It is my hope that parents will find the information in this book useful and that they will use it as a springboard to read more about the CPS approach. Parents should feel fully qualified to engage with their children in a collaborative way and still feel that they are providing the necessary direction and guidance to them.

Parents should also feel empowered to question caregivers, and they should expect to be educated and trained in the care needed to support their child. They should be recognized as true partners. Respect should be manifest in small ways as well as in big ways. Parents belong at the head of the table in treatment team meetings. What message are we sending when we call parents to a meeting to review our assessments or to hear our recommendations, and they are asked respectfully to wait in the lobby while the treatment team strategizes how the meeting shall be run? Starting meetings late and keeping parents waiting sends a clear message that the professional's time is more valuable than theirs. Meeting times need to balance the responsibilities of parents to other children at home and to jobs as well as to the busy schedule of therapists.

From another vantage point, parents need to understand that children are not placed in hospitals or other treatment programs to be fixed. A child needs the support, understanding, and love of his or her caregivers to function to his or her potential. Parents need to be intensively involved in the treatment provided by programs caring for their children. This should be a minimal expectation, and a clear commitment should be made at the front door as the child enters a program. This is just as true for substitute caregivers as it is for parents.

Looking at the bigger picture, policymakers are the lynchpins in creating better programs for children. They are the people who develop budgets that serve as the decision makers of chosen values for a society at a particular point in time. Those values are reflected in which programs are funded and which programs are not. Policymakers set standards of care and help society move toward new considerations and practices. If new programs show promise or raise the bar in how children should be treated, and policymakers are convinced of the efficacy of new programming—or if they believe that new programming shows promise (although not yet proven)—then these influential people need to pave the way for the spread of these new ideas by providing treatment dollars.

Lastly, we need coordinated care of children's services. What occurs now is a fragmented, departmentalized, and often dysfunctional system. Children and families need holistic programming, and we have much to learn from our brothers and sisters in other parts of the world who may not be as sophisticated but who intuitively understand that it takes a village to raise a child. Funding streams need to be developed that provide coordinated, intertwined care, and a child's needs should be considered in one comprehensive package that includes medical, educational, protective, and emotional needs. Bureaucratic divisions need to be overcome, and funding and planning should be shared.

SECTION FOUR

Results and Toolkit

This section contains information that may be useful to programs that are considering changes in programming. It begins with some information and charts about the results our unit has achieved to date. The remaining appendices are materials, policies, and forms that I developed in building an infrastructure to support the changes we made. My hope is that some of this information may be useful to others, and they are intended to be shared, used, and amended as needed.

A CASE STUDY:
Our Adaptive Challenge— The Big Picture and the Role of Leadership

When I took this job, I felt a strong a sense of purpose. I wanted to do something that would improve the care and services children and their families received. I perceived that this job would afford me the opportunity to make a difference. I had a clear sense of what did not seem right to me and the need for a shift in thinking about the treatment of children. I did *not* initially have a clear sense of what needed to be done; rather, it was a sense that something *did* need to be done, and I wanted to be a part of making that happen.

As the journey unfolded, I trusted my instincts, and I trusted my vision and belief that there was a better way to provide services to children and families—even if I did not see exactly what that would look like. I learned to trust and rely heavily on the staff with whom I worked. They earned my respect and my caring early on.

The journey led me to learn more about the process in which we were engaged and to have a deeper understanding of the dynamics of change and all that it entailed.

From Malcolm Gladwell's book *The Tipping Point*, I learned about concepts important to facilitating change, such as: the criticality of reaching a tipping point; recognizing the people who are critical to influencing others and jump-starting the change process; the importance of an idea being able to move others to action; and recognizing that people are heavily influenced by their immediate context. Examining our process in the light of these concepts enriched my perspective and helped me recognize the individuals with whom I needed to be on board to facilitate the changeover successfully.

I learned so much about the nature of the change process in its global definition and its structural components from Ronald Heifetz's book, *Leadership Without Easy Answers*. As I read his book, I was struck by the many parallels in our undertaking, and by the depictions and explanations given in this great resource. It proved to be my bible in understanding the big-picture issues involved in the process we were developing and implementing on the unit. I found it reassuring when I was directing processes in a particular direction, when I was in the position to take unpleasant stands, and when I was pushing an issue that I thought whose time had come to be reckoned with in full— that what I was doing had a context and was not just a personal whim—it was part of a pattern of change, and my action was related to one of the steps involved in implementing a change process.

I thought our small unit was replicating something specific to us and to our area of expertise, but it had a larger context—it was also a reflection of the way adaptive challenges play out in the real world in real time. Reading Heifetz's book proved reassuring. I found Heifetz's principles helpful in building a strategic plan. Putting our experiences in a larger context depersonalized it and, in times of struggle, it helped sustain my perseverance in forging ahead.

Heifetz states that "if we define problems by the disparity between values and circumstances, then an adaptive challenge is a particular kind of problem where the gap cannot be closed by the application of current technical know-how or routine behavior. To make progress, not only must invention and action change circumstances to align reality with values, but the values themselves may also have to change. Leadership will consist not of answers or assured vision but of taking action to clarify values."[16]

Clearly, this was our case. When I arrived on the unit, the circumstances, the routines, and the culture did not mesh with the values of child-centered care, of trauma-sensitive care, or of a nurturing environment. The culture and circumstances had dictated a reactive, somewhat rigid atmosphere. This was not just a gap with the values that I held dear, it proved to be a gap with the values the majority of staff working on the unit believed in and held dear. They may not have been consciously thinking in terms of child centeredness or trauma-sensitive care, but they were thinking in terms of helping children and supporting their strengths and had a strong desire to convey to the children for whom they cared that they cared about them greatly.

Another way Heifetz explained adaptive work was to state that the "adaptive challenge is the gap between aspirations and reality. Adaptive work is focusing attention on the specific issues created by that gap"[17]

That was our task. The reality was that the unit staff, upon my arrival in March 2001, were reacting as if they were besieged. Their core values of safety, security, and structure were being threatened. Staff did not feel safe; they felt endangered. This feeling influenced their ability to be child-centered and nurturing. They fell back on traditional practices for containment and imposed more structure and more rules. This did not increase the comfort level and reduce assaults; it was actually making the problem worse. Their technical solution was not working. Almost all of the staff had chosen to work on the unit because they enjoyed working with children and because they wanted to learn how to care for children who had experienced tremendous stress and loss in their young lives. They weren't here for the salary or for the great working conditions or for the career ladder available to them. They were a special type of worker—they had dedication and commitment, and they wanted to have a job that had meaning and did some social good. They wanted to contribute to society in some personal way.

At this point in time, those values were in conflict with the reality of the day-to-day care that they were providing. They were increasingly put in the role of being enforcers, limit-setters, and consequence-givers. The children liked most of the staff and were also dependent upon them to have their daily needs met. It was at times confusing for them to need these people and often to be struggling with them. The rules and structure imposed solutions to everyday occurrences, but they also predisposed the staff and children to having interactions that created conflict and often resulted in power struggles. The atmosphere was not consistently friendly or relaxed. The staff were often hyper-alert and hyper-vigilant to the potential for aggression, and they reacted quickly to put out fires by setting consequences as a child began to escalate.

Adaptive work begins with defining the problem. The problem was not an easy one to define, nor was the solution clear-cut. It would not lend itself to a simple technical solution. My assessment of the unit initially was that the staff, as well as the patients of the unit, had suffered trauma. The staff's trauma was related to the assaults that had been taking place over the prior year or so. In addition, there was the cumulative trauma of being involved in numerous restraints and seclusions. These were intense events evoking strong emotions that often were stuffed down during the event itself. This was compounded by witnessing the intensity of the child's anger and rage and an awareness of severity of the intervention itself ("taking a child down," containing the child by holding four limbs, often followed by witnessing a child crying disconsolately, screaming, and sometimes banging at the door, or banging his or her head or hands into the wall. Sometimes the intervention would progress further to mechanical and chemical restraints if the child did not calm quickly.) Almost all staff persons reported that even if they felt the intervention was warranted under the circumstances, they left the unit at the end of their shift feeling awful. There was no sense of satisfaction as having accomplished something worthwhile if they had been involved in a restraint or seclusion. And these events were occurring frequently. It had become part of the routine.

Heifetz identified seven areas of using authority as a resource for leadership:

- Creating a holding environment for containing the stresses of the adaptive efforts.

- Commanding and directing attention—toward the issues that are generating the distress.

- Having access to information.

- Controlling the flow of information.

- Having the power to frame issues—the major interpretive task of identifying which issues were close enough to the surface to warrant discussion and which were as yet unripe.

- Being able to orchestrate the conflict and contain disorder.

- Choosing the decision-making process—autocratic, consultative, participative, or consensual.[18]

In our process, we created a holding environment in several ways. Initially, staff meetings were used to talk about the problems on the unit so that we could develop a diagnosis of the problem that was reached by consensus. These meetings served to encourage brainstorming and created an opportunity to take the time to imagine how things could be better. They provided a place to think about and develop goals for our future development.

As a preliminary step to preparing for the changes ahead and in my efforts to get to know each staff member and his or her strengths, talents, and interests, I had initial meetings with each one. I used these one-on-one meetings as an opportunity to hear directly from every staff person what his or her own individual goals were and to hear any suggestions. After listening to the staff member, I talked about my perspective and my values. I discussed my vision of what the unit could be and my desire to work with each of them to bring about this vision.

Creating a holding environment also meant at times remaining calm in the midst of very stressful events that highlighted our inexperience with the techniques we were trying to master. Conveying a sense of conviction that this was but an interlude along the way to better times and exuding confidence in our ability to pull it off during the shaky, early phases of our changeover helped us move beyond our fears and doubts.

In commanding attention to issues that needed to be put on the table, it proved easy to begin discussions about questioning what we were doing by pointing out the reality that the staff were not happy with the state of things as they were at present; thus, there was nothing to lose by considering alternate ways to manage the milieu and to consider concepts that might even appear or seem radical at first glance. Supporting group supervision sessions as the vehicle for working out the problems and bringing up issues for discussion at these meetings served the purpose of focusing attention on difficulties as they arose. The sessions also facilitated our problem solving together and helped us identify with one another in our struggles to gain mastery over a new approach. In paraphrasing the words of Heifetz, it was an attempt by the leadership to hold steady during times of discomfort and seeing the discomfort as a reflection of our moving along the continuum of change.

As we moved through the processes of creating major change and a paradigm shift, the group supervision sessions were the vehicle for holding attention on issues that were ripe, and it was also the place where decisions were deferred on issues that were deemed unripe.

As one of the major coordinators or facilitators of the change process, I had access to much information. I was coordinating with Ross and Stewart regarding what needed attending to next, while they were providing advice on which issues were ripe and which should be deferred for awhile. I was in a position to be receiving lots of information from the staff about their take on how things were going. This included various individuals' opinions on which staff members were trying, which staff members were undermining efforts, and which individuals were still on the fence. I was coordinating with my boss the changes we were undergoing and their potential implication or impact for the organization at large. The medical director and I talked several times a week in the initial stages, and during that time we agreed on the approach to be taken.

Controlling the flow of information was an integral part of facilitating the process. When individuals would come to me with a particular issue or concern, I was able to suggest that they bring the issue to the next group supervision session, especially when I thought the issue was important for the group—i.e., the concern reflected a broader issue that would benefit from group discussion.

As one of the leaders, I supported the decision to suspend a meeting on the unit that we called our multidisciplinary staff meeting. This meeting had been designed for staff to discuss issues that had a bearing on the functioning of the unit or on staff interactions and working together. In practice, however, it had become somewhat dysfunctional and was perceived as being mainly clinical in nature. Very few milieu staff attended, and when I urged them to go to represent their concerns, it was clear that they did not view the meeting as helpful. The milieu counselors and many of the nurses reported that they did not feel comfortable or valued in these meetings. Their perception was that it had become a vehicle where clinical staff sometimes made negative comments about the milieu staff. The clinical staff were using it to discuss unit issues, but in reality the meeting had become bogged down.

When I arrived, there was a series of departures of clinical staff. My perception was that this staff meeting was not particularly effective as a leadership meeting, nor was it a true multidisciplinary meeting, as there was little representation of the milieu staff. Since this had been the most recent history of the meeting, a decision was made to suspend these meetings during the change process. We wanted all the staff to take any issues they had with our evolving changes to the group supervision sessions, which had been set up as the place to work things out as a group. It would also avoid having two meetings running concurrently, where dissenters of the changes could go to one meeting and complain but not mention these issues at the group sessions. It was important that the group work on problems together when they agreed with the concerns being raised.

We resurrected the multidisciplinary staff meetings two years later at the urging of the social work supervisor. She was very convincing in her advocating that the group restart, and it has been helpful to have a time and place to discuss issues that impact all the staff of the unit that cannot be explored in clinical meetings such as rounds. This meeting also has a broader staff scope than the nursing staff meetings.

Having the power to frame issues is a vital component of succeeding at major change efforts. This involved moving discussions from assumptions that change needed to occur within a structure that upheld traditional values to discussions that posed the question as to what values were the most important for us to have to provide superb child-centered care. Heifetz describes the need to talk about the elephant sitting on the table in the meeting. And he states that "leadership often involves helping groups make difficult choices that involve giving up something that they value on behalf of something that they care even more about"[19]. This was true in our discussions about our core values. We were questioning the validity of being preoccupied with the standard values of safety, security, and structure. We were talking about moving them down in our hierarchy of importance from first, second, and third place to fourth, fifth, and sixth. We were discussing placing the values of nurturance, teaching, and learning and the provision of choices in the first, second, and third place. This seems at first glance as not very significant, but *it was a major shift in thinking.* When problems or issues presented themselves, the staff had to force their thinking to consider these new values ahead of problem solving from a perspective of safety, security, and structure as the values that dictated decision making. They had to think about how to respond to a child's behavior in light of the individual child's needs, not the rules developed for a group norm or standard. That did not mean that we stopped considering safety issues. Our old values still played a role, but the driving force shifted from that perspective. The primary focus now was on creating a nurturing environment and considering a child's individual needs and having reasonable expectations for each child.

Framing issues also involved assessing the change process and the timing for bringing up new issues to explore, and the encouraging of decisions to try interventions to see if they brought positive results. It also meant forestalling group decisions that seemed premature at the time. The initial request by some staff to eliminate the level system in our initial stages of mastery is a case in point. At that early stage, it was an unripe issue and had the potential to increase distress and confusion. When it resurfaced several months later, it was ripe—we were at a very different level of functioning and expertise—we were ready for a group decision to eliminate the point system and levels. Now it was genuinely in the way and impeding our work.

Being able to orchestrate conflict and contain disorder is a sophisticated skill that develops over time and is something that is forever in a state of continued mastery. It is a skill set that is not unlike mastering the game of GO, where people spend a lifetime further honing their strategy and skills. Dealing with conflict is usually uncomfortable to some degree. You are often dealing with heated emotions and differing values that are held passionately by people. It is important to be able to mediate when staff are having conflicts and to confront people who are increasing the level of stress by a negative outlook. One of the most difficult issues for me was to confront directly the staff about whom I would hear had done things when I was not present on the unit. Usually these incidents involved preventing other staff from trying out new behaviors and interventions by imposing the will of the staff person from a position of power and asserting his or her authority. Frequently, but not always, this would occur with a nurse telling a milieu counselor that he or she was not to do "x and such" on "my" shift. She would add that she was in charge and it was her decision. The ultimate phrase for stopping any further dialogue was, "It's my license and my liability."

In a few instances, a milieu counselor would escalate a situation by jumping in to set a limit on an escalating child when another milieu counselor was dealing with the situation. The rejoinder, when the counselor was questioned, would be, "It's for safety and it's the way I was taught." It sometimes required that I keep my cool in confronting a situation and try to mediate a resolution after my clinical competence would be called into question. On occasion, I would finish the meeting and then rush to speak with my boss for support and a place to ventilate the feelings I had contained during the previous confrontation. Thankfully, those were few and far between.

Containing disorder is also a high-level skill in that it takes the ability to tolerate disorder and to intuitively know the difference between increasing disorder and impeding chaos. Much constructive learning can take place during a period of heightened and increasing disorder. Fearing that it is impending chaos can prevent the push ahead into new levels of mastery.

This was brought home clearly in our episodes with Pablo and Ramon and their episodes of continued aggression that lasted seventy-two and forty-eight hours, respectively. We learned we could push the envelope and that we could withstand our anxiety that things would get out of control beyond our ability to pull them back. We learned that, even with the best of abilities from highly trained staff, the unit as an entity could only withstand forty-eight hours of continued distress and then the milieu itself would start into a decline. We would then enter the phase we had learned to avoid and prevent—a messing up of the milieu. We learned from that experience that our expectations of adding more bodies to the unit to calm things down was not effective. It was the *mix of staff* that was the critical issue in containing ongoing aggression.

We also learned that it was not a reasonable expectation to request the clinical staff to enter into the fray undirected. We learned that we needed to have realistic expectations for who could and should be expected to do particular tasks when we were in emergency mode. As much as we worked to be a team, it did not mean that our roles were interchangeable, especially when we moved into emergency mode. To maintain our gains and move through a difficult period, it meant that the staff best equipped to manage intense aggression were the staff on the front lines. Extra help could provide assistance in other ways—e.g., answering phone calls, making calls to parents, and taking other children out of the area and engaging in activities with them.

The group sessions that occurred after the prolonged episode of Ramon's aggression were also an example of working to resolve conflict. Here the conflict involved the strong emotions and difference of opinion between clinical and milieu staff regarding the end limit for considering the use of restraints. In the first session, we attempted to confront the conflicting points of view and were not successful in resolution. Things felt heated and personal, and a lot was going unsaid. There was a palpable undercurrent of tension. The second attempt was more successful and was due to the care taken in reframing the issue in a more abstract way that allowed us to discuss differing points of view without feeling challenged personally.

Choosing the decision-making process was an ongoing part of the evolution of our change. For us, it involved more than one style of leadership. Many decisions were participative or consensual. They were decided in our group supervision sessions together. Some were consultative. We depended heavily on Ross and Stuart to help us internalize a different perspective and develop new lenses in which to view a child's aggressive behavior.

At other times, I relied on an autocratic style. When to bring an issue up for discussion sometimes was planned and not discussed or voted on ahead of time. The decision to use CPS as the model of care was autocratic based on my having been exposed to a seminar on the approach and my assessment that it had the potential to be a good fit with our population and my belief that the staff would ultimately accept this model as consistent with their own values. Another autocratic decision was deciding when a particular staff person had been given ample opportunity to learn new skills and, based on his or her resistance to implementing the model, the beginning of a process of confrontation and counseling regarding that particular person's ability to move on with the rest of us. There were some people for whom this approach was difficult; certain personality types had a more difficult time than others in their ability to be open to trying the model. I believed that reaching a tipping point sooner rather than later was vital to our success.

The decision to begin Open Hours for parents was autocratic. It was discussed in staff meetings, but the discussion centered on concerns and how they would play out. I answered questions, but it was not put to a vote or delayed until a majority of the staff came around to thinking it was a good idea. A date was set for us to begin.

Heifetz talks of the importance of giving the work back to the people. This was every step of the way a group effort. The staff did the work and developed mastery in the skills and thinking processes we needed to be successful. People helped one another and confronted one another tactfully and, on occasion, less tactfully. The process bound most of us together. New staff have entered and joined us. At times it was hard for the newer staff who missed our experience of learning together through the six months of group supervision. But the new staff have been hired with our new values in the forefront, and they have chosen to work with us based on their personal commitments to the values we share. They have mastered the skills needed without the benefit of being one of many learning together. Some have been with us long enough that we forget they were not here for the changeover. They worked as hard and are as proud as the original staff. Their skills and style enriched us and provided more cement to the structure we have built.

We are now more than three years into our change. It has been an exciting experience. We are now in the maintenance phases, and we continue to look for ways to improve our care. We are proud of the changes we have made, and we enjoy sharing what we have done with others who express an interest in our work. It has been a group effort, and it was only made possible due to the talents, strengths, intelligence, and commitment of a truly extraordinary staff group who continue to amaze me on a daily basis. Everyone should be as fortunate as I have been to be part of this great crew and this exciting and enriching endeavor.

My hope is that our story will encourage other groups of people to take on the change process and work on improving their services to children and families in a way that embraces the values of child- and family-centered care.

— Kathy Regan

THE RESULTS SO FAR

This appendix displays in graphic detail some indicators we measured as we altered the way in which we interacted with children and worked to create an environment that was child centered.

Graph 1 is labeled Restraint/Seclusion Events on the CAU, and the time period covered here is from 1/02 through 12/04. This graph measures the restraint and seclusion events on the CAU in aggregate terms, that is, events per 1,000 patient days. The Massachusetts Department of Mental Health uses this designation to compare all Child Units within the state. This is based on a formula that is calculated by

$$\frac{\text{Numerator}}{\text{Denominator}} \times 1,000$$

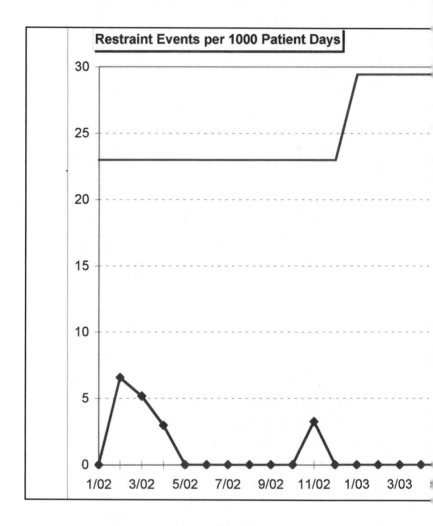

GRAPH 1
Restraint/Seclusion Events on the
Child Inpatient Service (CAU)
CAMBRIDGE HEALTH ALLIANCE,
DEPARTMENT OF PSYCHIATRY

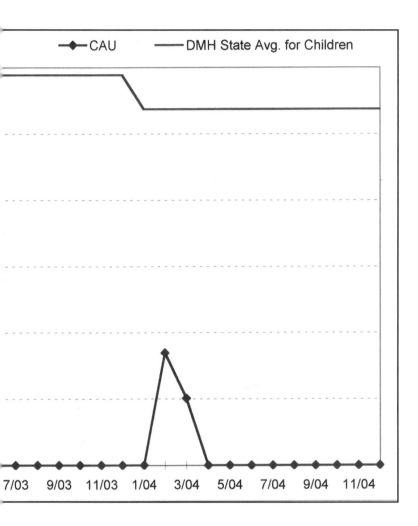

The numerator is the total number of mechanical, physical and chemical restraints per month. The denominator is the average daily census × 24 hours × the number of days in the month.

Graph 1 also compares the CAU with the DMH six-month average for children on all child psychiatric units within the state. This graph allows us to look at our decrease in these interventions as compared to the average of all child units within the state. Here we are well below the average for all child units.

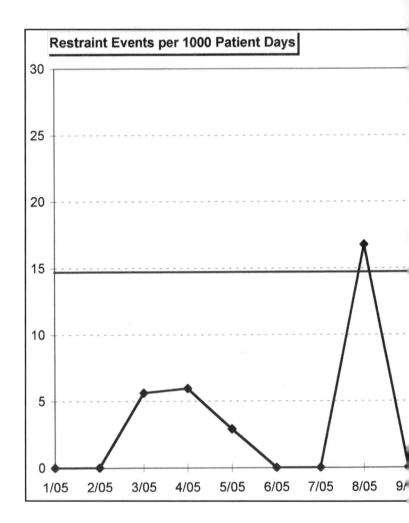

GRAPH 2
Restraint/Seclusion Events on the
Child Inpatient Service (CAU)
CAMBRIDGE HEALTH ALLIANCE,
DEPARTMENT OF PSYCHIATRY

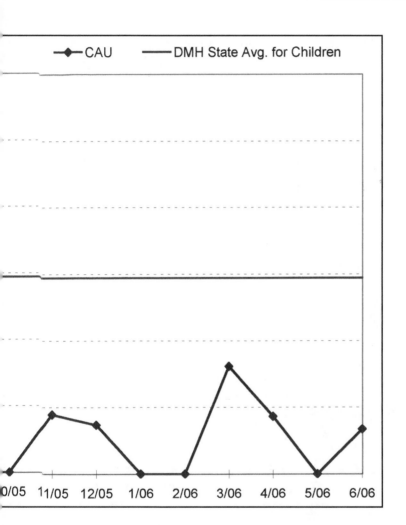

Graph 2 uses the same formula and comparison but extends the time period up to and including July 2006. As you can see, the statewide initiative is well underway, the child average has gone down significantly, and the CAU is still below the state average except for one month (August 2005).

The graphs are separated because in January 2005, we began to count any physical hold as a physical restraint. We adopted CMS (Center for Medicare and Medicaid Services) criteria. Up until that time, we used the DMH criteria, which separated out physical holds

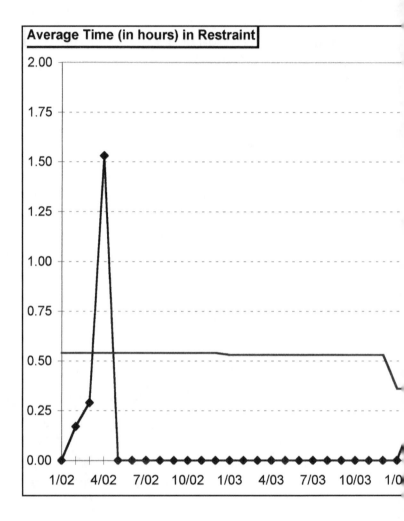

GRAPH 3
Restraint/Seclusion Events on the
Child Inpatient Service (CAU)
CAMBRIDGE HEALTH ALLIANCE,
DEPARTMENT OF PSYCHIATRY

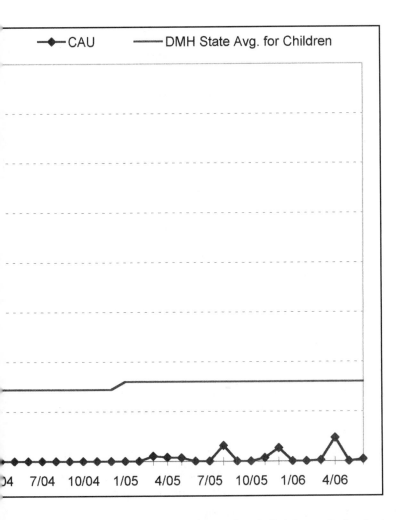

less than five minutes from the definition of physical restraints. As of April 2006, the Massachusetts DMH required that all child units adopt the CMS criteria and definition of physical restraints.

Graph 3 depicts the average time in hours of restraint events. This includes physical and mechanical restraints and locked-door seclusion. Of interest to me is that the outlying event in 3/2002, where we were above the state average by a large degree, was a restraint event for a child who had been restrained many times at home and at his school setting. He was one of our very last mechanical restraints. He was one of the children who had several admissions on our unit, and his last two admissions occurred at points when we had developed confidence in our model, resulting in his not being restrained. He was able to talk to us about the difference in his experience and in his perceptions. He tended to have a suspicious bias, and he had suffered a brain injury as a young child; therefore, he had difficulty modulating his affect. He was able to report to us that he perceived the unit as less dangerous for him when he did not have to worry about the possibility of restraints.

The other factor that is interesting when looking at these graphs is that they provide specific information that can be used for other areas of improvement. For example, the event listed for 4/06 was a significant increase in time in a physical hold. We have been working on decreasing the time a child is in a physical hold since 2003, and most of our holds are over in less than thirty seconds. This child was held for seven minutes! What this event showed me was that one of our nurses, who worked at another psychiatric unit part-time as well as on our unit, was not fully onboard with our philosophy and had not mastered the skill set needed to make serious charge decisions such as this one—a decision to institute a physical restraint on a child. It was an opportunity for a discussion about the expectations for the charge nurse role and the need for her to receive further mentoring before she could return to the charge nurse role on any shift she worked. Granted, the child who was restrained was very challenging to us, but the rest of the nurses on the unit were more comfortable with alternatives, such as having him escorted to his room to calm down and removing from his range, the female staff he was assaulting at that time.

Table 1 lists the actual injuries due to assaults and the severity of these injuries. These assaults can be child-to-child or child-to-staff. The severity scale is listed at the bottom of the table. Level-

	Level 1	Level 2	Level 3	Total
2000	16	2	1	19
Jan-Mar	3	0	1	4
Apr-Jun	1	0	0	1
Jul-Sep	5	1	0	6
Oct-Dec	7	1	0	8
2001	28	9	3	40
Jan-Mar	9	5	0	14
Apr-Jun	8	0	3	11
Jul-Sep	2	0	0	2
Oct-Dec	9	4	0	13
2002	30	10	0	40
Jan-Mar	13	6	0	19
Apr-Jun	10	3	0	13
Jul-Sep	6	0	0	6
Oct-Dec	1	1	0	2
2003	7	2	0	9
Jan-Mar	1	0	0	1
Apr-Jun	2	0	0	2
Jul-Sep	1	2	0	3
Oct-Dec	3	0	0	3
2004	5	5	0	10
Jan-Mar	3	4	0	7
Apr-Jun	0	1	0	1
Jul-Sep	0	0	0	0
Oct-Dec	2	0	0	2
2005	1	1	0	2
Jan-Mar	1	1	0	2
Apr-Jun	1	1	0	2
Jul-Sep	0	0	0	0
Oct-Dec	0	0	0	0
2006	0	1	0	1
Jan-Mar	0	1	0	1
Apr-Jun	1	2	0	3

Severity Level: 1—No injury or minimal injury (simple first aid);
2—Minor injury (e.g., medical evaluation, X-ray, dressing, sutures);
3— Significant injury or potential for significant injury

TABLE 1

Assault and Injury Rates on the Child Inpatient Service (CAU)
CAMBRIDGE HEALTH ALLIANCE, MH/SA SERVICE LINE

three injuries usually involved significant time out of work and included injuries such as a broken nose, a back injury, and, in one case (2000), a serious concussion resulting in a nurse being out of work for several months. All of the level-three injuries listed were injuries to staff. As you can see, in 2002, as we began the process of changing our culture, there was an increase in level-one injuries to staff and children. By 2003, all injuries had significantly decreased and have remained in single digits for the year totals for level-one and level-two injuries.

There have been no level-three injuries due to assaults since 2001.

Table 2 depicts some of the domain scores for patient and family satisfaction based on questionnaires given to parents at different points that we did polling. Twice a year for a ten-week period, we asked parents to fill out a survey tool on the services they received while their child was an inpatient with us. The form was given to them on the day of discharge or a day or so before the discharge. In previous years, we had mailed out surveys and the response rate was very low. We found that even when we handed parents the survey to fill out, if they took it home to complete, the return rate was zero.

The domains listed in the table are the ones that most closely relate to our improvement efforts as we changed our care to children and families. We expected that having Open Hours for parents would be reflected in our scores, and it proved to be true. One of the questions that we are often asked about our Open Hours is, "How do you deal with the confidentiality issue with having parents on the unit for long periods of time?" As you can see, the parents themselves feel that confidentiality is respected, especially in the past two years. Basically, what one parent finds out about another parent or child is based on what they share with each other when they are on the unit with their child. Staff do not share personal information with parents about another child or

	12/04	11/03	12/02	2/02	8/01
Visitor and Family Domain Score	**92.4***	**81.8**	**82.0**	**90.4****	**79.2**
Staff courtesy toward visitors	91.3*	75.0	85.0	93.2	82.7
Adequacy of visiting hours	96.4*	87.5	90.0	90.9*	78.6
Respect for visitor confidentiality	93.2	85.4*	75.0	94.3*	78.6
Space to meet with family/friends	92.1*	79.2	77.5	87.5*	73.3

Notes
* Significant improvement from previous score at .05 level
** Significant improvement from previous score at .01 level

TABLE 2
CAU Patient/Family Satisfaction
CAMBRIDGE HEALTH ALLIANCE, MH/SA SERVICE LINE

parent. That was never the issue. And being on the unit with the children present is no different from the experience of a parent with a child on a medical unit or parents and children in outpatient medical office waiting rooms.

The problem with this survey is that the number of respondents is very low, because we have been surveying for only two ten-week periods a year. When the numbers are so low, the results can be skewed either positively or negatively by one respondent.

We are now in the process of using a different survey that is more relevant for psychiatric services, and we will be able to do continuous surveying. Also, we are taking a number of relevant questions on the parent survey tool and are rewording them in developing a child survey tool. Therefore, we will be able to capture the child's perceptions about the care he or she received from us, and we will be able to compare the child's responses with those of his or her parents.

NURSING SERVICE STANDARDS OF CARE— For the Child at Risk of Aggression

STANDARD: Care of the aggressive child at risk of restraint

OUTCOME CRITERIA:
The patient will:

1. Behave in a way that fosters collaboration with staff

2. Maintain safety without interventions that may be retraumatizing

3. Learn skills to manage frustration that will result in a decrease in aggressive behavior

4. Build positive, trusting relationships

PROCESS CRITERIA:
The nurse will:

1. Utilize the collaborative problem-solving (CPS) approach to:
    a. Identify antecedents to aggressive behavior
    b. Conduct situational analysis
    c. Determine the skill deficits that impact a child's behavior

2. Use the CAU designated tools (Parent/Guardian Assessment Tool, Child Tool) and Nursing Assessment to gather information regarding the needs and special concerns of the child and family related to
    a. Situations in which the child becomes aggressive or frustrated, or has difficulty maintaining control of behavior
    b. Coping strategies, skills, and individual strengths utilized to manage frustration and stress.

3. Develop a Nursing Care Plan that builds upon a child's strengths and identifies areas for teaching that have been identified in the CPS assessment.
    a. Develop a formulation of the child's behavior using the "CPS pathways"
    b. Incorporate information regarding treatment approaches and CPS strategies
    c. Plan interventions based upon the skill set of utilizing Baskets B, C, or A

4. Reassess on a daily basis any change in a child's behavior:
    a. After a "meltdown" (child escalates and frustration builds, resulting in a major outburst such as throwing objects, yelling and cursing, making verbal threats, attempts to assault staff or another patient)

b. After obtaining new information that would impact the child's behavior or coping strategies that have worked for a child

STRUCTURE CRITERIA:

CHA policies related to Assessment/Reassessment Policy
Department Assessment Policy
CAU Therapeutic Programming/Behavioral Policies
CPS Group Supervision Notebook
CAU "CPS" Competency Assessment

REFERENCES:

Greene, Ross W., and Doyle, Alysa E.. "Toward a Transactional Conceptualization of Oppositional Defiant Disorder: Implications for Assessment and Treatment." *Clinical Child and Family Psychology Review*, Vol.2 No. 3, 1999: 129-148.

Greene, Ross W. *The Explosive Child: A New Approach for Understanding and Parenting Easily Frustrated, Chronically Inflexible Children*. HarperCollins, 2001.

Greene, Ross W., et al. "Psychiatric Comorbidity, Family Dysfunction, and Social Impairment in Referred Youth with Oppositional Defiant Disorder." *American Journal of Psychiatry 2002*; 159:1214-1224.

Chief Nursing Officer   Date

APPENDIX 4

NURSING STANDARDS OF CARE: Child Assessment Unit Nursing Standard of Care—For Nursing Patient Education and Teaching Interventions

STANDARD: Assessment and care of children admitted to the Child Assessment Unit

OUTCOME CRITERIA:

The patient will:

1. Learn that there are ways and choices available to handle feelings of frustration and anger before the behavior begins to escalate

2. Learn through interactions with the staff that making choices to manage frustration in the early stages will prevent aggressive behavior

3. Learn skills that help manage frustration and have increased problem-solving abilities

4. Learn to interact with other children and adults by increased verbal expression of feelings and decreased displays of anger

PROCESS CRITERIA:
The nurse and milieu counselor will:

1. Utilize the collaborative problem-solving (CPS) approach to:
   a. Identify possible pathways that lead to aggressive behavior
   b. Identify specific steps within the pathway of specific skill deficits that can be used as teaching points
   c. Provide patient education regarding the steps needed to work around the skill deficits in Basket B interventions both "in the moment" and "out of the moment"
   d. Use Basket B interventions in interactions with parents, guardians, and caretakers, teaching and identifying specific skill deficits and pathways to aggression for their individual children
   e. Use Basket B interventions to demonstrate the Basket approaches and explain the differences between Basket A, B, and C approaches in helping their children deal with frustration and be better able to problem solve
   f. Patient education and parent education and demonstration are done using the collaborative problem-solving (CPS) approach, and education is done using Basket B interventions

STRUCTURE CRITERIA:

CHA Policies Related to Patient Education
CAU Therapeutic Programming/Behavioral Policies
CPS Group Supervision Notebook
CAU "CPS" Competency Assessments (I and II)

REFERENCES:

Ahmann, E., and Johnson, B.H. (2000). "Family-Centered Care: Facing the New Millennium." *Pediatric Nursing* 26(1): 87–92.

Bowlby, J. (1956). "The Growth of Independence in the Young Child." *Royal Society of Health Journal* 76: 587-591

Erikson, E. (1963) *Childhood and Society.* New York: W.W. Norton & Company.

Greene, R. (2001). *The Explosive Child: A New Approach for Understanding and Parenting Easily Frustrated, Chronically Inflexible Children.* Harper Collins.

CAU Physical Holds/ Restraint Policy

PURPOSE:
To provide and maintain a safe environment for child psychiatric patients and their families while ensuring that care of all children is humane, non-coercive, and trauma-sensitive

PERSONNEL:
All staff of the CAU

POLICY:
All physical holds of children to restrict movement shall be considered physical restraints.

1. Physical restraints are not done for destruction of property.

2. Physical holds are done as an emergency measure after all other less restrictive interventions have been tried unsuccessfully and

all staff present agree that no other alternative is left to prevent ongoing physical assaults of other patients or staff.

3. A physical hold should be a rare occurrence that is followed by an intensive review process. The leadership of the unit is to be notified immediately following such an event.

4. Physical holds/restraints shall be considered incident occurrences and require that an incidence occurrence form be filled out in addition to other restraint paperwork.

5. Physical holds are done for the least amount of time necessary with the least restrictive interventions tried first (basket hold, one wrist, two wrists, one ankle, two ankles, etc.) Take-down holds resulting in four limb holds are considered the most restrictive of interventions in the physical hold category.

6. The charge nurse is responsible for ensuring that all procedures, steps, notification, and documentation of all paperwork and forms are done by the end of the shift. The charge nurse will make herself or himself available within seventy-two hours for a review of the events leading to the decision to perform a physical restraint. Staff working during that shift and involved in the decision to implement a physical restraint should also be expected to attend a review meeting within seventy-two hours following the event.

7. Physical restraints should not continue one second beyond what is absolutely necessary in an emergency situation. Once restrained, all efforts immediately move to the fastest release possible. If not already done, attempted release should occur within a maximum of thirty seconds and continued release attempts every ten to thirty seconds thereafter.

8. Every child must have an individualized "safety plan" that is written up, with one copy in the record, one in the Pass-On Book, and one for the child. These plans should be developed

within twenty-four hours of admission, and the parent assessment sheet, as well as input from the child, should be used in developing the safety plan. The safety plan should identify what events and situations the child perceives as upsetting, what strategies help the child calm, what doesn't work, and the child's preferences for helping him or her when the child is aggressive.

STEPS:

1. A priority in the sequence of events as a child is escalating is that efforts are made to support the child (not set limits) to calm the situation down.

2. Every possible alternative must be tried exhaustively. There will need to be clear, specific documentation of each intervention to manage aggressive behavior without resorting to threats to restrain. The patient's safety tool should be consulted and referred to in designing interventions to de-escalate the situation and to prevent re-traumatization.

3. Staff are required to carry out a "huddle" with all teammates on the unit to see if anyone has suggestions that have not been tried, and all need to agree that the restraint is the only alternative left to remedy the situation.

4. A minimum of two people should perform the restraint. Whenever possible, another staff member should participate as a "witness" to the restraint.

5. A person who has been assaulted should not be the person making the decision to restrain. This is based upon the recognition that it is hard to be objective when you have just been hit, kicked, choked, or spit at. And recognizing that, we need to assure that the decision to restrain is make after calm thinking and by someone who is still able to "think out of the box" in considering alternatives.

6. When a restraint is done, it should not be assumed that all four limbs need to be held and that the child needs a "takedown." Although, this may seem the safest and easiest from our point of view, it is the most restrictive hold, and there is more likelihood of escalation and injury from a takedown and holding of all limbs. Decisions for types of holds should include prioritizing least restrictive holds before considering more restrictive holds. This would mean that least restrictive holds are those that involve only one limb, such as one wrist or ankle; next would be considering a "basket hold," then two-limb hold, next three-limb hold, and, more restrictive, a four-limb hold. The most restrictive hold is a four-limb hold that includes a "takedown."

7. If a child is spitting, using a sheet (holding it in front of you) as a protection for the staff is effective. It is dangerous to put anything in a child's mouth to prevent spitting or biting. Gentle positioning of the head and changing staff position to avoid being bitten is the safest intervention for biting.

8. A physician must be called immediately—at the onset of the hold—and the physician must arrive within one hour to review the situation, write the order, evaluate the patient, and write a restraint note.

9. Releases should occur as soon as possible, but the maximum time allowed before an attempt at release is thirty seconds. Continued attempts at release should occur rapidly, with the maximum interval between release attempts being thirty seconds. After two minutes with a child and no sign of calming, then the team holding the child should switch off with other staff members. A change of faces may be just what is needed for the child to be able to come around and calm down.

10. A full account of the hold and the handling of the hold must be documented. Holds must be documented on various forms and in notes:

- On the physical hold assessment sheet

- A detailed nursing restraint note that reflects all the items covered in this protocol as well as reference to the specifics of the safety plan that were attempted. The time of the hold and the length of time with release attempts times should be clearly designated with observations of the patient

- In addition, all the required state DMH paperwork must be completed and all forms filled in. Of particular interest are all the interventions that were tried as the child was beginning to escalate before a decision was made to initiate a physical hold.

11. Immediately after the hold, the charge nurse is expected to call the nurse manager (NM) and review the entire process. If the NM is unavailable, then the medical director should be contacted.

12. The charge nurse must ensure that all paperwork is completed by the end of the shift. The forms should be placed in the nurse manager's mailbox (upon completion) for initial review.

13. Every hold requires a formal debriefing of all the milieu staff before the end of the shift.

14. Every hold requires an apology to the child before the end of the shift. We are apologizing because we were unable to find any other way to handle the situation and because we regret any harm the hold may have had on the child. We also are expected to promise that the staff will work hard to rebuild a relationship of trust with the child and acknowledge that trust has been breached by the physical intervention.

15. All holds will be formally reviewed within seventy-two hours, and an informal review will be conducted at the next daily

rounds. Data will be compiled to look for trends regarding holds, including day of week, shift, staff involved, nurse making formal order for the restraint, etc., for review and for quality improvement purposes.

CONVENTION ON THE RIGHTS OF THE CHILD, GENERAL ASSEMBLY RESOLUTION 22/45

(November 20, 1990; reworded for display in living room of CAU)
(Asterisks added for emphasis)

- Every country shall respect and ensure the rights of children listed in this paper.

- The "best interest of the child" shall be the primary concern in all actions concerning children.

- All countries should take whatever steps are necessary to ensure all the rights listed here.

- All countries shall respect the rights and duties of parents to guide the child in the use of their rights.

- Every child has the right to life and to be able to survive and to develop and grow.

- Every child has the right to a name, a nationality, the right to know and be cared for by parents, as far as possible.

- Every child has the right to preserve his/her identity, nationality, and family relations without unlawful interference.

- Children will not be separated from their parents against their will, except when such separation is in the best interest of the child.

- Children separated from one or both parents have the right to maintain personal relations and direct contact with both parents, except if it is contrary to the child's best interests.

- Children or parents requesting to leave a nation for the purpose of reunification with thechild or parent shall have that request be viewed positively, humanely and in a timely fashion.

- All countries shall take action to prevent the illegal placing of children in another country.

- ***Children capable of expressing their own views have the right to express these views freely in all matters affecting them, and the child's views will be given due weight based on his or her age and maturity.

- ***Every child has the right to freedom of expression. This includes freedom to seek, receive, and give information and ideas of all kinds orally, in print, in art or any other media of the child's choice.

- Every child has the right to freedom of thought, conscience, and religion.

- Every child has the right to meet with other kids and to freedom of peaceful assembly (to get together in groups).

- Every child has the right to obtain information from a variety of mass media, especially for social, spiritual, moral, physical well-being, and for mental health.

- Both parents have common responsibilities for the upbringing and development of the child. The best interest of the child shall be their main concern.

- ***All countries shall take all possible steps to protect children from all forms of physical or mental violence, injury or abuse, neglect, exploitation, and sexual abuse while in the care of parents or any person who has care of the child.

- All countries are responsible for the protection of children who are unable to remain in the care of their parents.

- All countries shall protect the rights of children and the best interest of the child in laws and supervising programs for adoption.

- All countries will provide protection and assistance to children seeking refuge status.

- ***All countries shall recognize that all children with physical or mental disabilities should enjoy a full and decent life, with dignity, in conditions that promote self-reliance and the child's active participation in the community.

- ***All children with disabilities have the right to special care and to all available resources (education, health care, training, rehabilitation, job training, and recreation).

- Every child has the right to enjoy the highest degree of health possible and to treatment for illness and rehabilitation.

- Every child who has been placed out of his or her home has the right to periodic review of his or her care and treatment.

- Every child has the right to benefit from social security and social insurance.

- Every child has the right to a standard of living adequate for the child's physical, mental, spiritual, moral, and social development.

- Every child has the right to education.

- ***The education of children shall be directed to the development of the child's personality, talents, and mental and physical abilities to the fullest potential. This includes teaching a respect for human rights and freedoms, respect for parents and cultural identity, language, and values. It includes preparation of the child for life in a free society with a spirit of understanding, peace, tolerance, equality of the sexes, and friendship among all people.

- A child who belongs to a minority shall not be denied the right to enjoy his or her own culture, religion, and language.

- ***Every child has the right to rest and leisure, to engage in play and recreational activities, and to participate freely in cultural activities and the arts.

- Every child has the right to be protected from being made to work and from performing work that is dangerous or will interfere with the child's education or be harmful to the child's growth and development.

- All countries will take steps to protect children from the illegal use of drugs and to prevent the use of children in illegal drug operations.

- All countries will take steps to protect children from all forms of sexual abuse.

- Nations will take steps to prevent the abduction (kidnapping) of children or the sale of children for any purpose.

- No child shall be subjected to torture, cruel, or degrading behavior. There shall be no capital punishment or life imprisonment for any child who is jailed for offenses before the age of eighteen.

- All countries shall respect the humanitarian laws in armed conflicts (wars) in which children are affected.

- ***All nations shall take actions to help children recover from the effects of neglect, abuse, and cruel punishment. This recovery shall respect the dignity of the child.

- Children within the jail system will be treated in a manner that helps the child's dignity and self-worth and that helps the child become a helpful member of society.

- All countries will make the rights of children known to adults and children alike.

APPENDIX *7*

NEW VOCABULARY

New Vocabulary	Old Vocabulary
Cognitive language terms	affective, processing terms
Skills deficit	acting-out behavior
Identified pathways (to aggression):	personality style
Executive skills deficit	secondary gain
Language skills deficit	attention- seeking
Mood deficit, dysregulated mood	intentional, intentionally
Social skills deficit	splitting, staff splitting
Sensory/motor deficit	boundaries, no boundaries

New Vocabulary	Old Vocabulary
Difficulty shifting cognitive set	paid no attention
Difficulty with time and sequencing	flighty
Difficulty maintaining focus	provocative
Difficulty problem solving	manipulative
Difficulty managing frustration	purposely ignored staff
Difficulty communicating one's needs or problems	negative behavior
Difficulty recognizing impact of behavior on others	gamey
Difficulty with transitions	refused to, refuses to
Inaccurate interpretation of social cues	does his own thing
Poor repertoire of social responses	enjoys negative attention
Poor self-awareness	pretends
Poor or inaccurate self-perception	doesn't listen
Became frustrated	won't listen
Impulsive	does what he wants when he wants it
Intrusive	chooses not to comply with staff request
Hyperactive	undermined staff

New Vocabulary	Old Vocabulary
Receptive language	wants to be the center of attention
Expressive language	demanding
Inability to put words to feeling states	entitled
Poor language-based problem-solving skills	being unforgiving
Difficulty engaging in linguistic give and take	needy
Difficulty comprehending linguistic feedback	failing to (instead of unable, not able to)
Auditory processing	insolent
Irritable mood, irritability, cranky	inappropriate
Hypomanic	mean
Manic	
Sad, depressed	
Hopeless	
Anxious, anxious mood, socially anxious	
Lack of understanding social cues	
Isolative, withdrawn, detached	
Rigid, inflexible thinking	
Black-and-white thinking	

New Vocabulary

Ritualistic behavior

Quick to anger

Explosive

Basket A, B, C interventions

Negotiation

Collaboration

Choices

Problem solving

Observations

Situational analysis

-5, -30, -60

Meltdown

Precipitants

Stressors

Triggers

Surrogate frontal lobe

Thinking skills

Work it out

Empathy invitation

Talked with, discussed with

THE MILIEU AND THE MILIEU STAFF

While your child is on the CAU, he or she will be cared for by the milieu staff (the nurses and milieu counselors). We refer to the atmosphere and the environment within the CAU as the milieu. Most of the time your child spends on the unit is spent in the milieu. He or she will meet with clinicians involved in the care of your child for an hour or so a day. The rest of the time, your child is on the milieu and participating in group activities and groups and interacting with other children on the unit and with the milieu staff caring for them.

The role of the milieu staff is that of caretakers, observers, and teachers. They are directly involved in the twenty-four-hour care of your child. They assist with all the activities of daily living, and they assist your child with interactions with other children of the unit.

It is from observing your child in the milieu that we learn much needed information in trying to answer the question: What is this child's deal? It is only by answering this question that we are able to develop a formulation as to why your child is having difficulty. The milieu staff play a vital role in this formulation by being astute observers on the milieu, watching interactions and each child's response to different situations with which they are confronted. These observations are communicated to the other staff of the unit so that we can determine under what situations and in what circumstances your child becomes upset and frustrated. Staff members look for patterns in the antecedents that lead to frustration and "meltdowns."

When we have been able to identify the circumstances under which a child becomes frustrated, we can then help with the thinking skills the child needs to develop to successfully problem solve how to manage and overcome his or her frustration. The milieu staff have become adept at doing this and spend much of their time helping kids in their interactions in "collaborative problem solving." You will observe them in interactions with children in which they are trying to work with the child to come up with a solution that is mutually acceptable. They will assist two children having difficulty and attempt to have the children work collaboratively with each other. This problem solving looks different with different children and with different staff. What all interactions have in common is that when a child is asked to do something and the child refuses, the staff will intervene by trying to work with the child to find a solution rather than using the traditional method of just "setting limits" and warning about consequences. We have found this method to be very powerful and very effective. We have also found that this approach to managing behavior has allowed us to eliminate the need for mechanical restraints and seclusion.

Occasionally, you will see milieu staff hold a child briefly. This is an infrequent occurrence, and it is a last resort to help a child when he or she is out of control or attempting to hurt him- or herself or others. We try to avoid this intervention whenever possible and we are always looking for creative ways to manage aggressive behavior that do not scare or frighten a child. We are ever mindful of not wanting children to be hurt in any way by an intervention by staff of the unit. We also try diligently to intercede quickly so that no child on the unit is able to hurt another.

The milieu staff are dedicated and take their jobs seriously. They work very hard to assist the children of the unit and to do so in an atmosphere that is nurturing and lends itself to teaching. We believe that hard work can be done in an atmosphere that is playful and caring. We believe that it is important to teach children in an environment that is child and family centered.

While your child is on the CAU, you have an opportunity to watch others interact with him or her. You will be able to observe staff who are using the "collaborative problem-solving" approach. We encourage you to ask questions, seek out staff, and talk with them about this. Staff members want to aid your family and to pass on to you what we have found may work in assisting your child when he or she becomes frustrated. The milieu is a great opportunity to observe, to learn, and to try this approach yourself in the time that your child is here. We would like to work together with you as partners in caring for and learning about your child.

APPENDIX 9

THE BEHAVIORAL PROGRAM ON THE CAU

The CAU has been undergoing a number of changes related to the behavioral pProgram. We have adopted a new model of care called "collaborative problem solving" (CPS). It was developed by Dr. Ross Greene and is a cognitive, behavioral program that focuses on how the adults (staff and parents) interact with children to manage their behavior.

A basic premise of CPS is that "kids do well if they can." This means that if they are not doing well, it is because they are unable to do so. Then our job becomes finding out why they are not doing well and trying to help them. Many kids are with us for only a brief time, so we may only have the time to begin to identify why they are having difficulty. Helping them find a way to do well may be the work of the family and the outpatient psychiatrist or the program they go to after their stay on the CAU.

Another basic premise of CPS is that 98 to 99 percent of all children who arrive at the CAU already know that it is wrong to hit others, to swear, to act aggressively, etc. Since they already

301

know this, our job is not to find motivators to get them to stop swearing and hitting, but to understand when they are likely to hit or swear. We want to find out what it is about those situations that causes a child to consistently respond by becoming angry and having a "meltdown."

A third premise of CPS is that "meltdowns" are not good for kids. When a child has lost control and is enraged, we say that he or she is at "- 30." When a child is at −30, an opportunity to teach has been lost. A child who is very angry cannot be reasoned with and is more likely to hit or swear in that state. Therefore, our job is to calm the child down as quickly as possible. Then we may have the possibility of talking with him or her and learning why he or she became so upset.

CPS is a model that believes the greatest opportunity for learning a child has is when he or she is just beginning to become frustrated over something. We call this "-5." We are looking for opportunities to learn what makes a particular child frustrated, for this will tell us where the child is having difficulty. As a result, we are more interested in what happened (in lots of detail) *before* the child got upset, not all the detail regarding what the child did after he or she became upset. Traditional programs focus on what happened after someone was upset and then set consequences based on what the child did when he or she was upset.

We are more interested in learning *why* and *under what circumstances* a child becomes upset and then working with the child to find ways to handle that situation without the child becoming frustrated to the point of having a "meltdown."

Because of this approach, the unit may look somewhat different than other psychiatric units. It may not look as calm; in fact, it may look almost chaotic at times. Since many of the children we have on the unit have difficulty managing anger, we could have several children at one time becoming upset. If we kept everyone calm all the time, we would have learned nothing about what is frustrating these children.

The staff members determine what approach they will use with a child based on our priorities of what is most important for us with a particular child while the child is on the CAU. CPS describes the decision making that an adult uses to determine the approach as three separate baskets:

Basket A is imposing adult will. It is the traditional way kids learn what to do and what not to do. This works for about 95 percent of children. These are not children who end up being hospitalized on a locked psychiatric unit. The children we see do not usually respond cooperatively to Basket A approaches. So, on the CAU, Basket A is saved for serious safety issues that we can enforce. We still tell kids "No hitting," as we do not want them hitting each other or us.

Basket C is deciding to let something go. We do not care enough about it to make a big deal about it. We ignore it or we agree to what a child has requested. An example of a Basket C situation is a child who has not brushed his or her teeth. While we see hygiene as a value and want children to be able to perform their daily living skills, that is not why they are on a locked psychiatric unit. So we may suggest that they brush their teeth, but we will not struggle over it and insist that our expectation be met to the point of having the children experience a meltdown.

Basket B is where the learning takes place and where we want to concentrate our efforts. When a child is beginning to get frustrated (-5), we will try to have a Basket B intervention. We will show our empathy for the child being upset and ask to help solve the problem. Basket B is a willingness to negotiate with the child, and the adult does not go into the interaction with a preconceived solution that has to be met. It is agreeing to compromise and come up with a solution that both parties are comfortable with. In this scenario, the adult has to remain flexible. This is a teaching opportunity, and we are trying to understand how the child is thinking about the situation that is upsetting him or her and trying to teach alternative solutions to becoming increasingly angry.

A fourth premise of CPS is that "we do not want a child to mess with the milieu." This means that when a child is aggressive, it does not only affect him or her—it affects the whole unit. Each child needs to be "workable" so that we can help a child when he or she is frustrated. If a child is continually aggressive, we say that that child is "not yet workable." Our job is to assist him or her in becoming "workable." There are several ways we do this: we talk with the child, we may have to keep him or her away from large groups of kids on the unit so that we can keep the milieu calm, and we may talk with you about medication to assist your child in becoming "workable." Since we do not use locked-door seclusion or restraints, if your child becomes aggressive, medication will be an important aspect of his treatment.

In addition to CPS, there is another factor that impacts the way the unit may appear to you. We have eliminated the use of mechanical restraints and locked-door seclusion on the CAU. In the past, if a child was acting up and hurled a chair on the floor, he or she might have been given an opportunity to go voluntarily to the Quiet Room, and if the child did not respond, he or she would have been escorted there. If the child did not stay in the Quiet Room or continued to act up, he or she might have ended up in locked-door seclusion or restraints. Now, you might see someone become upset and start to throw a chair, and the staff will get everyone out of the way quickly. Then they will try to work with that child to calm him or her down by a variety of means: talking, putting a hand on the child's shoulder, rubbing the child's back, or making suggestions for working off some of that aggressive energy by rollerblading, shooting hoops, etc. Once the child is calm, then staff members will try to determine what happened earlier in the series of events that resulted in the child becoming very angry.

The CAU has "open hours," so parents have ample opportunity to see us in action. We welcome their feedback, questions, comments, etc. We also offer opportunities to explain this approach in detail and to model this approach for them.

APPENDIX 10

CAU PARENT ASSESSMENT SHEET

Child's Name: _____

Date: _____

Our job on the CAU is to better understand what makes your child upset and to help him or her with this. Often kids get upset when they become frustrated. Some kids have figured out ways to deal with frustration, and for other kids this is harder.

We would like to help your child when he or she is beginning to get "frustrated" before it becomes a big deal and ends in a "meltdown." "Meltdowns" are times when someone is so upset and frustrated or angry that he or she "can't even see straight." At these times, it is very difficult to figure out what to do to make things better. The feelings of being upset, frustrated, and angry may make it difficult to think clearly and make decisions to solve the problem. At times such as these, it is very hard to feel in control and to problem solve.

Many of the children who come to this unit have problems managing frustration and stress. When they become very upset and lose control, it creates problems for parents/caretakers in knowing how to manage the situation.

We want to get to know enough about your child so that we can help when he or she is first beginning to become frustrated.

And we want to work on a plan with you and your child to help with this.

Here are some questions that will help us find the answers we need to help you and your child. For the following, please answer as if you were answering this for your child.

Which of the following do you think is true for your child?
Put a Y for yes or an N for no.

It is very hard for me to sit still

It is very hard for me to be quiet and not talk out loud.

It is very hard for me to switch what I am doing in a hurry, especially if I am having a good time.

I can't think straight if I am given more than one direction at once.

I have a hard time listening if people talk too long.

I need help trying to decide what I should do next and how to do it.

I have trouble remembering things, especially when I am upset.

I have a really hard time thinking clearly when I am upset.

I have a hard time making and keeping friends.

I need people to tell me exactly what they want; I can't figure it out by myself by looking at them.

I am not good at taking hints or body gestures and knowing what they mean.

I know that I want friends, but I do not know how to play with them.

I have a hard time trying to imagine ahead of time what will happen if I do something to someone.

I have a hard time figuring out what someone means or wants just by looking at their face, or listening to their tone of voice.

I have a hard time finding the right words to say when I want to tell someone something important.

I often have a hard time figuring out what someone is saying to me.

It is very hard for me to describe my emotions in words.

I feel cranky, grouchy, and irritable most of the time.

The littlest thing can make me very grouchy.

I have a hard time getting out of a grouchy mood.

I always imagine the worst.

I don't expect good things to happen to me.

I think that I am stupid, or fat, or ugly.

I do think that people like me.

I don't like my life.

I feel I need to look out for myself or people will hurt me.

I worry about a lot of things.

I expect bad things to happen. I wait for bad things to happen to me.

I feel scared a lot of the time.

I am afraid of people.

I want the same things to happen over and over again.

I do not like changes in my routine. I want each day to be the same.

I am sensitive to:

Temperature: I don't like it too hot or too cold.

Clothing: I only like certain types of clothes, and it depends on the way they feel.

Food: I only like certain foods. The way food feels in my mouth is important.

Motion: I like to sit, stand, jump, move a certain way.

Sound: I do not like certain noises. I don't like loud noises.

Touch: I do not like people to touch me. I like it when people squeeze me a little.

Tell us what really "bugs" your child.
For example:
I can't stand it when someone interrupts me when I am speaking.
I don't like it when people get too close to me.

_____

_____

_____

_____

_____

When your child becomes really upset, what helps him or her calm down?

Being left alone.

Being given some time to go to my room.

I like to throw things when I am upset.

I like to yell when I am upset.

I like someone to stay with me until I am a little calmer.

I need to feel that grownups understand why I am upset.

I need someone to help me understand what I did but to tell me in a soft voice.

I need to wait until I am calmer to talk about what happened.

I don't like to talk about what made me upset.

I can write down why I am upset.

It helps me to calm down if I can talk to my mother, father, grandmother, aunt, foster mom, etc.

I like to read in my room.

I like to take a bath or shower.

I like to rub lotion on my skin.

I like to comb my hair.

I like to pace up and down the hall.

I like play with my toys (Gameboy, stuffed animals, cars).

I like to shoot hoops.

I like to rollerblade.

What else would help your child to calm down?

_____

_____

_____

_____

_____

_____

_____

What should we watch for as a sign that your child is beginning to have a "meltdown?"

I clench my fists.

I mutter to myself.

I curse.

I yell.

I argue with people.

I try to start a fight.

I try to throw things.

I start to sweat.

I turn red in the face.

I run as fast as I can.

I refuse to move.

I repeat what someone says.

I start to talk loud.

I talk faster.

I make faces.

I cry.

What other things would tell us your child is very upset?

_____

_____

_____

_____

_____

_____

_____

What things would make it worse for your child when he or she was very upset?

Closing the door to the room I am in.

Male staff coming close to me.

Female staff coming close to me.

Being in the dark.

Being in a room with bright lights.

Being held down by staff (all staff, male staff, female staff).

Warning me about the consequences.

Trying to talk to me.

Not letting me make a phone call to my mom, dad, etc.

Making me sit still.

What time of the day is harder for your child?

No time.

I have a hard time getting going in the morning.

I have a hard time at night.

I have a hard time in the afternoon, before dinner.

Are there times or places that make him or her afraid or scared?

I am afraid to fall asleep.

I am afraid to be in a room alone at night.

I am afraid to be in a room with other people.

I can't fall asleep without music being on.

I need the light on to fall asleep.

I am afraid of the bathroom.

I don't like having to go into a closet.

I get scared when someone yells

I am afraid of strangers

I am afraid of certain types of people (big men, big women, etc)

What else is important for us to know about your child?

Additional information that is very important for us to know about has to do with experiences your child may have had or witnessed. Please share with us this personal information so that we can help your child and ensure that we do not make things any worse for him or her.

Has your child experienced any physical, sexual, or emotional abuse? (If your are not sure what this would be, please ask the staff person who asked you to fill out this form.)

No

Yes, (Please explain)

Was this experiencing a one-time occurrence, or did this occur repeatedly?

No

Yes, (Please explain)

Has your child or family experienced other upsetting or traumatic events? (fire, flood, witnessed a death of relative or friend, etc.)

No

Yes, (Please explain)

CHILD'S PROTECTION PLAN

My Personal Protection Plan

Date: _____

Sign Name:

Things that really upset me!

1)

2)

3)

Things that help me to calm down when I am upset:

1)

2)

3)

When I am having a meltdown:

Please don't do this:

1)

2)

3)

Please do this:

1)

2)

3)

APPENDIX 12

KID'S HANDBOOK FOR THE CHILD ASSESSMENT UNIT

My Name:

_____

My clinician's name:

_____

My doctor's name:

_____

WELCOME TO OUR UNIT

This book will try to tell you some of the basic things that we think you would like to know about our unit and its routines.

We have a number of events that occur often on the unit—important things like breakfast, lunch, dinner, and snack times. We have groups so that the children all have activities and things to do to keep them busy while they are here. We also allow a lot of time for you to play, because we believe that it is very important for children to play and to be able to be with other children and to make friends.

We have movies for kids to watch in the evenings and we have lots of books for kids to read and for the staff to read to them.

A typical day on the CAU looks something like this:

7:30–7:35
This is the time when most of the children begin to get out of bed.

7:30–8:30
This is the time for showering, getting dressed, making your bed, putting your laundry in the laundry room in a basket, and doing a chore. It is also a time when many of the children take their morning medicine from the nurse.

8:00–9:00
This is the time breakfast is served in the living room.

9:00–9:30
This is room time. It is a time for quiet play or reading or playing Gameboy.

9:30–10:30
This is a group time. We have all different kinds of groups. Some are for physical activities like relay races or rollerblading. Some are for arts and crafts or other projects, and some are to help you learn how to solve problems because everyone needs to know how to solve problems so that they can be happy and succeed. We also have a wonderful teacher, and she runs three school groups each day. You will be in one of those groups. She helps you with homework and helps you with your learning in English and Math and Social Studies.

10:30–11:30
Room time.

11:30–12:30
Group time.

12:30–1:00
Lunch (some kids have medicine at noon time, too).

1:00–1:30
Room time.

1:30–2:30
Group time.

2:30–3:00
Snack time.

3:00–4:00
Group time (often outside).

4:00–5:30
Groups and activities.

5:30–6:00
Dinner.

6:00–7:00
Quiet time, start showers, straighten out rooms. Some kids have medication at bedtime.

7:00–7:30
Early Birds have snack and start settling routine, story time.

8:00–8:30
Centrals start snack and settling routine, story time.

9:00–9:30
Night Owls start settling.

During your day, you will also meet with your "clinician" and your doctor. You may have "family meetings" with your family and your clinician. You may also have some tests done that involve your meeting with a psychologist who will ask you a lot of questions and give you certain activities to do.

What to expect when you arrive on the CAU:

We want to make sure that you are healthy. We do our best to check that everyone on the CAU is healthy. Here are some of the medical things that you can expect while you are here. Often they occur the first few days you are here.

VITAL SIGNS: A nurse or milieu counselor will take your temperature, pulse, and blood pressure, and we will also obtain your height and weight. We may need to obtain a urine specimen, and if we do, we will give you a special plastic cup to use and someone will explain to you how to use the cup.

A PEDIATRICIAN (a doctor who works with children) will come by the unit to do a physical exam. He or she will look in your eyes, ears, and mouth, listen to your heart and your breathing, and may press on your tummy to make sure that you are feeling OK and in good health. You will be asked how you are feeling and if you sleep and eating are OK. A staff person will accompany you and stay with you during this exam.

LABWORK: This is usually done the first or second day. People from the lab will come to the unit to take some blood. We know that most kids do not like this, so we try and make it easier for them. The nurse will put some cream on your arms about one-half hour before the lab work so that your arm is numb and will not hurt much at all when the lab people  draw the blood. We do not want you to be scared or afraid, and we will help you get through this. We do not want you to feel pain, so that is why we give you the cream for your arms. We can also help with some medication ahead of time if you need it so that you will be able to get through the short procedure. A staff person will be with you during this time.

5-MINUTE CHECKS: We do 5-minute checks on all the children of the CAU. One of the staff will be assigned "checks" and you will see them walking up and down the unit checking where all the children are every 5 minutes. We do this 24 hours a day. If you want to go to your room you should let the checks person know so they know where to find you when they are doing checks. You will hear the staff when they take some kids off the unit say: "Checks, I am taking Johnny, Kim, and Joey over to the play space."

SLEEPING: Sleeping and bedtime can be scary for some kids. Sometimes bedrooms are scary for kids. We try to make it easier for you to fall asleep. We try and have some fun in the evening and then we may watch a movie and you may begin to get tired during the movie. A staff person will help you settle and relax, often by reading you a story and maybe a backrub if that is relaxing for you. When you are first admitted you will sleep out in the hall on a mattress so that the night staff can see you. Some kids like to sleep in the hall for a while if they are afraid to sleep in their bedroom.

WE HAVE "OPEN HOURS" FOR PARENTS, GUARDIANS AND RELATIVES WITH WHOM YOU ARE CLOSE. This means that you may see different children's parents on the unit at all times of the day and night. Some parents spend hours during the day, some parents take turns spending time on the unit, and some parents spend the night until they and their child are comfortable with the CAU and the staff. We believe that it is important to have parents around, as they know you the best and they can help us learn more about you so that we can help you and your family quickly. Sometimes parents cannot come to the unit often, and sometimes they are not able to come at all. The staff will spend lots of time with you so that you are not feeling so lonely, and they really like spending time with kids. We want you to feel relaxed so that we can get to know you and help you figure out how to solve problems that brought you here. We also like to talk with you and play with you.

PHONE CALLS: You have use of our phone during most of the day and evening. We do not restrict calls, but who you call and who calls you is a decision that your parents or guardian will make, and they will give us a list of people who can call or visit. Sometimes we are also given a list of people whom your parents or guardian do not want you to have contact with while you are here.

WE NEED YOUR HELP: We really like kids and we don't want to do anything that would possibly hurt them. We do not like to have to put "hands on" a child unless it is to shake their hand or give them a pat, or even better—to give them a big hug. But we do need you to help us and work with us. If you are upset, we would like you to let us know. If you cannot tell us in words then we will help you make up another way to tell us that you are upset (a certain look, a tap on our shoulders, a special word). We will give you space to be alone if that is what you need, we will stay with you and talk to you if that helps, or we will stay with you and be quiet if that helps.

What is hard for us is when a child is hitting, or biting, or spitting at the staff or another child. We have to keep everyone safe here, so we want to be able to help you when you are frustrated and angry so that you do not hit or hurt yourself or anyone else. Sometimes a child needs to leave the group and be by him or herself to calm down. We may direct you to go to your room, or some kids like to go to the Quiet Room when they are really upset and angry. Some kids feel that a walk helps them calm down.

We will help you find what works for you. We do not want to have to hold you to prevent you from hurting yourself or others. We don't like it when we have to hold a child even briefly—even for 10 seconds.

We do end up doing this once in awhile when everything else we have tried has not worked to help a child calm down. We would rather find anything else, so please work with us so that we don't have to resort to this. We have worked very hard to do away with some things that we felt hurt kids. This unit does not use mechanical restraints or seclusion. We have not used those methods of dealing with kids hitting for a long time, and we do not plan to use them ever again. But once in awhile, we end up having to hold a child briefly to stop them from hurting other people.

GETTING TO KNOW YOU: This is our job. We need to get to know you and to understand what you like to do, what you are good at, what games you like, your favorite activities, sports, school subjects, etc. We also want to learn where you have some problems and when things are hard for you. We want to know what makes you happy, what makes you sad, what makes you frustrated, and what makes you angry. If we can learn these things about you, we can try and figure a way to help you so that you have an easier time. We want you to succeed and to be happy.

Helping us learn all we can about you helps us do our work faster so that you can leave and go home or back to your program.

The most important thing for you to know is that you have rights. You have the right to know information about your plan. You have the right to be involved in decision making about your discharge. You have the right to express your views and opinions about your care and your plan. We can't

guarantee that your wishes will always be agreed to, but we will take seriously what you say and will place a lot of importance on your views. You can help us by letting us know how you feel about the important things in your life.

We hope that you enjoy your stay on the CAU.

—The CAU Staff

END NOTES

1. Redl, Fritz, and Wineman, David (1952). *Controls From Within, Techniques for the Treatment of the Aggressive Child*. Glencoe, Ill.: The Free Press.
2. LeBel, J., and Goldstein, R (2004). "Cents and Sensibilities: What Leaders Should Know." Presentation at the Massachusetts Department of Mental Health Special Forum on the Role of Leaders in the Restraint Reduction/ Elimination Initiative, March 20, 2004.
3. Pynoos, R.S., and Mader, L. (1990). "Children's Exposure to Violence and Traumatic Death." *Psychiatric Annals* 20: 334–344.
4. Ibid.
5. Ahmann, E., and Johnson, B.H. (2000). "Family-Centered Care: Facing the New Millennium." *Pediatric Nursing* 26(1): 87–94, 88.
6. *Ibid.*, p. 88.
7. *Ibid.*
8. *Ibid.*
9. Heifetz, Ronald (1994). *Leadership Without Easy Answers*. Cambridge: The Belnap Press of Harvard University Press, p. 116.

10. Gladwell, Malcolm (2000). *The Tipping Point: How Little Things Can Make a Big Difference.* Boston: Little, Brown and Co., p 9.
11. *Ibid.*, p. 18.
12. *Ibid.*, p. 258.
13. *Ibid.*, p. 259.
14. Fawcett, J. *An Analysis of Contemporary Nursing Models and Theories.* Philadelphia: F.A. Davis Company, p. 632.
15. *Ibid.*, p. 633.
16. Heifetz (1994), p. 35.
17. *Ibid.*, p. 99.
18. Heifetz, R., and Linsky, M. (2004). "Leading in Tough Times." *Educational Leadership*, April 2004, 61(7), p. 37.

BIBLIOGRAPHY

Ahmann, E., and Johnson, B.H. (2000) "Family-Centered Care: Facing the New Millennium." *Pediatric Nursing* 26(1): 87–92.

American Academy of Pediatrics Committee on Hospital Care and Institute for Family-Centered Care (2003). "Policy Statement: Family-Centered Care and the Pediatrician's Role." *Pediatrics* 112(3), 691–696.

Bower, B. (2000). "Raising Trust: Relation of Child-Rearing Ttechnique to Social Development of Children." *Science News,* http://www.findarticles.com/cf_0/m1200/1_158/63692736.jhtml

Bowlby, J. (1973). *Attachment and Loss, Vol. 2. Separation: Anxiety and Anger.* London: Hogarthe Press.

Bowlby, J. (1980). *Loss: Vol. 3. Attachment.* New York: Basic Books.

Brennan, A. (1994) "Caring for Children During Procedures: A Review of the Literature." *Pediatric Nursing* 20(5): 451–458.

Bricher, G. (1999). "Pediatric Nurses, Children and the Development of Trust." *Journal of Clinical Nursing* 8(4): 451–458.

Brown, J., and Ritchie, J.A. (1989). "Nurses' Perceptions of Their Relationship With Parents." *Maternal Child Nursing Journal* 18: 79–96.

Brown, J., and Ritchie, J.A. (1990). "Nurses' Perceptions of Parent and Nurse Roles in Caring for Hospitalized Children." *Children's Health Care* 19: 28–36.

Callery, P. (1997). "Caring for Parents of Hospitalized Children: A Hidden Part of Nursing Work." *Journal of Advanced Nursing* 26 (5): 992–998.

Claveirole, A. (2000). "The Most Vulnerable." *Nursing Standard* 14 (23): 58–63.

Critchley, Deane. (1982). "Interventions with Disorganized Parents of Disturbed Children." *Issues in Mental Health Nursing* 4:199–215.

DeBord, K. (1992). "How Children Learn." *Day Care Connections* 1(5): 4.

Delaney, Kathleen. (1999). "Time-Out: An Overused and Misused Milieu Intervention." *Journal of Child and Adolescent Psychiatric Nursing* 12: 53–60.

Delaney, Kathleen. (1991). "Nursing in Psychiatric Milieus Part II: Mapping Conceptual Footholds." *Journal of Child and Adolescent Psychiatric Nursing* 5 (1): 15–19.

Erikson, E. (1963). *Childhood and Society.* New York: W.W. Norton & Company.

Espezel, H. (2003). "Parent-Nurse Interaction: Care of Hospitalized Children." *Journal of Advanced Nursing* 44 (1): 34–41

Galvin, E., Boyers, L., Schwartz, P., Jones, M., Mooney, P., Warwick, J., and Davis, J. (2000). "Challenging the Precepts of Family-Centered Care: Testing a Philosophy." *Pediatric Nursing* 26(6): 625–636.

Gladwell, Malcolm (2000) *The Tipping Point: How Little Things Can Make a Big Difference.* Boston: Little, Brown and Co.

Greenblatt, M., Levinson, D., and Williams, R.H. (1957). *The Patient and the Mental Hospital.* Glencoe, Ill.: The Free Press.

Greene, R. (2001) *The Explosive Child.* New York: Harper Collins.

Greene, R.W., Ablon, J.S., Hassuk, B., Regan, K., Markey, J., Goring, J., and Rabbitt, S. (2004). "Elimination of Restraint and Seclusion and Reduction of Injuries on an Inpatient Psychiatry Unit," under review.

Groves, B.M., Zuckerman, B., Marans, S., Cohen, D. (1993). "Silent Victims: Children Who Witness Violence." *Journal of the American Medical Association* 269(2): 262–264.

Guiliano, K., Pottick, K., McAlpine, D.M.A., and Andelman, R. (2000). "Changing Patterns of Psychiatric Care for Children and Adolescents in General Hospital, 1988-1995." *American Journal of Psychiatry,* 157(8): 1267–1273.

Guliano, K. (2000). "Families First: Liberal Visitation Policies May Be in Patients' Best Interest.∏ *Nurse Manager* 31 (5): 46–50.

Heifetz, Ronald. (1994). *Leadership Without Easy Answers.* Cambridge, Mass.: The Belnap Press of Harvard University Press.

Heifetz, Ronald, and Linsky, Marty. (2004). "Leading in Tough Times." *Educational Leadership* 61 (7): 33–37.

Holmes, J. (1993). *John Bowlby & Attachment Theory.* New York: Brunner-Rutledge.

Hutchfield, K. (1999). "Family Centered Care: A Concept Analysis." *Journal of Advanced Nursing* 29(5): 1178–1187.

Kopelman, L.M. (1997). "The Best Interest Standard Threshold, Ideal, and Standard of Reasonableness." *Journal of Medicine and Philosophy* 22: 271–289.

Kristensson-Hallstrom I., and Elander G. (1997). "Parents' Experience of Hospitalization: Different Strategies for Feeling Secure." *Pediatric Nursing* 23: 361–376.

LeBel, J., and Goldstein, R. (2004). "Cents and Sensibilities: What Leaders Should Know." Presentation Delivered at The Massachusetts Department of Mental Health Special Forum on the Role of Leaders in the Restraint Reduction/Elimination Initiative, March 30, 2004.

Lyons, J.A. (1987). "Post-Traumatic Stress Disorder in Children and Adolescents: A Review of the Literature." In Chess S., and Thomas, A., eds. *Annual Progress in Child Psychiatry and Development.* New York: Brunner Mazel.

Meleski, D. (2002). "Families with Chronically Ill Children: A Literature Review Examines Helping Them Cope.∏ *American Journal of Nursing* 102(5): 47–54.

Miles, M.S. (2003). "Support for Parents During a Child's Hospitalization: A Nurse's Guide to Helping Parents Cope." *American Journal of Nursing* 103(2): 62–64.

Newton, M.S. (2002). "Family-Centered Care: Current Realities in Parent Participation." *Pediatric Nursing* 26(12):164–170.

Perry, B., Pollard, R., Blakely, T., Baker W., and Vigilante, D. (1995). "Childhood Trauma, the Neurobiology of Adaptation and Use-Dependent Development of the Brain: How States Become Traits." *Infant Mental Health Journal* 16: 271–291.

Perry, B. (2003). "Effects of Traumatic Events: An Introduction to Child Trauma Academy." *Interdisciplinary Education* 2 (3): http://www.childtrauma.org/ctamaterials/effects.

Pynoos, R.S., and Nader, K. (1990). "Children's Exposure to Violence and Traumatic Death." *Psychiatric Annals* 20: 334–344.

Redl, Fritz, and Wineman, David. (1952). *Controls From Within, Techniques for the Treatment of the Aggressive Child.* Glencoe, Ill.: The Free Press.

Regan, K. (2003). "When Daddy Hits Mommy." *Advance for Nurses* 3(22): 22–23.

Regan, K. (2003). "Loosening Restraints." *Nursing Spectrum* 7(7): 5.

Regan, K. (2005). "Paradigm Shifts in Inpatient Care of Children: Approaching Child-Centered and Family-Centered Care." *Journal of Child and Adolescent Psychiatric Nursing.*

Rickard-Bell, C. (1994). "The Impact of Critical Incidents in Paediatric Hospital: A Review." *The Australian Journal of Advanced Nursing* 12 (1): 29–35.

Sheilds, L., Kristensson-Hallstrom, I., and Krisljansdattir, Hunter J. (2003). "Who Owns the Child in the Hospital? A Preliminary Discussion." *Journal of Advanced Nursing* 41(3): 213–222.

Taylor, L., Zuckerman, B., Harik, V., and Groves, B. (1992). "Exposure to Violence Among Inner City Parents and Young Children." *American Journal of Diseases of Children* 146: 487.

Yingling, J. (2000). "Verbal Responses of Children and Their Supportive Providers in a Pediatric Oncology Unit." *Journal of Health Communications* 5(4): 371–377.

Zimberoff, D., and Hartman, D. (2002). "Attachment, Detachment, Nonattachment: Achieving Synthesis." *Journal of Heart-Centered Therapies* 5(1): 3–94.

INDEX